NATIVE PEOPLES, POLITICS, AND SOCIETY

IN CONTEMPORARY PARAGUAY

MAP 1 Map of Paraguay, indicating the location of indigenous settlements

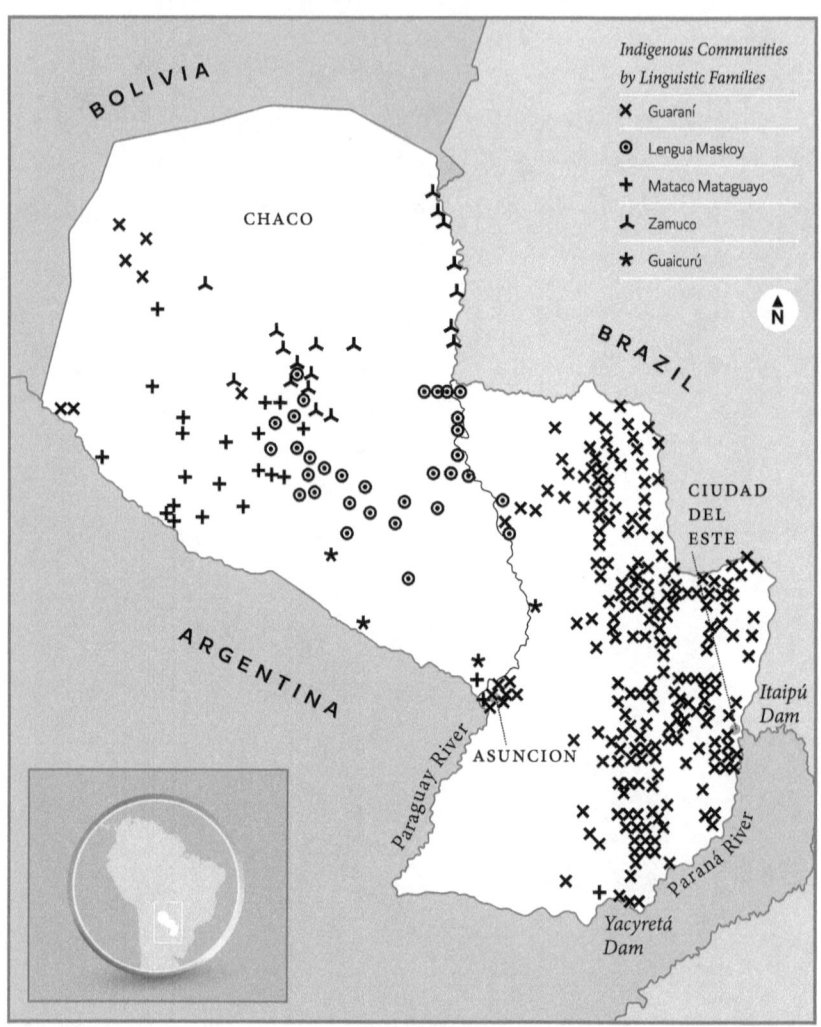

Sources: Map of Paraguay, depicting location of its indigenous peoples, 2012. Dirección General de Estadística, Encuestas y Censos, *Pueblos Indigenas en el Paraguay: Resultadas Finales de Población y Viviendas*, 2012. Fernando de la Mora: Gobierno Nacional, December 2014; Map of South America by National Geographic, 2016.

NATIVE PEOPLES, POLITICS, AND SOCIETY IN CONTEMPORARY PARAGUAY

MULTIDISCIPLINARY PERSPECTIVES

Edited by Barbara A. Ganson

University of New Mexico Press   Albuquerque

© 2021 by the University of New Mexico Press
All rights reserved. Published 2021
Printed in the United States of America

First paperback printing 2023

ISBN 978-0-8263-6257-5 (cloth)
ISBN 978-0-8263-6501-9 (paper)
ISBN 978-0-8263-6258-2 (e-book)

Library of Congress Control Number: 2021937815

Cover illustration courtesy of the author
Designed by Mindy Basinger Hill
Composed in 10/15 pt Minion Pro and Copihue

CONTENTS

List of Maps and Tables   vii

Acknowledgments   ix

Chronology of Major Events   *Melissa H. Birch, Paola Canova, Sarah Patricia Cerna Villagra, Barbara A. Ganson, and René D. Harder Horst*   xi

Introduction   *Barbara A. Ganson*   1

ONE   Indigenous People in Paraguay and Latin America's Move to Democracy   *René D. Harder Horst*   19

TWO   The Guaraní: From Forest People to Urban Refugees   *Richard K. Reed*   37

THREE   Rethinking Ayoreo Urbanity: Labor Relations and Land Claims in a Mennonite Colony of the Chaco   *Paola Canova*   53

FOUR   Paraguay's Political System from Authoritarian Hegemony to Moderate Pluralism, 1954–2019   *Sarah Patricia Cerna Villagra, Sara Mabel Villalba Portillo, Eduardo Tamayo Belda, and Roque Mereles Pintos*   73

FIVE   Gender Quotas and Women's Political Identities in Paraguay   *Brian Turner*   109

SIX   Paraguay and Mercosur: Unlocking Global Potential in a Regional Trade Agreement?   *Melissa H. Birch*   135

Contributors   163

Index   167

MAPS

MAP 1   Map of Paraguay, indicating the location of indigenous settlements   ii
MAP 2   Deforestation of eastern Paraguay   42

TABLES

TABLE 4.1   Ideological Displacement of the Traditional Paraguayan Political Parties   75
TABLE 4.2   Paraguay's Effective Number of Parties (Eff Ns, Chamber of Deputies)   78
TABLE 4.3   The Evolution of Effective Numbers in Paraguay (1989–2018)   79
TABLE 4.4   Performance of the Paraguayan Economy (1999–2008)   95
TABLE 5.1   Senate and Chamber of Deputies Elections in Paraguay, 1993–2018   118
TABLE 5.2   Party Distribution of Seats Held by Women in Congress   118
TABLE 5.3   Junta Departmental Elections   120
TABLE 5.4   Junta Municipal Elections and Gender (Im)balances in Juntas Municipales   121
TABLE 5.5   Mayoral Elections   123
TABLE 5.6   Gubernatorial Elections   123

TABLE 5.7 Legislative Production by Women Members of the Chamber of Deputies   123

TABLE 5.8 Gender-Sensitive Legislative Proposals by Political Party of the Proponent   128

TABLE 6.1 Growth of Paraguayan Exports to Mercosur, 1980–2018   143

TABLE 6.2 Paraguayan Exports to Mercosur by Country, 1980–2018   144

TABLE 6.3 Growth of Paraguayan Imports from Mercosur, 1980–2018   145

TABLE 6.4 Paraguay's Share of Mercosur FDI   147

TABLE 6.5 Paraguay Real Gross Domestic Product (GDP)   148

TABLE 6.6 Paraguay and Mercosur Gross Domestic Product   149

TABLE 6.7 Distribution of Income   150

ACKNOWLEDGMENTS

I would like to thank those individuals in Paraguay, Europe, and the United States, both friends and scholars, who stimulated my interest in the study of contemporary Paraguay from a multidisciplinary perspective. My appreciation goes to the staff of the Geography and Map Division of the Library of Congress for allowing me to view their fine collection of historical maps of Paraguay. The Department of History at Florida Atlantic University in Boca Raton provided travel funding to conferences, the Library of Congress, and the Benson Latin American Collection at the University of Texas at Austin. The School of Business at the University of Kansas and the Dorothy F. Schmidt College of Arts and Letters at Florida Atlantic University provided funding for the index. Contributors to this volume have recognized other foundations and institutions for support of their research in their notes.

Above all, I am extremely grateful to the director of the University of New Mexico Press, Stephen Hull, for securing excellent external readers who provided valuable comments. I greatly appreciate the meticulous efforts of senior acquisitions editor Michael Millman for suggestions to improve the book's final revisions. He is a first-rate editor and an exceptional individual in the scholarly world of publishing. Finally, many thanks to our highly competent copyeditor, Norman Ware, and the production staff of the University of New Mexico Press for their fine efforts and dedication. In particular, Alexandra Hoff helped with many details in the final manuscript.

Melissa H. Birch, Paola Canova, Sarah Patricia Cerna Villagra, Barbara A. Ganson, and René D. Harder Horst

CHRONOLOGY OF MAJOR EVENTS

1981 The Indigenous Rights Law 904 is enacted in Paraguay to counter accusations of human rights violations.

1987 The Maskoy people recover their homelands at Riacho Mosquito.

1988 Indigenous peoples in eastern Paraguay are evicted to clear land for agriculture. The Avá Guaraní hold an *aty-guasú* to discuss the loss of lands and outside threats.

May 17: Indigenous people from Paraguay, Argentina, Bolivia, and Brazil meet Pope John Paul II at Mariscal Estigarribia in the Paraguayan Chaco.

1989, FEBRUARY 2–3 General Andrés Rodríguez carries out a coup d'état to remove General Alfredo Stroessner from power, ending one of the longest dictatorships in the world, at thirty-five years.

1989, MAY 1 General Andrés Rodríguez is elected president as candidate of the Colorado Party. He initiates a process of democratic transition.

1991 Mercosur, the regional common market comprising Argentina, Brazil, Paraguay, and Uruguay, is created.

Constitutional Assembly in Paraguay.

Constitutional Assembly and reforms in Colombia.

Indigenous March for Territory and Dignity in Bolivia.

1992 The Columbus quincentenary commemorations are held.

1992, APRIL Paraguay includes a chapter on indigenous rights in the country's new constitution.

1992 Paraguay's new constitution is promulgated. It limits a president to serving only one five-year term.

1992, DECEMBER 22 Police archives from the time of the Stroessner regime are discovered, which shed light on the nature of political repression during that time.

1993 Paraguay ratifies the International Labor Organization's Indigenous and Tribal Peoples Convention, 1989 (no. 169).

1993 Colorado candidate Juan Carlos Wasmosy, a civil engineer, wins Paraguay's first free presidential elections and becomes the country's first civilian president, serving until 1998.

1994 The Yacyretá Dam goes into operation on the Paraná River, a binational hydroelectric project between Paraguay and Argentina.

1994 The Itaipú Dam, a binational hydroelectric project between Paraguay and Brazil that entered into operation in 1984, is designated one of the Seven Wonders of the Modern World by the American Society of Civil Engineers.

The Ouro Preto Protocol revises the original Mercosur Treaty in what is sometimes referred to as the "relaunch" of the common market project.

1995–1997 The Wasmosy government confronts Paraguay's worst financial crisis of the twentieth century.

1996 A political crisis erupts with an attempted military coup by Lino Oviedo, the commander of the Paraguayan army.

Chile and Bolivia sign "complementarity agreements" with Mercosur. Neither country is prepared to join Mercosur at this time, but the agreements establish preferential trading arrangements for these countries with the four Mercosur nations.

1998 Raúl Cubas is elected president; he resigns in the wake of the assassination of Vice President Luis María Argaña in 1999, which leads to riots. This crisis becomes known as Marzo Paraguayo (Paraguayan month of March).

1999–2003 Luis Ángel González Macchi serves as "caretaker" president; in 2006, he is indicted on corruption charges.

2002 Violent street demonstrations break out in protest against the privatization of public works undertaken by the government of González Macchi and political corruption. Peasant farmers and supporters of Lino Oviedo take to the streets in different parts of the country to demand the resignation of the president. The protests leave two dead and hundreds wounded, and lead to more than three hundred arrests. President González Macchi declares an Estado de Excepción for five days, temporarily suspending civil rights.

2003 President Óscar Nicanor Duarte Frutos of the Colorado Party is elected president and serves until 2008.

2004 The Mercosur Parliament, the legislative branch of the regional integration organization, is created.

The Ley de Adecuación Fiscal is passed, introducing an income tax for the first time in Paraguay. Most agricultural activities are exempt.

Seventeen Ayoreo-Totobiegosode people make contact with the surrounding society due to extensive deforestation of their ancestral territories in the Chaco region. Other members of their tribe remain in voluntary isolation.

The Law of Zero Deforestation slows the process of deforestation by requiring that a quarter of rural properties in the Chaco region be left alone in their natural state. Compliance with this law, however, remains an ongoing problem.

2005 President Duarte Frutos promises to crack down on organized crime.

The Enxet people win the lawsuit *Yakye Axa Indigenous Community v. Paraguay* filed before the Inter-American Commission on Human Rights. The court orders the Paraguayan state to restitute part of the Enxets' traditional land and submit it to the community at no cost.

The Enxet people win the lawsuit *Sawhoyamaxa Indigenous Community v. Paraguay* filed before the Inter-American Commission on Human Rights. The court orders the Paraguayan state to restitute part of the Enxets' traditional land and submit it to the community at no cost.

2006 General Alfredo Stroessner dies in exile in Brazil at age ninety-three.

Former president Luis González Macchi is sentenced to six years in prison for illegal bank transfers from Paraguay to the United States.

2007 The last two turbines are installed on the Itaipú hydroelectric dam, completing the project with a total of eighteen turbines, making it the largest hydroelectric dam in the world in terms of installed capacity.

2008 *August 15:* Fernando Lugo Méndez, from the Christian Democratic Party, is elected president. Lugo's victory puts an end to sixty-one years of Colorado rule. He is the first Catholic bishop to be elected head of state in Paraguay.

Margarita Mbywangi becomes the first indigenous woman to take the presidency of the Instituto Paraguayo del Indígena, the government agency for indigenous affairs.

2009, APRIL Scandals rock the country over paternity suits and accusations of child abandonment by President Lugo. Having illegitimate children is common in Paraguay; the issue here is that Lugo admitted that one child had been conceived when he was a Roman Catholic bishop.

2012 Mercosur votes to suspend Paraguay temporarily for violation of the democratic clause of the founding treaty, for the country's impeachment of President Lugo. Paraguay argues unsuccessfully that the impeachment followed democratic norms. Venezuela becomes the fifth member of Mercosur over the objections of Paraguay.

June 15: Seventeen people are killed in Curuguaty, northeastern Paraguay, including peasants and members of the police who sought to dislodge landless peasants on contested land occupied and belonging to Blas Riquelme, a Colorado politician and businessman.

June 21: The Paraguayan Chamber of Deputies votes 76–1 to initiate the impeachment of President Lugo for "poor performance of functions."

2013 Horacio Cartes wins the presidential election as the candidate of the Colorado Party.

2014 The Mercosur Parliament adopts Guaraní as an official language.

2015 The "UNA no te Calles" protests begin, led by students of the National University of Asunción in protest against corruption at the university. The protests result in the resignation and imputation of the rector, Froilán Peralta.

Bolivia formally starts the process of becoming a full member of Mercosur.

2016 Itaipú, one of the world's largest hydroelectric plants, built and jointly owned by Brazil and Paraguay, generates more than 103 million megawatts in 2016, a world record in power generation for a single dam.

Venezuela is suspended from Mercosur for violations of the democratic clause.

Law 5777/16, Integral Protection of Women, is promulgated with the objective of establishing policies and strategies for preventing any form of violence against women; and instituting sanctions and integral reparations, in both the public and private spheres.

The project of Ley de Paridad Democrática (Law for Democratic Equality), which seeks to modify the electoral system in the county to give women parity in opportunities in politics and the public sphere, is presented.

2017 Street protests erupt over a possible amendment to the constitution that would allow President Horacio Cartes to run for reelection. Senate offices are burned, and a young man dies as a consequence of police repression.

2018, AUGUST 15 Mario Abdo Benítez, the forty-six-year-old son of the former private secretary of General Alfredo Stroessner, is elected president of Paraguay, from the Colorado Party.

2019, JANUARY 11 People march in Asunción to protest the deforestation of the Chaco.

July 5: Dr. Joel Filártiga, whose family admirably fought against human rights violations in Paraguay under Stroessner, dies at the age of eighty-six.

Decades earlier, the Filártigas won a landmark case in the United States that extended a universal law against torture, following the 1976 murder by a Paraguayan policeman of seventeen-year-old Joelito Filártiga, a high school student who did deliveries for his father, Dr. Filártiga, to the latter's nonprofit medical clinic in Ybycuí, seventy-five miles southeast of Asunción. Since the ruling was handed down, the statute on which it was based has been the source of almost all significant human right rights litigation in the United States and the rest of the world.

Paraguay ties with Panama in 2019 as the happiest countries in the world, according to the Gallup 2019 Global Emotions Report.

MARCH 2020 Paraguay takes early action to impede the COVID-19 outbreak. The government closes its borders, imposes a strict lockdown, shuts down schools, suspends public events, and reinforces social distancing, well ahead of neighboring countries.

NATIVE PEOPLES, POLITICS, AND SOCIETY

IN CONTEMPORARY PARAGUAY

Barbara A. Ganson

INTRODUCTION

The year 1989 was a watershed in world history; it not only marked the fall of the Berlin Wall, officially ending the Cold War, but was the year one of Latin America's most enduring dictators, General Alfredo Stroessner (1912–2006), fell from power in Paraguay after thirty-five years. This collection of multidisciplinary essays provides depth in understanding recent developments in Paraguay, since General Stroessner fled into exile to Brazil after the coup. Breaking free from a long tradition of authoritarian rule and corruption as well as economic inequality, extreme poverty, and a large informal sector (a system of trade or economic exchange, including the barter of goods and services, practiced by street vendors and traders), however, has not been easy for Paraguay's emerging democracy, despite having established one of the fastest-growing economies in South America since 2003. Between 2004 and 2017, Paraguay exhibited some of the strongest economic growth in the region, averaging nearly 4.5 percent growth annually during that period. However, annual GDP declined from 5 percent to less than 1 percent in 2019 due to adverse crop weather and less favorable trade relations with Brazil and Argentina.[1] Much of the growth has been driven by the agricultural sector and its contribution of commodities exports to the global market. Paraguay has become the fourth largest exporter of soybeans in the world, and it ranks among the top ten exporters of beef by total tonnage.[2] The question addressed by this unique essay collection is, how has Paraguayan society fared since the overthrow of Stroessner's dictatorship? The essays included are exemplary in their scope and depth of understanding of various elements of Paraguayan society: indigenous peoples, politics, women's rights, the economy, and aspects of the natural environment, in one of Latin America's poorest countries, which is largely agrarian but is also one of the world's largest producers and exporters of hydroelectricity. Taken together, these essays serve as an important resource for comparative purposes with other countries that have also made the transition from dictatorship to modern democracy.

Historical Background: Spanish Expansion in the Sixteenth, Seventeenth, and Eighteenth Centuries

In the mid-sixteenth century, Paraguay became the center of Spanish conquest in the region of the Río de la Plata during the expedition of Pedro de Mendoza, within three months after the initial founding of Buenos Aires in 1536. In a letter written in 1556, doña Isabel de Guevara, a Spanish woman on the expedition, described the extreme hardship the Spaniards had endured during their journey, including the five hundred women who had accompanied them. One thousand Spaniards died of starvation, she noted, following attacks by nomadic indigenous peoples of the pampas. The men, she observed, became so weak that Spanish women assumed the work of sentinels by keeping watch at night, while armed with crossbows. Guevara also noted how women prepared the food, nursed the sick, and washed clothing.[3] Pedro de Mendoza, who suffered from syphilis, decided to return to Spain but died on June 23, 1537, and was buried at sea. Unable to adapt to the environment in the grasslands of the pampas at Buenos Aires, the Spaniards traveled more than a thousand miles along the Paraguay River to establish an outpost called Nuestra Senõra de Santa María de la Asunción in Paraguay in 1537. There, Spanish explorers under the command of Juan de Ayolas encountered some twenty-four thousand semisedentary indigenous Cario-Guaraní, who, following some minor military skirmishes, welcomed the idea of forming a military and kinship alliance with the Spaniards in order to confront their traditional enemies, the nomadic peoples in the arid western region known as the Chaco.

While Paraguay's first governor, Domingo de Irala, acquired seven indigenous wives, the daughters of caciques, other Spaniards married Spanish women or took Indian wives and concubines of their own. In 1541, Irala reported that there were seven hundred Guaraní women serving the settlers; another report, from 1545, noted that "one is poor who has only five or six wives, most having 15, 20, 30, and 40."[4] Guaraní women worked for them in the fields by growing corn, manioc, squash, sweet potatoes, and peanuts among other crops. They also made pottery and spun and wove cloth, besides taking care of their children and other domestic chores. The spinning of cloth and weaving of thread were central to women's work. The term *hilandera* (female weaver) appears in an early Guaraní dictionary, suggesting that proper work for women was weaving in the missions. Spanish women also dedicated much of their time in Asunción to spinning cotton and the fibers of a kind of wild pineapple, the *caraguatá*; weaving cloth; and making lace. Spider-web lace (*ñanduti*) was created using needles and a European-style handloom, incorporating intricate Native motifs such as coconut flower, fish bone, guava flower, and cornflower. Early Paraguayan lace was woven using only black-and-white thread; later female artisans introduced more colorful imported linen and silk or made their own colorful threads from the dyes of native plants.

In 1556, an estimated twenty thousand Cario-Guaraní were divided among 320 Spaniards to work in agriculture, construction, shipbuilding, and Spanish households under the encomienda (a grant of Indian laborers usually given to Spaniards for having performed services for the crown; it carried the obligation to Christianize the Indians). Indigenous men and women were required to work two months per year for their encomenderos, who held these grants for two generations; then they reverted back to the crown. The remaining ten months of the year, indigenous men and women worked on their own lands. The Spanish and their mestizo offspring, both men and women, also took part in expeditions to found new towns in the province, including Santa Cruz de la Sierra in what is today Bolivia, and the Argentine towns of Santa Fé, San Juan de Vera de las Siete Corrientes, and Buenos Aires (which was reestablished in 1580). A simple bronze plaque commemorates the second founding of Buenos Aires on Calle Florida near Avenida Corrientes, in which at least one mestiza, Ana Díaz, participated.[5]

Indigenous peoples of Paraguay may have named the large province of colonial Paraguay for the Paraguay River, adorned by *camalote*s, floating islands of aquatic plants. In the Tupí-Guaraní language, *para* means "variety," *gua* means "to adorn," and *y* means "water," so Paraguay possibly means "crowned river," referring to the shape of Lake Xarayes, the headwaters of the river.[6] Indigenous peoples brought their Native languages and cultural traditions to early Spanish missions founded by the Franciscans in the central region in satellite communities near Asunción beginning in 1580, and after 1610 to those established by the Jesuits in Guayrá in what is today southeastern Brazil, which were relocated southward along the Paraná River following Indian slave-raiding attacks by the Paulistas (the marauding inhabitants of São Paulo who engaged in this illegal activity) in the early seventeenth century.

Catholic missionaries directed the processes of cultural adaptation by providing the Guaraní with fishing hooks, metal knives, sewing needles, clothing, axes, and other new tools of European technology. Jesuits and Franciscans concentrated on the education of male Indian children, especially the sons of caciques, who would then indoctrinate their parents and later play influential roles in the administration of the missions. Boys learned how to read and write as well as do mathematics. Although Guaraní women provided extensive agricultural labor, girls' education was largely relegated to the performing of domestic chores, and the spinning of cotton and wool thread to make clothing for their families. Guaraní men, on the other hand, were trained to serve as riverboat sailors, blacksmiths, shoemakers, tailors, printers, sculptors, scribes, musicians, and pottery makers as well as to handle livestock.

Gender separation took place not only in the workshops and on the mission ranches but in the schools and during church services. While Guaraní boys and girls both studied catechism, the children filed into the church in separate lines. Boys entered first, followed by men. Then came the girls, followed by the women, all seated according to their gender. Catholic missionaries, moreover, confined elderly women, single women, and orphans in a separate compound or asylum.[7] These were shelters located next to the church where women's honor and virginity were protected, as well as their physical well-being. Usually, two or three elderly women raised the orphans and looked after the welfare of the young women. Women left these enclosures to work in the fields and then only in groups. Men exercised authority in the Indian cabildos or town councils, as well as in the militias established by the Jesuits to combat Indian slavery beginning in the 1620s.[8] There were no female members in these councils or constables to patrol the streets of the missions. Yet, women were not without some influence, and their voices can occasionally be heard in their testimonies in judicial records. While girls and women were taught catechism, there seems to be no evidence of them learning how to read and write, or to perform mathematics.[9] The little attention given to the schooling of Guaraní girls and women is not surprising in light of the patriarchal nature of society, which was reinforced by the teachings of the Catholic Church.[10]

Missionaries brought with them vital skills, including knowledge of the Catholic faith, science, architecture, and material culture. Indigenous peoples benefited from their knowledge and readily adopted new technologies and material goods for their own use. The Jesuits in exchange acquired knowledge of the natural environment, such as herbal medicine, which the Native peoples had acquired on the basis of trial and error over the course of centuries. Initially the Jesuits attempted to convert the Guaraní by preaching to them in their villages, accompanied only by an interpreter or several loyal Native individuals. They then established settlements or Indian towns of their own called *reducciones*. Music and song greatly facilitated the Jesuits' conversion efforts and served as a recruitment tool to attract Native peoples to these early settlements. The Guaraní adapted to living in the missions and responded to the missionaries in diverse ways. The Guaraní became vassals of the Spanish king by swearing their allegiance to the Crown. The formation of militias by Jesuits renewed the adult male Indians' sense of independence, power, self-worth, and warrior traditions. At the same time, Native peoples retained and preserved many of their own cultural traditions and language, often through the assistance of missionaries who served as their political advisers, physicians, and teachers. As laborers and recipients of European material goods and technology, the Guaraní built thirty reducciones in the area of the Paraná and Uruguay Rivers, as well as two settlements in northeastern Paraguay, in the mid-eighteenth century. According to the 1647 census, the first official census of the missions, twenty reducciones where the census was taken had a total population of 28,714. At their peak year in 1732, the settlements reached a total of 141,182, inhabitants, before their decline to 73,910 in 1740 and recovery to approximately 91,000 by 1750.[11]

For those Guaraní boys and men who learned how to read and write, the technology of writing exercised strong influences over their everyday lives.[12] The acceptance of this new technology enabled indigenous people to exercise more control over their everyday lives. The Guaraní gained knowledge of the colonial world by being able to read and write, which aided them in their resistance to colonial rule. After signing the Treaty of Madrid in 1750, which altered the territorial boundaries, with Spain ceding mission territory to the Portuguese in Brazil, the Spanish Crown offered 28,000 pesos to the Guaraní for their fine houses, churches, ranches, and plantations in this border region on lands belonging to ten missions. In response, Guaraní members of Indian cabildos and caciques wrote or signed letters of protest addressed to the governor of Buenos Aires and other Spanish officials, creating a voice for themselves in the negotiations, having been excluded from sitting at the diplomatic table in Madrid with Europeans. In their letters, the Guaraní refused to comply with the treaty because they had been asked to turn over their towns, churches, houses, and land to the Portuguese, their traditional enemies who had enslaved tens of thousands of Guaraní beginning in the late 1620s. The Treaty of Madrid was eventually rescinded in 1761 but only after the death of 1,511 Guaraní militia soldiers in 1756 and the relocation of more than 14,000 Guaraní to other settlements west of the Uruguay River in what is today northeastern Argentina and southern Paraguay.[13]

Attempts to suppress the use of the Guaraní language date back to the mid-eighteenth century, but these Spanish measures proved to be largely unsuccessful. In 1743, the Spanish Crown circulated a decree encouraging the eradication of Native languages spoken in the empire, requiring that only Spanish be spoken. King Philip V of Spain specifically ordered Jesuits in Paraguay to teach Spanish to Indian children that same year. Nevertheless, the Jesuits found it nearly impossible to put this decree into effect because the Guaraní language was so widely spoken, not only in the missions but throughout the entire province of Paraguay, even in the Spanish towns. Following a tour of the province in 1744, the bishop of Paraguay, José Cayetano Paravicino, observed: "The customs and language of the Spaniards born here as well as that of Negros and mulattos of which there are many, is that of the Indians, with few differences."[14] A Jesuit observed: "In Paraguay, many have forgotten the Spanish language and adopted that of the Indians, which they use in their homes in the towns and in the rural areas where as many live, as in the towns, and where no one knows another language other than that of the Indians."[15] Boys, he noted, studied Spanish in the schools but did not know it well, and they were punished if they spoke their native Guaraní language. Interestingly, Guaraní mission Indian fugitives, most of whom became day laborers or ranch hands living in Buenos Aires and Santa Fé in the mid-1750s, kept in touch with events in their mission towns "through the letters they received" from other mission Indians.[16]

The Crown circulated a similar decree in 1760, encouraging the eradication of the diverse languages spoken in the Spanish Empire and requiring that only Spanish be spoken. Charles III ordered that the "Indians be taught the dogmas of our religion in Spanish and that [they] be taught to read and write in this language only . . . in order to improve administration and the spiritual well-being of the natural ones (Indians) and so that they can understand their superiors, love the conquering nation, rid themselves of idolatry, and become civilized." Individual Guaraní appear to have had an incentive to learn Spanish, particularly those who were riverboat captains, sailors, and soldiers who came into periodic or extended contact with Spaniards outside the missions. It is still unknown how many or what percentage of the Guaraní population learned how to read and write in their native language or in Spanish. Literacy thus was not always reserved for members of the Indian elites; conversely, even some members of the elite were illiterate. There is evidence in documents showing that some caciques and members of Indian cabildos indicated that they could not sign their own names; they signed these documents with an *X*.

One purpose for Indian councilmen to learn to read and write was to administer their own towns. There is ample evidence that the Guaraní kept track of the community property they kept in their warehouses and the number of cattle on their ranches. One of the first Guaraní teachers, Andrés Arano, qualified himself to teach at Mission Apóstoles in 1801, having in turn passed examinations in reading, writing, mathematics, religion, and Spanish.[17]

In summary, the colonial Guaraní succeeded in deriving certain benefits from their relations with Spanish missionaries, having learned how to read and write and do mathematics. However, the formal education of Native Guaraní women was neglected, and indeed, girls and women were largely disadvantaged by limiting their life experiences, especially by keeping them illiterate. Through selective literacy of certain males, however, indigenous peoples could take more effective action and exercise greater control over their lives in what was a turbulent colonial world.

A Tradition of Authoritarian Rule Following Independence

Paraguay became a nation, separating itself from the control of the *porteños* (inhabitants of the port) in Buenos Aires by defeating troops under General Manuel Belgrano in the battle of Cerro Porteño on January 18, 1811. On March 9, 1811, Paraguayans defeated the Argentine militias a second time near the Taquary River, a tributary of the Paraguay River. A leading member of the revolutionary junta, José Gaspar Rodríguez de Francia (1766–1840), seized power in 1813 as one of two consuls of the new Republic of Paraguay, and then as "Supreme and Perpetual Dictator" from 1814 until his death in 1840. He largely closed all of Paraguay's borders to ensure the country's political independence and territorial integrity. His successor, dictator Carlos Antonio López (1790–1862), in contrast opened up the country to commerce, looking toward Europe to develop Paraguay's infrastructure by contracting European engineers to build one of the first railroads in South America, obtain modern steamships and ironclads (warships), and establish an iron foundry at Ybycuí. In 1846, 42 percent (100,314 persons) of Paraguay's population of 238,862 lived in or within the radius of its capital of Asunción.[18] López improved the status of slaves by enacting the Free Womb Law of 1842, which declared the freedom of children born to slave mothers after they had served their masters until age twenty-five for males and twenty-four for females. The 1846 census listed 17,212 blacks, representing less than 8 percent of the total population, of whom 532 were *libertos* (freed children) and the remainder were either enslaved or free blacks and mulattos.

López's deranged and paranoid son, General Francisco Solano López (1826–1870), who succeeded his father as dictator, plunged his country into South America's most devastating war, against Brazil, Argentina, and Uruguay, from December 1864 to March 1870.[19] The Paraguayan War (also known as the War of the Triple Alliance or the "Great War") remains Latin America's only total war; it was a struggle over territorial boundaries, natural resources, navigational rights, and power between the forces of conservatism and liberalism. Paraguayan women and children even fought in some of the final battles.[20] By March 1870, Paraguay had largely become a land of women, widows, invalids, and orphans, a country in despair. Paraguay lost more than a third of its prewar territory to Brazil and Argentina and nearly half of its population, although the extent of Paraguay's demographic losses in Latin America's most catastrophic war remains controversial.[21] Patterns of female heads of households became more common (although their presence had been listed in censuses prior to the war, especially in rural communities). Baptismal records for the year 1887 show that the illegitimacy rate for all of Paraguay was 64.1 percent. Of the 8,170 children baptized, 5,244 were illegitimate that year. These birthrates of illegitimate children are higher than those recorded in the cities of Córdoba and Buenos Aires, Argentina, and São Paulo, Brazil, where rates ranged from 23 to 54 percent in the mid- to late eighteenth century.[22]

In the aftermath of occupation by Argentina and Brazil for six years and the adoption of the country's first constitution in 1870, which abolished slavery, Paraguay's first main political parties emerged.[23] The conservative Colorado Party dominated Paraguayan politics from 1887 to 1904; then the Liberal Party dominated much of the early twentieth century. Some brilliant Paraguayan Liberal intellectuals came to govern Paraguay in the early twentieth century, such as President Manuel Gondra Pereira (1871–1927), but they had great difficulty remaining in power for very long.[24]

From 1870 to 1929, population gains from immigration were only slight. The Paraguayan government opened up vast tracts of land in the Chaco beginning in 1880. The most significant immigration took place among the Mennonites, who arrived from Germany, Canada, Manchuria, Russia, and the United States (mainly Pennsylvania) beginning in 1927, some five thousand of whom lived in thirty-six communities by 1933.[25] Mennonites came in search of religious freedom and were attracted by the availability of free land in the Chaco offered to them by the Paraguayan government. Mennonites in Paraguay speak Plattdeutsch, a Low German dialect, among themselves, but also Spanish. Neighboring indigenous peoples who work for the Mennonites in the Chaco have also learned to speak Plattdeutsch.

Paraguayans fought another territorial conflict, this time against Bolivia in the Chaco War (1932–1935). Supported by their *madrinas de guerra* (godmothers of war; usually wives or sisters who would send care packages to their loved ones), peasant soldiers fought bravely and victoriously on the battlefield, nearly expelling the Bolivians entirely from the disputed territory. Paraguay, however, was less successful at the diplomatic table that determined the new territorial boundaries of the Chaco in a signed treaty, which granted Paraguay three-quarters of the Chaco.

A decade of instability broke out following the Chaco War. On February 17, 1936, Chaco War hero Colonel Rafael Franco tried on the presidential sash, only to have it removed the following year by a new Liberal president, Félix Paiva. Having nearly driven the Bolivians militarily out of the Chaco but chafing at the diplomatic setbacks in settling the territorial conflict, many of the veterans of the Chaco War were discontent. Military leaders formed the semifascist Revolutionary Febrerista Party and ended Liberal rule, claiming that the Liberals were corrupt and had forced Colonel Franco's exile to Uruguay. In August 1939, General José Félix de Estigarribia, another Chaco War hero, who was popular among university students, veterans, and cadets, became the new Paraguayan leader. General Estigarribia used the press, the radio, and mass meetings to indoctrinate his followers, and he soon imposed government censorship to rule almost singlehandedly, as any dictator. A new 1940 constitution replaced the 1870 constitution, creating a single house of Congress that only met once a year.

In 1947, General Franco tried to reinstall himself in power during an unsuccessful military revolt. From 1948 to 1954, five different men governed Paraguay, including two elected presidents, two provisional presidents, and the leader of a military revolt. Only in the aftermath of civil unrest did a young artillery officer, Alfredo Stroessner, rise through the ranks of the military to become Paraguay's new authoritarian leader in 1954. In 1961, Paraguayan women over the age of eighteen earned the right to vote for the first time. Suffrage, however, did not mean much in a country where fraud was common in elections and where few elections took place in which there was more than one candidate. The new 1967 constitution had 239 articles, and established a Congress with a Senate and House of Representatives. Voting became mandatory for all citizens in all elections using a secret ballot; Paraguayans accordingly could not easily demonstrate any disapproval by not showing up to vote.

Backed by the military, the conservative Colorado Party, the police force, and other conservative elements in the country, Stroessner was a staunch anticommunist and a strong supporter of the United States in regional organizations such as the Organization of American States (OAS). He admittedly did bring about some improvement in the quality of life of many Paraguayan peasants by introducing electricity and running water to many rural areas for the first time. Yet Paraguay remained one of the poorer countries in the hemisphere. The gap between rich and poor was apparent in the contrast between the mansions along Avenida Mariscal López in Asuncion, and the houses with dirt floors in La Chacarita, a shanty neighborhood of the same city; the wealth gap fueled a large informal economy. The political reality of the country under Stroessner was one in which human rights were not well respected; corruption, contraband, and domestic abuse ran rampant; and journalists and those rare individuals who were outspoken political critics occasionally were subjected to political intimidation, torture, and even murder. Concerns about continual reports of human rights violations and corruption were heightened during a visit by Pope John Paul II in May 1988, which undoubtedly undermined Stroessner's ability to govern.[26] In 1989, the aging dictator was overthrown in a bloody coup and sent to Brazil in exile by his own son-in-law, General Andrés Rodríguez (1923–1997). Elected as president on May 1, 1989, General Rodríguez, one of the richest men in the country and a Stroessner collaborator, wished to see Paraguay embark on becoming a democracy following a period of transition. He freed political prisoners, welcomed home exiles, restored civil liberties, and conducted open presidential elections.[27] Today, Paraguayans remain optimistic and undoubtedly are much more willing to participate in politics through fair elections and by occasionally demonstrating in the streets.

The Physical and Cultural Landscape

Paraguay is dwarfed in size by its neighbors Brazil and Argentina; approximately 157,047 square miles (406,752 square kilometers), the country slightly smaller than the state of California (163,696 square miles or 423,970 square kilometers) but larger than Italy (116,339 square miles or 301,318 square kilometers) (see map 1). Northern Paraguay lies in the tropics, while southern Paraguay is subtropical. It shares borders with Portuguese-speaking Brazil and the Spanish-speaking countries of Argentina and Bolivia, where Native languages are also spoken. The Paraguay River, which is 1,580 miles (2,550 kilometers) in length, along with hundreds of small rivers and streams that flow into either the Paraguay or Paraná Rivers, underscore Paraguay's great potential in the development of hydroelectric energy. The Paraguay River at its southwestern tip flows into the Paraná River, which continues southeastward to the estuary of the Río de la Plata, making the Paraná–La Plata one of the longest rivers in the world, extending 2,769 miles or 5,550 kilometers.[28]

To the west of the Paraguay River is the Chaco, a large area of about 95,000 square miles of grassy plains, scrub forests, and marshes, which supports less than 2 percent of Paraguay's population but accounts for 61 percent of the country's land mass. Small bands of hunters and gatherers in the Chaco once designed their own tattoos and body decoration, for both men and women. Most of these bands readily adopted the horse, while others, such as the Payaguá (Evueví), were riverine and well adept at handling their paddles and canoes on rivers, which they used for fishing, hunting, and raiding.[29] Indigenous peoples and Mennonites make up much of the sparse population. Semisedentary Guaraní reside in eastern Paraguay, which is subtropical and contains plains, hills, and plateaus. Agriculture and forestry currently employs nearly one-third of the population in eastern Paraguay.

Sadly, Paraguay has earned the distinction of having one of the highest rates of deforestation in the world. Between 2001 and 2014, nearly 3.5 million hectares have been cleared in the western region of the Chaco. In southeastern Paraguay, far more acreage has been cleared for agriculture (see map 2, in chapter 2 below). Deforestation harms not only indigenous peoples but Paraguay's varied species of plants, birds, mammals, reptiles, and amphibians. Indeed, through loss of habitat, many animal species have become increasingly threatened, such as the jaguar (whose name originated from the Tupí-Guaraní language, *jaguareté*), the fox-like, long-legged maned wolf (*aguará guazú*, meaning "large fox" in Tupí-Guaraní), golden lion tamarin monkeys, woolly spider monkeys, maned three-toed sloths, giant anteaters, and red-tailed parrots.[30]

Although Paraguay is often referred to as the "Guaraní nation" (its currency is the guaraní), the country's indigenous population remains quite small (less than 2 percent); 95 percent of the country's total population of seven million are mestizo.[31] According to the latest census taken of Paraguay's indigenous peoples, the 2012 census, the Guaraní linguistic groups in the country—the Paĩ-Tavytera, Mbyá Guaraní, and Avá Chiripá—numbered 53,961. The 2012 census identified nineteen distinct indigenous groups totaling 117,150 people, or 1.8 percent, out of a total population in the country of 6,435,218.[32] Like their ancestors, the Guaraní today experience a clash over new social values with a dominant culture, conflicts over land and religious beliefs, and the need to defend their cultural identity and independence. These indigenous peoples also face serious problems such as deforestation, the loss of hunting and fishing sites, the decimation of fish populations, urban migration, and even suicide among some of their youth, especially among the Guaraní-Kaiowá, who reside near São Paulo in Brazil.[33] The Brazilian-Italian film *Terra Vermelha* (2008; directed by Marco Bechis), released in 2010 in the United States as *Birdwatchers*, depicts the problem of suicide among young Guaraní and tensions in contemporary society when a group of indigenous people attempt to reclaim their ancestral lands from a Brazilian farmer and rancher.

Despite extreme poverty and other issues facing Paraguay's indigenous peoples in their continual struggle for survival, problems that are common in other parts of South America, Paraguay is considered one of the most content countries in the world. According to Gallup's 2019 Global Emotions Report, Paraguay ties with Panama as the world's happiest and most positive country; the poll was conducted in 140 countries, based on extensive interviews in which people daily reported their positive emotions. This is due in large part because Latin Americans are family oriented. Paraguayans typically work from 7:00 to 11:00 a.m., before returning home for lunch and relaxation with family. They finish working from 3:00 to 7:00 p.m. This family-work balance is quite different from what people experience in the United States and in many other countries around the world.[34] The transition from dictatorship to newly emerging democracy since 1989 undoubtedly has contributed to Paraguayans' positive opinions about the quality of their everyday lives. The use of the Guaraní language on television and radio, especially in the early morning hours, is widely welcomed, too, and represents an inclusive change in the presentation of mass media and popular culture.[35]

Paraguay is the only country in the Western Hemisphere where an indigenous language, in this case Guaraní (part of the Tupí-Guaraní language family in South America), is more widely spoken than a European language, in this case Spanish. In 2020, some 90 percent of Paraguayans speak Guaraní. According to the 2002 census, which covered 86.6 percent of the country's population of about six million people, 58.3 percent of the population were bilingual Guaraní and Spanish speakers; 27.6 percent were monolingual Guaraní speakers; and 8.2 percent only spoke Spanish.[36] The richness of expression in the Native language makes it a favorite to be spoken in the streets of Asunción, but especially in the rural areas of the country. Although Guaraní is now a required subject in middle schools and is even a college major, Spanish remains the predominant language of government, the courts, the professions, schools, and the news media. Paraguayan citizens gained the legal right to have access to public information in Spanish and Guaraní under the new 1992 Paraguayan constitution, which declared Guaraní and Spanish to be Paraguay's two official languages. Other Native languages spoken by some seventeen different ethnicities were also recognized in the 1992 constitution as part of the country's cultural heritage. After three years of work in 2018, Paraguay's Academia de la Lengua Guaraní (Academy of the Guaraní Language) published its first official grammar, which utilized grammars and dictionaries dating back to 1640, written by Jesuits who relied on Guaraní village elders as informants in the early reducciones of colonial Paraguay.[37]

The following chapters pay tribute to Paraguay's cultural characteristics and serve to enlighten us how Paraguayans have embraced their new spirit of democracy. Like *ñanduti* (intricate spider-web lace) woven by artisans in Paraguay, this collection of essays underscores important patterns and threads that enable us to understand the texture of the country's society, economy, natural environment, and political culture, which earlier was overwhelmingly dominated by strongmen and the conservative Colorado Party, along with the military and large landowners. The son of a German immigrant and a Paraguayan mother, General Alfredo Stroessner (who spoke Guaraní and Spanish) came to govern through a military coup d'état in 1954. The story of Dr. Joel Filártiga as depicted in the Hollywood film *One Man's War* (1991), directed by Sérgio Toledo and featuring Anthony Hopkins, portrays well how under Stroessner the political reality of the country was such that human rights were not well respected and individuals who were outspoken political critics along with their family members were subjected to political intimidation, torture, and even murder. The film is an excellent starting point for those wishing to understand aspects of modern Paraguay, the impact of authoritarian regimes on society, and the Filártiga family's courageous struggle for human rights and justice under a brutal dictatorship.[38]

Stroessner ruled through fear and intimidation. On one occasion, a school principal in Ybycuí was rumored to have raised questions about the president's declining health; she was removed from her position and banned for life from employment in public service. Tossing political opponents from airplanes alive without a parachute was a known practice among security agents of Paraguay and other military regimes in the Southern Cone during the mid- to late 1970s, which murdered political opponents and filled clandestine cemeteries.[39] On a lighter note, plays such as *El comisario del Valle Lorito* (The police chief from the Valley of the Little Parrot), written by Mario Halley Mora as a satire of Stroessner's authoritarian rule during the 1960s and 1970s, have been performed in Guaraní in major venues in Asunción and Buenos Aires, and in community theaters and schools, with success.

The essays in this volume are a rich sampling by both junior and well-established scholars from a variety of academic disciplines. The volume provides an important link between 1989 and 2019, moving beyond the period of transition aptly analyzed in *The Transition to Democracy in Paraguay* (1993), edited by Peter Lambert and Andrew Nickson, and the fine work by René D. Harder Horst, *The Stroessner Regime and Indigenous Resistance in Paraguay* (2007).[40] General Stroessner left a strong authoritarian legacy, which still has an impact on Paraguay's political culture today, in which the conservative Colorado Party continues to dominate much of the political landscape. Yet, the country has transitioned to a modern democracy. How has political change affected Paraguayans, especially the country's small indigenous population?

The opening chapter by René D. Harder Horst demonstrates how Paraguay's indigenous peoples have been participating in national society and politics to a greater extent than ever before. Based on interviews, he shows how indigenous people influenced legislators in the preparation of the 1992 constitution and thereby contributed to the vision of a multiethnic society in a new, democratic Paraguay.[41] His valuable chapter enables us to understand how the encounter between indigenous peoples in the Chaco and Pope John Paul II in May 1988 contributed to the collapse of the Stroessner regime. In chapter 2, American anthropologist Richard K. Reed examines the migration of the Guaraní to urban settings by telling the story of a young Guaraní woman, Lali-puku, and her family. Reed looks at strands in a larger pattern in which greater numbers of Guaraní and Ache peoples have migrated into the three major urban centers of Paraguay—Asunción, Encarnación, and Ciudad del Este—to seek greater employment opportunities. His important essay enables us to understand how land tenure inequalities and deforestation have had a disproportionate impact on Paraguay's indigenous population, whose lives are intricately tied to their physical environment.

In chapter 3, Paraguayan anthropologist Paola Canova examines the relationship between indigenous urbanity and land claims of the Ayoreo, indigenous peoples in a Mennonite colony in the Chaco, Paraguay's arid western region. She enables us to appreciate the political strategies of the Ayoreo to secure an urban space in Filadelfia, where these indigenous peoples can put forth their land claims by having a greater presence in the community. Her outstanding essay demonstrates the complexities of the urban experiences of indigenous peoples in the Chaco in today's world. She also carefully traces the labor history of the Ayoreo since the early twentieth century. In chapter 4, Paraguayan scholars Sarah Cerna Villagra, Sara Villalba Portillo, Eduardo Tamayo Belda, and Roque Mereles Pintos provide an overview of the major political trends in the country since 1989. The coauthors note the similarities between the two major political parties and the key features of the major political changes that took place in 2008. Their essay provides a meaningful examination of the 1992 Paraguayan constitution, which reshaped the institutional structure of the country's society as well as its authoritarian culture. American political scientist Brian Turner, in "Gender Quotas and Women's Political Identities in Paraguay," helps us understand Paraguayan women's continuing struggle for political rights and equality; Paraguay was indeed the last country in the Americas to grant women the right to vote, in 1961. Paraguayan women, he shows, have since then built successful political careers and gained positions at the top of political parties. Finally, American economist Melissa Birch analyzes the regional organization of Mercosur, which enables us to understand how Paraguay has benefited economically from its participation in the largest trading bloc in Latin America, as its poorest member. Together, these chapters provide new understandings of how Paraguay has become more integrated in the economies and societies of Latin America, and changed in unexpected ways.

Notes

1. World Bank, Databank for Paraguay, Global Economic Prospects, https://data.worldbank.org/country/paraguay, accessed March 16, 2020. According to the World Bank, Paraguay's per capita income in 2018, the most recent year for which data are available, is $5,821.80, about one-third of the per capita income in Chile.

2. "In Paraguay, Rapid Deforestation Is the Price of an Economic Boom," interview with Joel E. Correia, *World Politics Review*, February 1, 2019, https://www.worldpoliticsreview.com/trend-lines/27344/in-paraguay-rapid-deforestation-is-the-price-of-an-economic-boom.

3. Doña Isabel de Guevara's letter of July 2, 1556, was published in Luis G. Benítez, *Historia cultural: Reseña de su evolución en el Paraguay* (Asunción: Editorial El Arte, 1966), 75–76.

4. Philip Raine, *Paraguay* (New Brunswick, NJ: Scarecrow Press, 1956), 9–28; and Elman R. Service, *Spanish-Guaraní Relations in Early Colonial Paraguay* (Ann Arbor: University of Michigan Press, 1954), 54.

5. Pastor Urbieta Rojas, "Una paraguaya en la segunda fundación de Buenos Aires," *Revista del Ateneo Paraguayo* 3 (March 1970): 7.

6. Jesuit Pierre François Xavier de Charlevoix (1682–1761) mentions that in the language of some indigenous peoples, the word "Paraguay" came from the shape of the lake from which the river begins, as if it were a crown, referring to the lake of the Xarayes. Pierre François Xavier de Charlevoix, *Histoire du Paraguay*, 6 vols. (Paris: Ganeau et al., 1757), 1:5.

7. Barbara Ganson, *The Guaraní under Spanish Rule in the Río de la Plata* (Stanford, CA: Stanford University Press, 2003), 72–79.

8. Antonio Ruiz de Montoya, *The Spiritual Conquest: Early Years of the Jesuit Missions in Paraguay* (1639), trans. Barbara A. Ganson and Clinia M. Saffi (Boston: Institute of Jesuit Sources, Boston College, 2017), 229.

9. Paraguayan historian Olinda Massare de Kostianovsky, in her work *La instruccíon pública en la época colonial*, contends that the schools in the missions were for boys and girls and that girls were educated in cooking, weaving, and other subjects at separate times. She writes: "La permanencia del niño era generalmente tres horas a la mañana y tres horas por la tarde, admitiéndose niñas pero enseñandoles por separado" (The boys generally studied three hours in the morning and three hours in the afternoon; the girls studied apart from them). Olinda Massare de Kostianovsky, *La instruccíon pública en la época colonial* (Asunción: n.p., 1975), 110.

10. For further analysis, see Barbara Ganson, "A Patriarchal Society in the Río de la Plata: Adultery and the Double Standard at Mission Jesús de Tavarangue, 1782," in *Cultural Worlds of the Jesuits in Colonial Latin America*, ed. Linda Newson, 91–110 (London: Institute of Latin American Studies, School of Advanced Study, University of London, 2020).

11. Ernesto J. Maeder and Alfredo S. C. Bolsi, "La poblacion guaraní de las misiones jesuíticas: Evolucion y características, 1671–1767," *Cuadernos de Geohistoria Regional*, no. 4 (1985): 5; and Ganson, *The Guaraní under Spanish Rule*, 53.

12. The term in early modern Europe was "mechanical arts," as "technology" is a more modern word that first appeared in print in 1831. Pamela O. Long and Robert C. Post, introduction to *Technology and Society in Ming China (1368–1644)*, by Francesca Bray (Washington, DC: American Historical Association, 2000), vii–ix.

13. Ganson, *The Guaraní under Spanish Rule*, 108–11.

14. José Cayetano Paravicino, "Carta a Su Majestad dando informe de la visita pastoral hecha a todos los pueblos de la provincia," Asunción, November 21, 1744. Gondra Collection, MG 1035a, Benson Latin American Collection, University of Texas at Austin.

15. José de Cardiel, S.J., *Compendio de la historia del Paraguay* (1780) (Buenos Aires: Secretaría de Cultura de la Nación, 1994), 202.

16. Bernardo Nusdorffer, S.J., "Segunda parte de lo sucedido en las doctrinas . . ." Biblioteca Nacional de Rio de Janeiro, Coleção de Angelis, Seção de Manuscritos, Roll 31846, Defensa de los Jesuítas, 1.2.34, Guerra de los Guaraníes, 8.2.25, fol. 17.

17. Ganson, *The Guaraní under Spanish Rule*, 141.

18. John Hoyt Williams, "Observations on the Paraguayan Census of 1846," *Hispanic American Historical Review* 56, no. 3 (August 1976): 424–37.

19. James Schofield Saeger, *Francisco Solano López and the Ruination of Paraguay: Honor and Egocentrism* (Plymouth, Devon, England: Rowman and Littlefield, 2007). Solano López is a highly controversial figure. See Bridget María Chesterton, *The Grandchildren of Solano López* (Albuquerque: University of New Mexico Press, 2013).

20. Barbara Ganson, "Following Their Children into Battle: Women at War in Paraguay, 1864–1870." *The Americas* 46, no. 3 (January 1990): 335–71.

21. Vera Blinn Reber, "A Case of Total War: Paraguay, 1864–1870," *Journal of Iberian and Latin American Research* 5, no. 1 (1999): 15–40; Vera Blinn Reber, "The Demographics of Paraguay: A Reinterpretation of the Great War, 1864–70," *Hispanic American Historical Review* 68, no. 2 (May 1988): 289–319; Thomas L. Whigham and Barbara Potthast, "Some Strong Reservations: A Critique of Vera Blinn Reber's 'The Demographics of Paraguay: A Reinterpretation of the Great War, 1864–70,'" *Hispanic American Historical Review* 70, no. 4 (November 1990): 667–76; Thomas L. Whigham and Barbara Potthast, "The Paraguayan Rosetta Stone: New Insights into the Demographics of the Paraguay War, 1864–1870," *Latin American Research Review* 34, no. 1 (1999): 174–86; Jan M. G. Kleinpenning, "Strong Reservations about 'New Insights into the Demographics of the Paraguayan War,'" *Latin American Research Review* 37, no. 3 (2002): 137–42; and Thomas L. Whigham and Barbara Potthast, "Refining the Numbers: A Response to Reber and Kleinpenning," *Latin American Research Review* 37, no. 3 (2002): 143–48.

22. Historian Susan Migden Socolow notes that birthrates for illegitimate children were generally higher for *castas* (peoples of mixed race); see *The Women of Colonial Latin America*, 2nd ed. (Cambridge: Cambridge University Press, 2015), 80. We have no comparable data for the nineteenth century for this region.

23. Harris Gaylord Warren, *Rebirth of the Paraguayan Republic: The First Colorado Era, 1878–1904* (Pittsburgh: University of Pittsburgh Press, 1986); and Harris Gaylord Warren, *Paraguay and the Triple Alliance: The Postwar Decade, 1869–1878* (Austin: Institute of Latin American Studies, University of Texas, 1978).

24. The Benson Latin American Collection at the University of Texas at Austin acquired President Gondra's vast library, including more than seven thousand books, several hundred maps, and written or typed copies of manuscripts from the Archivo General de Indias in Seville, Spain (which have been catalogued) concerning Paraguay's claim to the Chaco but also a variety of other topics since the sixteenth century.

25. Harris Gaylord Warren, *Paraguay: An Informal History* (Norman: University of Oklahoma Press, 1949), 269.

26. Miguel Carter, "The Role of the Paraguayan Catholic Church in the Downfall of the Stroessner Regime," *Journal of Interamerican Studies and World Affairs* 32, no. 4 (Winter 1990): 67–121.

27. "Andrés Rodríguez Dies at 72; Overthrew Paraguay Dictator," *New York Times*, April 22, 1997.

28. *Oxford Atlas of the World*, 26th ed. (New York: Oxford University Press, 2019), 56, 82.

29. Barbara Ganson, "Contacto intercultural: Un estudio de los payaguaes del Paraguay, 1528–1870," *Suplemento Antropológico* (Centro de Estudios Antropológicos, Universidad Católica de Asunción) 24, no. 1 (June 1989): 79–121; and Barbara Ganson, "The Evueví of Paraguay: Adaptive Strategies and Responses to Colonialism, 1528–1811," *The Americas* 45, no. 4 (April 1989): 461–88.

30. "In Paraguay, Rapid Deforestation Is the Price of an Economic Boom," interview with Joel E. Correia.

31. Miguel Chase Sardi, "Situación de los indígenas en el Paraguay," *América Indígena* 44, no. 3 (July–September 1989): 419–30. In 1982, Paraguay's Native peoples represented less than 2 percent of the population, or 38,703 persons.

32. Dirección General de Estadística, Encuestas y Censos, *Pueblos indígenas en el Paraguay: Resultados finales de población y viviendas, 2012* (Fernando de la Mora, Paraguay: Gobierno Nacional, December 2014), 49–51. Currently, there is no indigenous census in Paraguay; the last was in 2012.

33. José A. Perasso and Jorge Vera, *La cultura Guaraní en el Paraguay contemporaneo (etnografía ava-kue-Chiripá)* (Asunción: RP Ediciones, 1987), 90.

34. Josh Hafner, "The Misery Is Real: A Third of the World Is Stressed, Worried and in Pain, Gallup Report Finds," *USA Today*, April 25, 2019.

35. Joan Rubin, *National Bilingualism in Paraguay* (The Hague: Mouton, 1968). The popularity of the Guaraní language today is reflected in the 2015 film *La Chiperita* (directed by Hugo Cataldo), a love story, which has garnered international attention.

36. Lenka Zajicova, "La ley de lenguas paraguaya de 2010: Evolución y análisis," *Revista Internacional de Lingüística Iberoamericana* 10 (2012): 110.

37. The Spanish Crown instructed Catholic missionaries to study indigenous languages and cultures, and to teach Guaraní males how to read and write in their native language using the Roman alphabet, thus helping to preserve the language. Franciscan missionary Luis de Bolaños (1539?–1626) produced the first Guaraní dictionary, grammar, and catechism in Paraguay, which was approved in Lima in 1583. Jesuit missionary Antonio Ruiz de Montoya (1585–1652) published a Guaraní-Spanish dictionary in 1640. Ruiz de Montoya relied on the works of Jesuit José de Anchieta (1534–1597), who published a grammar of the Tupí language in Coimbra, Portugal, in 1595, for the writing of his works *Arte y vocabulario de la lengua Guaraní* (Art and vocabulary of the Guaraní language, 1722) and *Arte de la lengua Guaraní* (Art of the Guaraní language, 1724); and his memoir, *Conquista espiritual hecho por los religiosos de la Compañía de Jesús: En las provincias del Paraguay, Paraná, Uruguay, y Tapé* (The spiritual conquest accomplished by the religious of the Society of Jesus in the provinces of Paraguay, Paraná, Uruguay, and Tapé, 1639). A bilingual edition of *The Spiritual Conquest* (2017), translated by Barbara Ganson and Clinia Saffi, furthers our understanding of Paraguay's rich Native past, problems of Indian slavery, and the origins of the region's distinctive cultural hybridity.

38. Graziella Corvalán, "La vitalidad en la lengua guaraní en el Paraguay," *Población y Desarrollo* 30 (December 2005): 1–16; and Capucine Boidin, "La política de educación bilingüe guaraní español en el Paraguay de los años 90," *Revista Paraguaya de Sociología* 36, no. 105 (May–August 1999): 147–58.

39. Antônio Augusto Cançado Trindade, "Recollection of the International Adjudication of Massacre Cases: In Relevance for Transitional Justice and Beyond," in *The Role of Courts in Transitional Justice: Voices from Latin America and Spain*, ed. Jessica Almqvist and Carlos Espósito (Abingdon, Oxon., England: Routledge, 2012), 17–30.

40. Peter Lambert and Andrew Nickson, eds., *The Transition to Democracy in Paraguay* (Basingstoke, Hants., England: Macmillan, 1997); and René D. Harder Horst, *The Stroessner Regime and Indigenous Resistance in Paraguay* (Gainesville: University Press of Florida, 2007).

41. Harder Horst, *The Stroessner Regime and Indigenous Resistance*, 166.

René D. Harder Horst

---

one INDIGENOUS PEOPLE IN PARAGUAY AND LATIN AMERICA'S MOVE TO DEMOCRACY

A Momentous Encounter

On the evening of May 17, 1988, hundreds of Indigenous people and Bishop Lucio Alfert welcomed Pope John Paul II to the small Paraguayan town of Mariscal Estigarribia. Located in the dry, western Chaco, the small community was just about as far from anywhere that still had an airstrip to receive the papal entourage. Mariscal, as locals call the village, featured an army base and a Catholic mission to the local Nivaclé Indigenous people. In front of the large assembly of hundreds of Native people from Paraguay, Brazil, Argentina, and Bolivia who had arrived to meet the pope, the bishop quickly took his seat and instead invited Enenlhit leader René Ramírez to the podium. Just the year before, Ramírez had led his community and people through a difficult, long, but ultimately successful legal battle to recover their ancestral territory at Riacho Mosquito in the lower Chaco. The positive outcome of the Maskoy struggle for land led Catholic authorities to choose Ramírez to address the pontiff. The leader had traveled for a year, asking other Native people around the country: "If you could talk with the pope, what would you want to say to him?"[1] Ramírez and church authorities then assembled his collection of testimonies into a moving oration.

Confidently delivering the most significant speech of his life, Ramírez explained to the surprised pontiff that in his country there was more land available for cows than for the Indigenous people.

> We are a living testimony to the people who have lived in these continents before they were called "Americas." We are the inheritors of their cultures and their spiritual richness. We feel strongly united together with you. We speak different languages and have different cultures and religions, yet we share the same history,

the same sufferings, and the same concerns.... The Whites tell us that we must become civilized. We invite the Whites to be civilized and respect us as people, respect our communities and our leaders, respect our lands and our forests, and return to us even just a little of what they have taken away from us. We wish to be friends of all the Paraguayans. We want them to let us live in peace.[2]

John Paul II began to cry when he realized that the abrupt change in the program was purposeful, and he listened attentively to the Indigenous testimony. The pontiff then responded compassionately in Guaraní, "Ymá guivéma aimese penendive; ha peina âga, aimema pendeapytepe" ("For a long time I have wanted to be with you. And now here I am, I am with you"). Then the pope asked if they could understand him. When the assembly shouted back with a resounding shout of "heẽ," or "yes" in Guaraní, John Paul II completely won over the crowd by declaring that he then should also become a missionary in the Chaco.[3]

Continuing in Spanish, the pontiff expressed his support and called on those in power to respect Native peoples and lands.

Your desires for general improvements are just. Most importantly, you desire respect as persons and that your human and civil rights be recognized and protected. I know the serious problems that you face, particularly in reference to your land ownership and property titles. For these I appeal to the sense of justice and humanity by those responsible so they defend the have-nots. From the beginning of evangelization in these lands, the Church defended the liberty and dignity of the Indigenous people, and missionaries often spoke against the abuses to which your ancestors were at times subject.... You desire to make your own choices about your people's development, and request respect for your cultures and free decisions to develop your economic and human levels by way of education that joins your traditional values with advances in today's world.[4]

The large gathering with the pontiff turned into a pan-Indigenous celebration. People discussed and compared their situations over the next three days and long into the nights as they danced, talked, and celebrated their eventful meeting. The gathering reveals the way in which, by the late 1980s, Native people throughout Latin America were organizing themselves, pushing authorities to respect their legal rights and government legislation, and networking with Indigenous people elsewhere throughout the hemisphere.

Embarrassed by the unexpected media victory that Indigenous people had scored, the Paraguayan dictator, Alfredo Stroessner, immediately tried to assassinate Ramírez. The Enenlhit leader fled into hiding, living in the woods near his home at Puerto Casado, on the western banks of the upper Paraguay River, 180 nautical miles north of the capital, Asunción. He explained later that while regime assassins searched for him, his community clandestinely supplied him with food and news about developments in the capital. Not until Stroessner's thirty-five-year regime finally collapsed eight months later, in January 1989, was Ramírez able to return home. My interview with the Enenlhit leader, in May 2001, took place during the first time in over ten years that Ramírez had ventured to return to Asunción, the center of political activity in the nation.[5] Even though by that time Paraguay boasted a democratic government, civil liberties, and a new constitution, fears of retaliation still haunted Ramírez daily and kept many Native people living in fear.

René Ramírez clearly understood that his presentation to the pope had been part of the groundswell of popular opposition to the Stroessner regime and a milestone for Indigenous people throughout southern Latin America who desired greater participation in government. Authorities at the time recognized that the encounter between the pontiff and the Indigenous people played a role in furthering Paraguay's political change. Ramírez later emphasized to me, "My virtuous protest was that we wanted liberty in democracy and that Indigenous people be treated as humans, as people who were the original inhabitants of this country. We wanted our land, our territory, since we were no longer able to practice our culture."[6]

Scholars support this leader's declaration about growing Indigenous desires for political participation and a democratic opening. Political scientist Donna Lee Van Cott includes the Paraguayan example in her study of nations in which the militarization of relations with Native people and the resulting Indigenous responses have helped move nations away from authoritarian rule.[7] In his study of the Catholic Church and the end of the Stroessner regime, political scientist Miguel Carter notes the Indigenous meeting with Pope John Paul II as an important step in the erosion of public support for the dictator.[8] Paraguayan lawyer Esther Prieto shows that Catholic Church support for Indigenous people moved Paraguay toward a democratic future through their lobby for and inclusion in the new constitution of 1992.[9] The Native presentation to the pope brought together Indigenous people throughout the Southern Cone of Latin America and symbolized their growing participation in national and continental events. No longer would Latin American leaders easily marginalize Native people in their midst.

An Indigenous Awakening in Latin America

The Indigenous meeting with the Catholic pontiff in the western Chaco is an example of the awakening of Indigenous activism and protests that punctuated the last decades of the twentieth century in Latin America. From Chile to Colombia to Brazil, from Paraguay to Guatemala to Mexico, Native people took every available opportunity to communicate their voices and anger over difficult living conditions and lack of political representation. Only a few months later, in February 1989, an even more impressive assembly of three thousand Kayapo people and their allies converged on the Brazilian town of Altamira to protest plans for the construction of hydroelectric dams along the Xingu and Iriri Rivers. The project would have displaced twenty-five thousand people in eighteen Native groups from dozens of communities. Plans to develop the forest in Brazil had earlier passed unnoticed. This time, though, led by Kayapo leader Raoni with his notable lip plug and his rock star ally Sting, the massive demonstration captured widespread media attention, recruited ample international support, and finally put the dam projects on hold. It seemed as though the world had woken up and suddenly realized that there were still Indigenous people in Latin America who were enduring difficult conditions. Those people were now doing something about their plight by using the media to publicize their interactions with the states within which they were enveloped. These dramatic events serve as good examples of ways that Indigenous people in Latin America have recently captured world attention. Yet Indigenous people have been adapting to and reacting against non-Indigenous people since they first made contact with outside peoples. This chapter explains how Indigenous people in Paraguay participated in the popular movement that ended the Stroessner dictatorship, represented an example of Native protests taking place throughout Latin America, and helped move the nation toward a different political future.

Growing International Connections for Indigenous Peoples in Paraguay

Given the traditional insular perception of Paraguay and the isolated Indigenous communities within its boundaries, it might seem logical that Native leaders in rural areas of the nation would have been isolated from Indigenous movements and political developments taking place elsewhere in the hemisphere and the world. The meeting with the pontiff reveals that, on the contrary, Indigenous people were aware of broader currents of Native organization that were changing Latin America. What connected international movements with Native people in rural Paraguay? Throughout the 1970s and 1980s, important opportunities exposed Indigenous people in Paraguay to Native movements and political transformations outside of their country. As Alison Brysk has shown, the Native rights movement "was born transnational," encouraged by anthropologists who first met at the Barbados Conference in 1971.[10] Two anthropologists from Paraguay, Georg Grünberg and Miguel Chase Sardi, attended the conference and contributed that Native people in their nation were in danger of imminent extinction.[11] The assembly widely disseminated its Declaration of Barbados, which promised to improve Native conditions, and the Catholic Church in Paraguay publicized the work to Native communities by sponsoring a congress in Asunción that disseminated the Barbados conclusions to Native people in Paraguay.[12]

Anthropologists in Paraguay promptly organized an NGO named Marandú, Guaraní for "information," and the team visited Native communities throughout Paraguay to explain how to secure documentation and health care, and to encourage broader Indigenous organization. In 1974, Marandú hosted Native leaders from Argentina, Bolivia, Brazil, Venezuela, and Paraguay at their center in Asunción, further linking people in Paraguay with Native organizations abroad. Following intense deliberations, the assembly finally declared: "We Proclaim the Validity of our Cultures before the men of all the earth.... [S]trangers of Indigenous communities need to realize that we are united, and that in the future it will be more difficult to continue the extermination of our brothers."[13] Indigenous leaders accused missionaries and governments of perpetrating five centuries of abuse, and they demanded health care and legal protection.

The following year, Marandú sent Nivaclé leader Alberto Santacruz and Western Guaraní Severo Flores to an international congress for Native people in Florida, in the United States. Native representatives from Paraguay also visited Indigenous gatherings in Canada and Washington, DC.[14] These examples show that, because of modern communications and the awakening of Indigenous political activism, Native people even in Paraguay were aware of and exposed to international Indigenous movements on a continental and international level.[15]

Concerned about deteriorating Indigenous conditions and growing attacks on their resources and communities, thirty-five Indigenous people and anthropologists from throughout the continent met again in 1977 at the Second Meeting of Barbados. This time, Native people from Guatemala and Páez representatives from Colombia risked their lives to travel secretly to Barbados. Some of the participants were already in hiding or in exile. Indigenous leaders quickly made clear their desire to take charge of their own ethnic affairs and political goals, which caused tensions with non-Indigenous advocates who saw Native participants as only advisers. Indigenous delegates declared themselves victims of physical and cultural domination and rejected educational efforts by outsiders as attempts to divide their peoples. They pushed to unite Indigenous peoples and for an analysis of ways outsiders had colonized, dominated, and exploited their peoples. Native representatives pushed for Native participation in politics as a way to improve their conditions and secure broader international support.[16] Native people began to speak as a united bloc.

These gatherings made Indigenous organizational goals and the limitations that Native activists faced abundantly clear: it was difficult to convince even their advocates to recognize their desire to achieve self-agency, self-representation, and self-determination in their own way, through their own choices and systems of knowledge. The Indigenous leaders from Paraguay who had participated in Barbados, Santacruz and Flores, described the ways in which Native people in Paraguay were organizing themselves. Their references to self-management and respect for cultural diversity reveal that they had acquired new tools to build ethnic consciousness and now demanded equal treatment before the law.[17]

The Last Year of Dictatorship for Indigenous People in Paraguay

Indigenous organization in Paraguay continued to grow over the next decades, even as the dictator prolonged his regime. By 1988, Stroessner's last year in power, however, the dynamics that had created the Cold War between the two world superpowers had changed. The general secretary of the Communist Party of the Soviet Union, Mikhail Gorbachev, diminished Soviet control over Eastern Europe, began gradual democratization of the Soviet Union, and ultimately even met with US president George H. W. Bush in December 1989. Waning Soviet power made US military allies in Latin America, including dictators such as Stroessner, irrelevant and inconvenient to their erstwhile northern ally.[18] Shifting geopolitical relations inevitably influenced even social and political relations in far-off Paraguay.

Even as they established broader liaisons within the nation in which they lived and forged international connections, Indigenous people in Paraguay mobilized broadly to demand the return of the lands they claimed as homelands; their struggles grew desperate throughout the countryside during those tense years.

In eastern Paraguay especially, conditions were dire: non-Indians displaced more than two dozen Guaraní communities in 1988 alone. Well organized by then, Native groups joined forces, and their protests focused attention on the regime's corruption and human rights abuses.

Stroessner emphasized the expansion of agricultural production in rural areas to build his nation's export production, and it was this extension of ranching and crops that especially threatened Native lands. On January 19, 1988, the Campos Morombí ranch tried to evict a community of Mbyá Guaraní from their homes at Arroyo Mbói, which was located within the ranch's property. Ranch owner Blas Riquelme was a formidable threat: he had earlier been the president of the national Chamber of Industry and wielded significant political power. When burning the Mbyá homes to the ground did not force their occupants off his land, the rancher tried to bribe the people to leave. The Mbyá leaders joined neighboring communities and denounced Riquelme at the Institute of Rural Welfare and the National Indigenous Institute, to certain NGOs, and finally to the Catholic Church itself.[19] The vigorous Mbyá lobby finally convinced Stroessner to expropriate 1,200 hectares from Riquelme for the Indigenous community.[20] News about threats to Indigenous lands bolstered groups opposing the dictator in the capital. In preparation for national elections in February, the Catholic Church published the *Diálogo Nacional*, a call for a democratic opening that featured Native rights.[21] Indigenous people prominently demanded, in this document, to be considered "authentic nations" within a free Paraguay, an unprecedented and bold claim that reveals a high level of awareness about international events and Indigenous movements abroad.

A more violent conflict over land took place in northeastern Paraguay in August 1988, at the Paï Tavyterã community of Takuaguy Oygue. An armed cavalry division suddenly burst into the community, located in Amambay Province, the site of one of the last virgin forests in the area. Colonel Lino Oviedo and eight of his soldiers, dressed in camouflage and shouldering automatic weapons, threatened to kill the frightened people if they fled in search of help. Sixty army peons began to cut down trees with chainsaws and drag the logs out of the community's woods with bulldozers. Within only one week, the workers had taken down so many trees that twenty army trucks were needed to haul the logs, twice daily, to sell in the state capital of Pedro Juan Caballero.[22] Community leaders escaped under cover of darkness and denounced the attack in Asunción, adding that soldiers had also ravaged their fields of manioc, corn, and beans.[23]

Hitting a virtual brick wall in the capital at regime agencies when publicizing the attack, sixteen neighboring communities decided late in September that they had nothing to lose by resorting to fear and force to defend their people's natural resources. "On that occasion," leaders recalled, "we affirmed, 'either us or the end of the world,' and we decided, given the authorities' indifference, to expel the invaders from our lands."[24] A few days later, seventy Paï Tavyterã men, including allies from surrounding communities, painted themselves for battle. Carrying bows and arrows and screaming, the warriors fell upon the *paraguayos* clearing the trees. The terrified soldiers fled in disarray, frightened nearly to death by the horde of yelling warriors. The attackers took and held a few prisoners for a few days but released them when the army pledged to leave.[25]

The Paï Tavyterã victory, like so many empty regime promises of the past, again proved illusory. Even in Stroessner's weakened position, opportunities for his subordinates to enrich themselves at the expense of impoverished peasants were too tempting. Six days later, a militia troop entered Takuaguy Oygue again, firing into the air with automatic weapons to disperse the terrified people. Soldiers detained seven men and threatened to kill any other leaders they could catch. The invaders next destroyed Native corn and watermelon plantations and burned down community houses. The entire Paï Tavyterã community fled for good. Mobilizing heavy earth-moving equipment, soldiers leveled the woods and sold the lumber, assessed at over US$400,000, to Brazilian businesses.[26]

Another conflict over land that year culminated in the neighboring department of Caaguazú, where for many years Mbyá communities had struggled over land with Mennonite settlers at their colony of Sommerfeld. The immigrants, originally from Canada, harassed and pressured Natives to abandon their homes, by then encircled and cut off from their resources by the settlers' farms and fields. Native people were obviously clearly aware of both their legal rights and of the regime's refusal to enforce its own legislation. After settlers destroyed six communities, three Mbyá communities in desperation took the regime's National Indigenous Institute to court for not having defended their interests. Leader Nemecio Flores declared:

> We can no longer live in peace because they are constantly harassing us. Not long ago they opened a ranch and put cattle on the land one of us had used. They cut down all the trees and planted grass, because they say they are the owners and can do what they wish. Yet we also have rights here. . . . We realize that Law 904 [the Native Rights law passed in 1981 to appease foreign critics

of the regime's social policies] does not serve the *Indígenas* but only the Mennonites, because it seems like only they have rights here.[27]

By this time, Indigenous people were calling into question the actual legal foundation of the Paraguayan government and society and strongly showing their disagreement with the regime's social and economic goals that disadvantaged them.

Active Resistance Strengthened by Indigenous Cultural Heritage

One notable feature of Indigenous resistance during the last years of the regime was the way in which Native organizers grounded their opposition to outside threats in their cultural heritage, the perceived notion that they carried on a legacy of resistance from their ancestors. Avá Guaraní political and religious leaders from nine communities in the department of Alto Paraná, for example, gathered during August 25–27, 1988, for an *aty-guasú*, an extraordinary assembly. Together they declared:

> All the members of the Alto Paraná communities have come together . . . so that we can live in our traditional system as our God and our grandparents have left us our way of life. . . . We have prayed much and have talked about our way of life. We have also debated . . . the needs we have to secure our lands. We have seen that no outsider to our communities can stay with us because they influence us negatively. All the Chiripá [Avá Guaraní] communities . . . need to live as true Guaraní by our traditional way of life. . . . In sacred dances, white perfumes and decorations should not be used.[28]

There were in reality few visible cultural differences anymore between the Avá Guaraní and the Paraguayan peasant majority, both originally of Indigenous ancestry. The ongoing defense of their resources and way of life, though, encouraged these people to protect what they identified as important cultural distinctions. The most important of these ethnic markers was agroforestry. The Guaraní still harvested and sold forest resources for cash, even as they gathered, gardened, hunted, and raised domestic animals for subsistence.[29] The Guaraní's economy had traditionally strengthened their own communal fabric without destroying the actual forest canopy that allowed their way of life to endure. By the 1980s, Native people in Paraguay worked for cash on ranches and sold forest resources through commercial exchanges to the *okapeguá*, the "people of the outside."[30] Both religion and location, as well as a perceived communal cultural heritage, strengthened Guaraní determination to keep a Native identity and way of life.

The Maskoy people, who had mobilized to recover ancestral territories at Riacho Mosquito in previous years, for instance, relied on authority structures they had re-created at Puerto Casado. As René Ramírez recalled, it was the elders (*los ancianos*) at their community of Pueblito Indio who had led their struggle. Insightfully, the elders insisted that the people themselves initiate, fund, and support their push for land in order to avoid creating dependencies on outsiders who might subvert their original goals. Los ancianos grounded their decisions in what they understood to be their community's traditional ways. Ramírez recounted: "The elders were always my consultants and advisers. They guided and awakened me to the need to know our culture and way of thinking" to support the struggle.[31]

While group elders may have directed the process, the Maskoy wisely also sought alliances with opponents of the regime to bolster their political claims. The tribes found their primary advocates in the Catholic Church. Even after bishops toned down their criticism of the dictatorship following the Third Latin American Episcopal Conference (1979) in Puebla, Mexico, they still supported Indigenous land claims, because this advocacy allowed the church to be involved with the lower classes without endangering its tenuous relations with the regime.[32]

By 1988, international support for Native conditions worldwide had increased. The NGOs Cultural Survival, OXFAM, and the Inter-American Foundation all supported the creation of local Indigenous organizations and enabled networking during these years, first with international supporters and then with national organizations. Native leaders then secured support from the Organization of American States and the International Labor Organization (ILO) of the UN, sparking a movement that by the Columbus Quincentenary of 1992 included hundreds of Native organizations.

Indigenous People and Democracy in Paraguay

Despite the regime's attempt to quiet René Ramírez after his encounter with the supreme Catholic authority, the political changes that followed the collapse of the regime in January 1989 presented an opportunity for both the Maskoy leader and Native communities throughout Paraguay to advance their people's political organization.

Indigenous people mobilized together as never before to claim the first constitutional recognition of their existence when General Andrés Rodríguez, the son-in-law who had deposed Stroessner, enacted a new code of law in 1992. A total of 134 Indigenous leaders, the largest such pan-Indigenous meeting ever recorded in Paraguay, gathered for three days late in May 1991 and requested participation in the constitutional assembly.[33] Leaders demanded that the new body of laws construct national unity "on a foundation of respect for the cultural diversity of the autochthonous peoples of the country."[34] Initially completely unsuccessful in Asunción, even more delegates from seventy communities met a second time on September 11 and 12 to demand land reform.[35] Contacts with Indigenous allies in Ecuador and also in Colombia, where Native people had won recognition in the 1991 constitutional reforms, encouraged Indigenous people in Paraguay to apply the 1992 antiquincentenary sentiment to their situation.[36] In a risky gamble, Indigenous leaders demanded that four Native representatives be allowed to participate directly in the constitutional convention and even requested the creation of a new cabinet ministry to represent Indigenous affairs.

The unprecedented gathering highlights the degree to which the struggle against the regime had forged a pan-Indigenous identity in Paraguay. By this time, Native peoples identified themselves as "nations" that had existed prior to European arrival. Their appropriation of Western political terminology and the collective name "the Indigenous peoples of Paraguay" shows the degree to which the struggle to protect and recover lands had changed Native people, and exactly how aware they were of Indigenous organization and movements taking place elsewhere in the continent. Clearly pragmatic, the Native move toward broader identification forced the state to entertain Indigenous demands. Pan-Indigenous organization additionally indicates the importance of church advocacy, because Catholic Church activists pressured the government to accept tribal rights in the constitution. The persistent Indigenous lobby finally bore fruit.[37] In February 1992, legislators agreed to include Indigenous rights and to allow Indigenous representatives to speak on the convention floor.

Meanwhile, René Ramírez, leader of the Maskoy recovery of Riacho Mosquito in July 1987 and the celebrated speaker who had addressed the pope, participated in the constitutional convention as a delegate for the Liberal Party, despite pressure from the local Colorado Party chapter, because of his dislike for the former regime. Liberal Party members respected him highly, Ramírez recalled, because he tried to hold them to the party regulations, which he had dutifully studied.

For the Enenlhit leader, there seems to have been no contradiction in representing the Liberal Party instead of the Native bloc. Nor did his political ambitions appear in his view incongruous with his former advocacy for communal land claims.[38] Ramírez's choices demonstrate a significant degree of familiarity with local politicians and close alliances with the national political system.

At last, on April 30, 1992, Paraguay's constitutional convention finally added a chapter on Indigenous rights. The Indigenous delegates explained in emotional voices how the articles would protect their people. Severo Flores thanked politicians for excluding Indigenous people from military conscription in the constitution.[39] The novelty of Indigenous participation in such an important national event charged the chamber; delegates punctuated each Indigenous statement with long rounds of applause.

The six articles that congressional delegates agreed to include as the fifth chapter of the new constitution marked a significant legal achievement for Indigenous peoples in Paraguay. The law guaranteed their right to "preserve and develop their ethnic identity within their respective habitats" and to practice their own political, social, economic, cultural, and religious organization. What is more, the state promised to provide enough property for communities to secure a living as they chose, and to respect "cultural peculiarities" in relation to formal education. Finally, the law pledged to defend Indigenous people from economic exploitation.[40] Indigenous peoples thus achieved their demands for greater legal recognition.

During the following days, the four Indigenous representatives, briefly celebrities featured by major media throughout Paraguay, took advantage of the public attention to reiterate their peoples' need for "more respect and better treatment" from those they still referred to as *paraguayos* and *blancos*.[41] The public merging of both Paraguayans and immigrants into one large non-Indian "other" shows the way in which the entire constitutional struggle had reinforced the Native sense of autonomous identity. Indigenous participants in the constitutional debates obviously regarded the new law of the land as a significant victory. They publicly expressed hope that the constitution would finally put an end to "white" discrimination."[42]

René Ramírez himself also clearly regarded constitutional inclusion as a step in the right direction.[43] Legal recognition of Indigenous rights, in his view, laid the foundation for Indigenous participation in national politics and increased the chance of improved conditions in the future. Still, the conflict over Riacho Mosquito, his presentation to the pontiff, and the constitutional struggle had clearly brought this leader closer to non-Indian political structures. Although he helped his people move back to Riacho Mosquito following their territorial victory, for instance, Ramírez remained behind at Puerto Casado among the people who chose to stay and work among the Paraguayans. The leader apparently felt no inconsistency in his choice to settle on a permanent basis in town rather than join his people on the land he had fought to recover. While Ramírez still identified with his Enenlhit people and their future, the struggle for land and political activism had also drawn him more closely into Paraguayan society.

Even as Indigenous people celebrated their victory, Paraguayan politicians also lauded the chapter on Indigenous rights. The new constitution repeated many of the earlier promises made in the Indigenous rights bill, Law 904 of 1981, to provide enough land for Indigenous communities to live on tribal territories according to their customary laws and religions. Politicians knew that, much like the earlier legislation, the new articles might serve to appease foreign critics of their nation and yet would have little application in reality, so they emphasized the guarantees for education and state assistance.[44] By the conclusion of the process, the Colorado politicians declared that Paraguay had finally achieved its elusive goal of Indigenous integration.[45]

Paraguay's New Constitution and the Continental Indigenous Movement

Paraguay's new constitution and similar legislation elsewhere during the 1990s marked Latin America's transition from military rule during the Cold War to democratic governance. Foreign human rights advocacy and international attention made it more difficult for national governments to sidestep Indigenous people and their growing organization. As a result, states developed new, politically correct strategies of control to manipulate their Native populations. To explain the strategy that emerged, Bolivian sociologist Silvia Rivera Cusicanqui developed the concept of "indio permitido," or "authorized Indian." This concept best explains the shift in attitude throughout the continent during the 1990s, in which governments tried to employ the use of cultural rights to divide and domesticate Indigenous movements. Governments framed Native rights during this time as a reward for cooperation from Native people, to allow them to organize as they wished as long as they did not call into question the fundamental privileges of the state. During the 1990s, then, nations updated their early twentieth century *indigenismo* by incorporating the current catchphrases "Indigenous rights" and "pluricultural tolerance" into their legislation in an attempt to tame the growing Indigenous militancy and placate national critics and foreign observers.

Paraguay had used this strategy back in 1981 with its Indigenous rights bill, but Colombia was the first country to apply the "authorized Indian" strategy to a national constitution. In its 1991 constitution, Colombia included significant Native rights. Indigenous participants in the constitutional convention included lawyer Francisco Rojas Birry from the Embera people, Guambiano leader Lorenzo Muelas, and Páez lawyer Alfonso Peña Chepe, who participated in the deliberations without legislative power. Their presence symbolized the image that Colombia was projecting: tolerance of minorities, pluralism, a rediscovered national identity, and national political effectiveness that was inclusive of broad popular participation, even of Native rights. The constitution employed minority rights to show how inclusively Colombia had incorporated the most marginalized into the nation by offering even Indigenous people legal protection.

Indigenous people also pushed for greater legal recognition in other nations. By the early 1990s in Bolivia, Native people who spoke at least one of thirty-four recognized Indigenous languages in the country formed 57 percent of the population. Highland Aymara people numbered 1.6 million, while there were 2.4 million Quechua also in the mountains; members of these peoples by now worked as farmers, miners, teachers, truck drivers, urban merchants, and even national congressional delegates. Native speakers in the Bolivian eastern lowlands numbered 260,000 in the Indigenous census of 1995; smaller groups there were the Araona, Paikoneka, and Yukuí; the Canichana, Chácobo, and Esse Ejja numbered from 2,000 to 3,000; larger groups included the Guarayu, Ts'iman, and Movima; while the largest groups of 40,000–60,000 included the Moxeño, Chiquitano (Besiro), and Guaraní. These peoples were largely agrarian but also included teachers, merchants, artisans, evangelical ministers, and national bureaucrats. During 1991, the lowland and highland Indigenous people joined in the March for Territory and Dignity, a seven-hundred-kilometer trek from the lowland jungle to La Paz to demand the defense of their property from logging interests and legal protection of their communal lands. This movement led to national recognition of four Indigenous territories and Bolivia's 1991 ratification of the ILO's Indigenous and Tribal Peoples Convention on the rights of Indigenous peoples.

Building on the example of these other nations, President Juan Carlos Wasmosy of Paraguay finally ratified the ILO statement on the rights of Indigenous communities into Law 234/93 in 1993 to demonstrate his nation's successful transition to democracy. Paraguay thus committed to "protect the rights of the Indigenous peoples to guarantee their integrity," and to defend their right "to use lands that have not been exclusively occupied by those groups, but to which they have had traditional access for their traditional and subsistence activities."[46] While the legislation was similar to Law 904, which Stroessner had passed in 1981 to quell foreign criticism, it is an example of another state response to increasingly organized and assertive Native populations in Paraguay, and throughout the Americas.

Conclusion

This chapter has shown that even though Alfredo Stroessner's regime discriminated against them and tried to clear them out of the path of rural economic development, Native people in Paraguay mobilized broadly and joined the popular opposition against the dictator. Linking forces with Indigenous movements elsewhere in Latin America by the late twentieth century and building on support by anthropologists, NGOs, and even some religious advocates, Indigenous peoples drew international attention to human rights abuses and the negative effects of regime development policies on the lower classes in Paraguay. Organizing broadly, Indigenous activists successfully pressured the nation to include Native rights in the new Paraguayan constitution that followed the collapse of the dictatorship. The transition into a different future for the nation would not prove easy for Indigenous people in Paraguay, and many of the regime's programs and policies continued to challenge their communities and people. The last years of the Stroessner regime promised, however, that Indigenous people would continue to help shape the future of the country in which they lived.

Notes

1. René Ramírez, personal interview by René D. Harder Horst, Asunción, Paraguay, May 21, 2001.
2. Ramírez, "Discurso de bienvenida."
3. Ibid.
4. Ibid.
5. Ramírez, personal interview.
6. Ibid.
7. Van Cott, *Indigenous Peoples and Democracy*, 2.
8. Carter, *El Papel de la Iglesia*, 138–39.

9. Prieto, "Indigenous People in Paraguay," 240–41.
10. Brysk, "Acting Globally," 32.
11. Harder Horst, *The Stroessner Regime and Indigenous Resistance*, 79.
12. *ABC Color*, "Habrá reunión," 8; *ABC Color*, "Concluye hoy consulta indígena," 26; and Colombres, *Por la liberación del indígena*, 38–39.
13. *ABC Color*, "Parlamento indio," 9.
14. *ABC Color*, "Retornaron indígenas que participaron."
15. Harder Horst, *The Stroessner Regime and Indigenous Resistance*, 93.
16. Ulloa, *The Ecological Native*, 36.
17. "Retornaron indígenas," 11.
18. Mora and Cooney, *Paraguay and the United States*, 231.
19. "Denuncia del Ecocidio Cometido," 225.
20. *Patria*, "IBR solicitará 1,200 hectáreas," 10.
21. *Última Hora*, "Conclusiones del *Diálogo Nacional*," 16.
22. "Denuncia del Ecocidio Cometido," 225.
23. Ibid.
24. Ibid., 227.
25. *Última Hora*, "Se saben más detalles," 28.
26. "Denuncia del Ecocidio Cometido," 227.
27. *Última Hora*, "Ésta es nuestra tierra," 19; and *Última Hora*, "Nos quieren dar tierras feas."
28. "Los Chiripá se Reunen," 9.
29. Reed, *Forest Dwellers*, 128–29.
30. Harder Horst, *The Stroessner Regime and Indigenous Resistance*, 45.
31. Ramírez, personal interview.
32. Stunnenberg, *Entitled to Land*, 110.
33. *Última Hora*, "Constituyente: Indígenas quieren participar."
34. *Última Hora*, "Nativos presentan propuestas," 16.
35. *Noticias*, "Indígenas desean ser protagonistas," 2.
36. Frutos and Velázquez; and Varese, *Pueblos indios, soberanía y globalismo*, 208.
37. *Hoy*, "Buscarán dar representación," 8.
38. Ramírez, personal interview.
39. *Noticias*, "Dan fín a discriminación."
40. Paraguayan constitution of 1992, chapter 5, "About Indigenous Peoples," 14–15.
41. *Última Hora*, "Constituyente: Indígenas quieren participar."
42. *Noticias*, "Satisfacción por capítulo indígena."
43. Ramírez, personal interview.
44. *Hoy*, "Analizarán capítulo."
45. Harder Horst, *The Stroessner Regime and Indigenous Resistance*, 138.
46. Paraguay's Law 234/93 approving ILO Convention 169, the Indigenous and Tribal Peoples Convention.

Bibliography

ABC Color. "Concluye hoy consulta indígena." March 10, 1972.
———. "Habrá reunion de indigenistas latinoamericanos en Asunción." February 22, 1972.
———. "Parlamento indio pidió se devuelva tierras a tribus con títulos de propiedad de las mismas." October 16, 1974.
———. "Retornaron indígenas que participaron." November 8, 1975.
Brysk, Alison. "Acting Globally: Indian Rights and International Politics in Latin America." In *Indigenous Peoples and Democracy in Latin America*, edited by Donna Lee Van Cott, 29–54. New York: St. Martin's Press, 1994.
Carter, Miguel, *El Papel de la Iglesia en la caída de Stroessner*. Asunción: RP Ediciones, 1991.
Colombres, Adolfo. *Por la liberación del indígena: Documentos y testimonios*. Buenos Aires: Ediciones del Sol, 1975.
Decreto #1,343 (1958). *Por el cual se crea el Departamento de Asuntos Indígenas*, Asunción, 1; DAI documents, 20, INDI Archives, Asunción, Paraguay.
"Denuncia del Ecocidio Cometido en el Tekoha Paï Tavyterã de Takuaguy-Oygue," *Suplemento Antropológico* 23, no. 2 (December 1988): 225.
Frutos and Velázquez, Colorado deputies, to Dr. Antonio Ruffinelli, September 19, 1991, Paraguayan Congressional Archives, Asunción.
Harder Horst, René D. *The Stroessner Regime and Indigenous Resistance in Paraguay*. Gainesville: University Press of Florida, 2007.
Hoy. "Analizarán capítulo referente a los pueblos indígenas." June 6, 1992.
———. "Buscarán dar representación a los indígenas." September 17, 1991.
"Los Chiripá se Reunen," *Diálogo Indígena Misionero* 9, no. 20 (October 1988): 9–11.
Mora, Frank O., and Jerry W. Cooney. *Paraguay and the United States: Distant Allies*. Athens: University of Georgia Press, 2007.
Noticias. "Dan fín a discriminación de los pueblos indígenas." May 1, 1992.
———. "Indígenas desean ser protagonistas." September 16, 1991.
———. "Satisfacción por capítulo indígena." June 7, 1992.
Patria. "IBR solicitará 1,200 hectáreas para indígenas mbyá apyteré." April 18, 1988.
Prieto, Esther. "Indigenous People in Paraguay." In *Indigenous Peoples and Democracy in Latin America*, edited by Donna Lee Van Cott, 235–58. New York: St. Martin's Press, 1994.
Ramírez, René. "Discurso de bienvenida dirigida a su santidad Juan Pablo Segundo." Unpublished mimeograph, May 1988. Mariscal Estigarribia, Catholic Church Archive, Asunción.
Ramos, Alcida Rita. *Indigenism: Ethnic Politics in Brazil*. Madison: University of Wisconsin Press, 1988.
Reed, Richard. *Forest Dwellers, Forest Protectors: Indigenous Models for International Development*. Boston: Allyn and Bacon, 1997.
Stunnenberg, P. W. *Entitled to Land: The Incorporation of the Paraguayan and Argentinean Gran Chaco and the Spatial Marginalization of the Indian People*. Saarbrücken: Verlag Breitenbach, 1993.
Ulloa, Astrid. *The Ecological Native: Indigenous Peoples' Movements and Eco-Governmentality in Colombia*. New York: Routledge, 2005.

Última Hora. "Conclusiones del *Diálogo Nacional*: Indígenas aspiran a que se reconozca su presencia." January 21, 1988.
———. "Constituyente: Indígenas quieren participar." June 7, 1991.
———. "Decretan ocupación de tierras para asentamiento de indígenas." October 11, 1980.
———. "Esta es nuestra tierra y no queremos mudarnos." June 29, 1988.
———. "Nativos presentan propuestas para la nueva Constitución." June 18, 1991.
———. "Nos quieren dar tierras feas y con muchos esteros." July 1, 1988.
———. "Se saben más detalles del incidente con los nativos paï." October 14, 1988.
Van Cott, Donna Lee, ed. *Indigenous Peoples and Democracy in Latin America*. New York: St. Martin's Press, 1994.
Varese, Stefano, ed. *Pueblos indios, soberanía y globalismo*. Quito: Ediciones Abya-Yala, 1996.

Richard K. Reed

---

two **THE GUARANÍ** FROM FOREST PEOPLE TO URBAN REFUGEES

Introduction

I first met Lali-puku when she was probably eleven years old—a button-nosed Guaraní girl with sparkling brown eyes living in the forests of eastern Paraguay. In the picture I snapped at the time, she is giggling self-consciously, friendliness leaking through her shyness. She is proudly wearing the white smock of a Paraguayan schoolgirl, clutching a pencil in her hand and holding her notebook under her arm. Lali is the daughter of Ava-ka'é and Kunajeju, a young Guaraní couple who befriended me when I entered their little hamlet in the rolling hills of the lowlands near Brazil. I had followed a trail twenty-five miles into the forest to do anthropology research in their midst. The young couple were among the few Guaraní to speak a few words of Spanish. They became friends and teachers in my effort to learn their language and enter their world.

Lali, in the photograph, stands under the roof of her father's house, which like in most Guaraní houses is a simple thatch roof without walls. There is a fire smoldering on the dirt floor in the center, and the family's few possessions are affixed beneath the rafters. Ava-ka'é had cut a small clearing in the forest not far from the homes of friends and relatives in a place called Itanaramí, "the place of the little white stone." They had planted a garden and collected most of what they needed in the nearby forest. A wall of greenery surrounded their little sunlit world with a sense of self-sufficiency and security, and a narrow trail led into the forest, past the houses of friends and family, to the one-room school where Lali was headed.

At the time I took the photo, some thirty years ago, the forests of eastern Paraguay stretched east from Itanaramí to the Atlantic Ocean and north toward the Amazon River. Over the decades, both the landscape and Lali have changed, and the process of my research has documented both the environmental destruction and the Guaraní struggle for a place in their rapidly changing world.

Mata Atlantica

Itanaramí is set in a region of "Atlantic Forest," a subtropical deciduous forest notable for its high level of natural biodiversity. A towering canopy stretches overhead, orchids and liana vines hang from the branches, and palm trees grow in the humid, warm air below. Twenty thousand species of plants spread in a tangled mass over the region, with up to 450 tree species found in a single hectare. Spider monkeys scamper and three-toed sloths lumber through the branches, while tapir and deer tread the forest floor below. Studies in Brazil record over 140 different mammalian species in the region, and research continually adds to the thousands of known insects and amphibians. Not surprisingly, the region has been identified as one of the world's hotspots for diversity, second only to the Amazon basin.[1]

The natural abundance of flora and fauna in eastern Paraguay is more striking in that the natural elements create what is otherwise an inhospitable environment. In the rainy season, hard rain pummels the region; in the dry season, direct sunlight scorches the landscape. If the ground is exposed, the soils are washed of their nutrients and baked to hardpan. Despite this, over time an ecosystem has developed strategies to defend itself from these harsh factors, fostering one of the world's most diverse biomes. The thick, high canopy is composed of trees with large, waxy leaves that throw a blanket over the region. The covering protects all below from the brutal force of the rain and keeps the air beneath moist and cool during the hot, dry weather. The complex system below this canopy has adapted to this environment with interspecies symbiotic relationships. Epiphytes, plants that grow on other plants without damaging them, flourish without contact with the soil. Liana vines weave a network among the high trees, stabilizing them in the fierce summer rainstorms. Insects fertilize the flowering trees, and monkeys eat the fruit and disperse the seeds through the region. In short, plants and animals exchange nutrients and protection in a series of ecological zones under the canopy and above the harsh soils of the forest floor.

Guaraní of the Forest

The Atlantic Forest of Paraguay shelters more than natural diversity. The forest provides the resources and refuge that allow the Guaraní to maintain their self-sufficient lifestyle. Guaraní farm in the forest, using the abundant foliage to fertilize the weak soils. Trees are felled and burned, which releases potassium, phosphate, and nitrogen into the soil to allow crops to flourish. Working with the natural world as a model, they plant manioc (*Manihot esculenta*), a woody shrub with large, thick leaves to create a canopy over the soil, then cultivate more fragile plants like sweet potato (*Ipomoea batata*) and squash (*Cucurbita pepo*) in the shade underneath. After several years, as the fertility of the soil is washed away and weeds invade the garden, the Guaraní abandon the field, cut a new garden, and start the process once again. And their fallow field eventually returns to forest. Thus, the Guaraní use the forests without undermining their basic integrity, a practice of sustainable horticulture that has allowed their society to flourish for thousands of years.

In addition to providing the resources for gardening, the forest provides the Guaraní with a dependable supply of meat. Hunting and fishing allow forest peoples to supplement their root crops and vegetables with animal protein. The Guaraní are masterful trappers. Using vines, saplings, twigs, and logs, the men construct snares and deadfall traps to kill armadillos (*Dasypus novemcinctus*) and agouti (*Dasyprocta punctata*), and a range of other small forest animals. After the rainy season, when there is little to eat in the gardens, a night of fishing in nearby oxbow lakes would provide a dependable meal.

The self-sufficiency of the Guaraní in the forest does not isolate them from the larger world, however. In addition to gardening and hunting, Guaraní families sell products they harvest from the forest to buy market goods. Most families buy salt, soap, cloth, and machetes—things that they cannot make themselves. Without leaving their home in the forest, men gather a range of products around their homes and sell them to patrons who come into the forest. Most important among these is *yerba mate*, the leaves of a species of holly tree (*Ilex paraguariensis*). The yerba tree is endemic to the forests of Paraguay and Brazil, and its foliage has a caffeine content that rivals that of tea. Harvested, dried, crushed, and soaked in hot water, the infusion produces a stimulating drink that has become a traditional favorite in Paraguay, Brazil, and Argentina. For more than five hundred years, the Guaraní have harvested the wild leaf and traded it for goods from the market.

In addition to self-sufficiency, the forests have provided the Guaraní with a modicum of security. Even as the rivers of South America were explored, and even as distant towns grew into cities and colonies developed into nation-states, the forest allowed the Guaraní to retain their independence. Few colonists ventured into the dense growth, and when they did they were more interested in buying yerba than in creating settlements. Sporadic relations between the Guaraní and the larger system were advantageous for both. Patrons carried yerba to Asunción and Buenos Aires. If a patron was unjust or there was little market for yerba, men found other goods to sell. Animal skins, distilled essential citrus oils, and split fence posts all could be sold for cash. And, in a worst case scenario, given the food and shelter that could be found in the natural world, the Guaraní could always retreat into the depths of the forest.

In sum, the dense forest of South America's Southern Cone covers a vast region and protects an extremely diverse biome. In addition to this natural world, contact with outside societies has allowed the Guaraní access to the larger world without being dominated by it. The forest has offered the indigenous Guaraní a place to be self-sufficient without being isolated from the national society and international economy.

Changes in the Forest

My research in Itanaramí in the three decades since 1990 has recorded considerable change, both in Lali and in the forests she lived in. Each time I returned to Itanaramí, I took pictures of Lali and her family, and on my next return I brought them a copy. The assembled clutch of photos shows them growing as a family, recording Lali-puku growing from a little girl to a big one, an adolescent to young woman, and eventually getting married and raising her own family. As time went on she followed her husband to a new village, and we lost contact.

Just as Lali changed over the years, the forest of the Guaraní underwent dramatic changes. The path through the forest became a jeep track, bridges were built across the rivers, and soon Caterpillar tractors were pushing into the far corners of the forest. The sound of chainsaws broke the forest silence, and logging trucks lumbered through the village to carry the valuable timber to world markets.

Eastern Paraguay has experienced one of the world's most rapid processes of deforestation. As late as 1973, 73.4 percent of the region was covered by forest. But bridge- and road-building projects financed by USAID in the 1970s were rapid and devastating. Colonists and loggers flooded into previously inaccessible forests. As early as 1980, Paraguay ranked as high as fourth in global rates of deforestation, with 3.5 percent of the cover being removed each year (Allen and Barnes 1985).[2] Rates increased in the subsequent two decades. As shown by Landsat images, the proportion of forested area in Paraguay was reduced to 40.7

percent by 1989 and further down to 24.9 percent by 2000 (Huang et al. 2009).[3] From 1980 to 1996, the destruction was second only to Indonesia's in terms of rate of deforestation and total portion of cover removed, with up to 170,000 hectares being cleared annually. In 2020, it is estimated that only 14 percent of Paraguay's original forest canopy remains, and half of that has been seriously degraded by logging. The remaining forests exist as small and isolated parcels that retain little of the biodiversity of the original expanses.

Roadbuilding opened up the valuable forests to logging, but three additional factors destroyed Paraguay's forests. First, cattle ranching transformed vast areas from forest to pasture. Dramatic Brazilian economic growth in the 1960s pushed land sales and clearing across the southern highlands to the Paraguayan border. World demand for beef increased, and Brazil became the world's largest exporter of beef. Brazilian cattle ranchers and their laborers found cheap land and easy access across the *linea secca*; the pastures and people of Brazil moved fluidly into eastern Paraguay's unbroken forests.

Second, in this same period, forest destruction was facilitated by the demand of the rural poor for more land. Paraguay's land is largely controlled by a few families who own vast tracts. Rapid population growth in the latter decades of the twentieth century led to shortages of land among the masses of small farmers. Rather than redistribute the extensive large estates of the rich, the military dictator, Alfredo Stroessner, sought to mollify the landless masses by distributing vast forested acreages inhabited by indigenous peoples to poor peasants from the densely settled regions near Asunción. As the logging trucks left, buses and pickups took their place, dropping immigrants into the heart of the forest.

Finally, and most profoundly, the world demand for soy created an explosive and land-hungry agroindustrial economy. The soybean was first grown in Paraguay in 1967, but by 1970 the country had 54,600 hectares planted. This first wave of soy was planted in established wheat fields, and it was found to rejuvenate the region's weak topsoil. Quickly, however, the export potential of the crop became clear, and corporations and investors began to snatch up the cheap land; aided by the massive roadbuilding projects, they converted the region into one of the world's premier soybean exporting zones. While US production stagnated, Brazilian production grew at twice the world rate of increase—and Paraguay's rate of production increase was even higher. By 1987, soybeans covered some 718,800 hectares in Paraguay, more than any other crop, with an annual output of one million tons and export revenues of approximately US$150 million. As the world market strengthened, roads were improved, drying and storage facilities

MAP 2 Deforestation of Eastern Paraguary

Source: ABC Color / WWF

sprang up, and the dense forest was pushed into massive windrows, with fields replacing the forest canopy. Today, Paraguay ranks fourth in world soybean production, with corporations increasing their fields by approximately 100,000 hectares of soy each year to reach almost three million hectares planted by 2012 (Markley 2012).

The forest destruction has wider environmental impacts. As the protective cover is removed, it increases the quantity and force of the rainfall that reaches the unprotected soil surface. Soybean cropping on the cleared land prevents the regrowth of soil cover. Over time, the baking creates a hardpan that restricts the ability of the earth to absorb the water. Consequently, rainfall and runoff on the Paraná plateau have increased significantly, measured both in the frequency of rain events and the water levels in the major river systems, characterized by periods of up to a 50 percent increase in stream flow in the Uruguay, Paraná, and Paraguay Rivers (Barros, Menéndez, and Nagy 2005). As the water runs off over the barren ground, it carries soil away. According to data from the Global Land Degradation Assessment and Improvement project of the Global Environmental Facility, 16.4 percent of Paraguay's territory has been degraded by erosion. As the population is concentrated on arable land, over two-thirds of the Paraguayan population has been affected by this soil degradation, occurring at a faster rate than anywhere else in the world (Bai et al. 2008).

Deforestation and the Guaraní

As logging, ranching, and farming destroy the forest canopy, it also exposes Guaraní communities to forces that make a self-sufficient life untenable. Most had access to extensive forests until the 1970s, with families farming and foraging in the region surrounding their communities. As noted, even the scattered settlements of Paraguayan mestizos in the region were accommodated without greatly disrupting indigenous economies. This latter fact was greatly facilitated in that most of the development of the economic potential of the forests depended on the harvesting of yerba mate, timber, and essential oils, activities that did not undermine the basic integrity of the forest. Indigenous peoples entered into the extractive economy to supplement subsistence production with items that could only be acquired from the market. This is not to idealize the conditions of indigenous peoples in these times. They were defenseless against the violence and institutional racism of the larger society. But given the vast stretches of unbroken forest, communities could often escape and live beyond the purview of the larger system.

As forest development began to impinge on Guaraní communities in the 1970s, anthropologists and missionaries joined forces to identify and guarantee lands to indigenous people. The Stroessner government was willing to meet the demands, in part to improve the government's international image, which had come to be known for brutality against peasants and dissidents. By 1980, roughly three-quarters of the Guaraní communities identified by *indigenistas* had acquired some guarantees to their land (UNPFII 2010). Many of them, however, remained without land guarantees. Less than a third of the Mbyá communities that had been identified received any assurances. Even then, many were too small, too isolated, or resistant to official contact. Moreover, perhaps half the total indigenous population remained unaccounted for and unprotected in the forest. Exacerbating the problem, the most devastating land clearing proceeded in those areas where land control by indigenous residents was the most tenuous. They were either overlooked or escaped official recognition and land demarcation (López 2015, 1).

Even indigenous communities with land found their self-sufficiency undermined as cattle ranches, soybean fields, and mestizo colonization devastated the region. Although they could continue to farm the land they had, they lost use of the surrounding forests for hunting and gathering. They were forced to increase the size of their gardens with cash crops to buy the food and material they had previously gathered in the vast forests. To accommodate larger gardens, the rate of clearing on reservation land increased dramatically, often rendering major sections of these reservations as barren fallow. Groups that had maintained stable relations with the mestizo population for decades, or perhaps centuries, became dependent on the brutal commercial system.

Outside these reservations, new landowners, interested in capital investments and agricultural profits, had nothing to gain from accommodating Guaraní groups on land they had purchased. Guaraní houses were removed, their food gardens destroyed by soybean fields, and the forests hauled off to sawmills. When houses were allowed to remain on an undeveloped corner of a new landholding, the forests that had previously provided food for foraging, space for gardening, and goods for commercial collecting were expropriated and destroyed—leaving the Guaraní on small, dry, dusty patches of earth, without any means of making a living. To add insult to injury, the highly mechanized soybean farms brought in imported heavy equipment and had little interest in hiring indigenous laborers.

From the early years of this process, there were reports of Guaraní being driven off their lands and camping along Paraguay's few roads. Generally, these groups sought plots near water that offered the possibility of wage labor for the men. The paving of the highways created a wave of economic activity. Settlements sprang up around highway construction sites, which quickly turned into gas stations and commercial centers for the rapidly expanding transportation infrastructure. Tenuously holding onto their house sites nearby and their few possessions, the Guaraní had little opportunity or incentive to plant gardens. Most subsisted on what they could scrounge. Guaraní individuals became a common sight hanging around the edges of these frontier settlements to panhandle or just for the entertainment of watching the rough life of the *transportistas* and highway crews. Men worked in the new fields when they could. Young people were attracted to the bright lights of these highway camps, some finding access to scarce cash in petty crime and prostitution. Guaraní began to show up on the shoulders of the roads, the women to sell produce and the kids running in a gaggle, calling to speeding cars and trucks.

Not all the destruction can be attributed to agriculture and ranching. Another process of environmental destruction dislocated indigenous people as well. Between 1980 and 2000, two major dams were constructed on the Paraná River. The world-famous Itaipú Dam, north of Ciudad del Este, was opened in 1981 to become the world's second-largest operating hydroelectric facility. It impounds a reservoir of 23.5 million acre-feet of water, rising 100 meters off the original forest floor. The lake extends 125 kilometers upstream, eventually flooding the famous Sete Quedas Falls, covering over 520 square miles of forest. A second major dam, the Yacyretá Dam, was opened downstream on the Paraná River in 1993 near the city of Encarnación. This dam, although only a quarter the size of Itaipú in vertical drop, nevertheless ranks among the top twenty hydroelectric dams in the world. And although a narrower reservoir is impounded by the dam, the area inundated is even larger than that of Itaipú, covering over 650 square miles.

The two dams caused considerable disruption of indigenous communities, both Guaraní and Aché. Small indigenous hamlets have generally clustered along riverways, making them particularly vulnerable to hydroelectric dam flooding. In total, the dams dislocated more than one hundred thousand people, the majority being Paraguayan and Argentine mestizos and Brazilian peasants. Although small in relative population, a total of thirty-two indigenous settlements were lost to the flooding as residents were forced to find land for houses, gardens, and hunting elsewhere. Many of these small hamlets further dispersed into smaller collections of homes of close relatives living on the last vestiges of forested land in the region.

The Guaraní were hemmed in on two sides, caught between two advancing waves of deforestation and environmental devastation. Many communities suffered a process of serial displacement. Finding that their lands had been titled to a rancher, the government, or corporate agriculture, they would retreat farther into the forest or onto lands that were less desirable for farming and pasture. Eventually, these lands, too, fell victim to chainsaws and tractors. When indigenous residents failed to give ground, rural developers quickly resorted to violence, invading the vulnerable hamlets with men, guns, and dogs and using bulldozers and fire to destroy houses and fields.

Finally, forced onto the major roads for whatever work or handouts they could find, the Guaraní were drawn into the three major urban centers of Paraguay: Asunción, Encarnación, and Ciudad del Este. Guaraní were soon walking, hitchhiking rides on trucks, or buying passage on the buses that plied between the three towns. Many of these families had previously had tenuous, sporadic contact with the capital city. Younger people had gone to have identity cards issued in government offices; older men to purchase goods only available in the urban markets; or families for visits to the public hospitals. Emboldened by these brief visits, families without resources in the countryside boarded buses or trucks and found themselves on the road to Asunción. They arrived without food, money, or family, descending from cargo trucks along the busy main streets or from buses at the metropolitan bus station.

Dressed in threadbare rags, unwashed and unkempt, the Guaraní were immediately evident at traffic lights, panhandling in traffic. Young mothers carrying their infant children would sit disconsolately on the curb as their young children moved between the rows of vehicles looking woefully into the stopped cars. At night, these groups camped in vacant lots or slept on city sidewalks, becoming an extremely visible (and extremely vulnerable) sector of the urban environment.

Forest People in the City

Engaged in long-term ethnographic research with forest Guaraní, my studies logically followed the families to the cities where they found refuge. I began to stop Guaraní on the street and engage them in conversation. They wandered rather than walked the city streets. As they begged for food from middle-class Asunceños, they lifted their hands and met the questioning looks of the Paraguayans with vacant eyes. I sought out small clusters of families, often found sitting on the curb outside urban stores, begging from shoppers as they left with bags of groceries. In the vacant lots to where they retreated, I shared their beggars' meals from Styrofoam clamshell containers and drank from the dirty plastic bottles in which they hauled their water. At first impression, the scenes seemed oddly similar to meals in the forest, the adults squatting around and eating out of a single cooking pot, kids leaning over their shoulder to grab a bite or a bone. Here, however, the tiny groups were incongruously embedded in a world of asphalt and engine exhaust. They seemed to have lost routine and goals, sitting in the midst of traffic and sidewalks, their lives having become bereft of meaning.

Curiously absent from many of these groups of straggling urban nomads were young people. The urban families were predominantly parents and little children. After asking, I learned that the young people hung out together in separate encampments. They were known in the city as *niños del calle*, literally "street children." With just a little effort, these little groups disappeared into abandoned buildings, drainage culverts, and empty lots. Beyond the reach of their elders and almost invisible to passersby, they entered a hard and dangerous world. As I got to know these groups, I discovered that the young people were heavy users of dangerous drugs, often crude cocaine paste or *cola de zapatero*, shoemakers' glue. Either drug, which many young people used almost incessantly, could provide a cheap and intense high. The grounds of their small encampments were littered with feces and plastic bags used to sniff glue. Young people slept fitfully in the middle of the day, unconscious to their surroundings.

My research with urban Guaraní led me to a safe house for Guaraní children run by a local NGO. Indigenistas working with Native peoples explained how young Guaraní gained the money for drugs from prostitution. Both boys and girls often started when they were quite young. At their encampments, taxis with men could be seen pulling up to a corner or a doorway; youngsters emerged and crawled in, often ushered by an older hustler who had arranged the transaction by phone. To help these lost children, the NGO had rented a safe house where young people could get a good meal, clean up, play games or music, and hang out with staff. Nevertheless, by the time most kids showed up at the safe house, they were severely addicted. Moreover, they were embedded in a difficult world that led them on a downward spiral. Drugs offered small respite from their reality of sexual exploitation and also brought on the addiction that compelled them to continue to sell their bodies.

To my great surprise, I discovered an old friend working with addicted kids in the safe house. Angela Sales, Lali's little sister, had attended grade school in the forest and come to Asunción for high school. She had now finished college and was devoting herself to helping Guaraní street children. Her understanding of Guaraní culture and familiarity with Asunción gave her a privileged position in working with Guaraní young people in trouble. Angela informed me that her sister Lali was also living in Asunción. But while Angela was drawing a salary and had rented a house in a middle-class neighborhood, Lali had not been as fortunate. She was living with her husband and three daughters in the city's dump, where other Guaraní refugees in the city had gathered.

Cerro Potý

Today, indigenous refugees can be found at seventeen different locations in and around Asunción (UNPFII 2010). These groups altogether include approximately five hundred families and perhaps as many as four thousand people. Although some exist as small clutches of wandering vagrants, others have carved out small spaces in the city itself. New residents activate their networks of family and community to find familiar faces in the strange urban world. Thus, they come to be defined loosely as kin groups of similar ethnicity who attempt to reterritorialize their new environment. Many have ended up in more organized groups living near the regional bus station, in the city's poorer neighborhoods, or along the river at the edge of town.

Angela and I found Lali camped along the river near the mountains of garbage in the settlement called Cerro Potý ("Flower of the Hill"). Lali, her husband, and her three daughters were in a small house on the edge of a massive pile of rancid garbage. The putrid air was filled with dust, flies, and a swirl of paper and plastic. Hungry dogs and cattle nosed the waste for rotten food. The Paraguay River flowed slowly past, filled with trash and dead fish and covered with an iridescent oil slick. We shared cold *terere* and caught up on the years since we had seen one another. I was struck by how far this little group had come, conceptually, from the isolated clearing in the vast forest to this hellish spot in a postapocalyptic environment

Asunción's city center is bounded on the west by the Paraguay River, and Argentina on the far side of the water. Suburbs spread over the highlands to the east. Squatters looking for a place to build shelter must move onto unclaimed land on muddy shores of the slow-moving river. The first Guaraní families came to the spot in 1990 from the department of Guairá. Undisturbed on unoccupied marshy lowlands near the city dump, they quietly constructed houses from scavenged material and adopted a sense of stability in the urban environment. Friends and relatives joined them from other desperate Guaraní communities, gravitating to this "safe zone" along the river. Originally attracted to the proximity of the refuse for foraging, the group had grown to more than three hundred people, with a preponderance of women and children, making up some sixty Native families.

Several of the first families at Cerro Potý arrived from a Guaraní community near Itanaramí. Although their land was recognized by the state, they had been granted only 980 hectares for the entire group. By 2009, there were eighty families in the forested reservation, with about 420 individuals—allowing an average of only 12 hectares per family. Later, a paved road was constructed linking the area with the Brazilian border. The surrounding forests were cleared and soy planted to the very borders of the *colonia*. Soon thereafter, community members began to report that crop dusting of herbicides and pesticides was applied without attention to winds, natural barriers, or proximity to houses and schools. Chemicals drifted into the colonia school, sickened domestic animals, and fouled the community's water; residents suffered diarrhea, fever, and nausea (López 2015). Families abandoned their land and moved toward Asunción, finding their way to Cerro Potý.

While others are living as vagrants on the streets or hiding in empty lots, the Guaraní of Cerro Potý have begun to assert a semblance of order in their chaotic new world. The location in Los Bañados del Sur is convenient to the most important source of income: the landfill for scavenging. Even while it overflows and spills into the marshy river, the refuse continues to accumulate at a rate of over 1,200 tons per day, or a kilo per person in the city. In the midst of the flies, dust, toxic effluent, and flooding, Guaraní can earn a living by recycling a wide variety of materials. The lucky forager can find lead, copper, or construction materials. But even without these, Guaraní can gather plastic bottles to wash for resale. On a good day, residents earn as much as eight dollars, allowing a family to provide for basic food needs—if little else.

The second principle source of income for urban Guaraní is begging. In the morning, as men head into the mountains of fetid trash, women with babies in arms take the bus to the center of town. There, they stand on street corners, raising their hands to the busy crowds, plaintively and silently asking for help. While to the Asunceños they seem to appear from nowhere, these women have developed a highly organized system, dispersing to busy corners of residential areas where traffic is slower and where they can avoid competition among themselves.

More than earning cash, the people of Cerro Potý have organized as a community, solicited government recognition, and accepted considerable public assistance in their efforts to establish a community. Refugees from various Guaraní communities assembled near the landfill, elected a leader, and won certification from the Instituto Paraguayo del Indígena (INDI) as a *comunidad indígena nacional*. With government assistance, the group of families have built a primary school, and erected a religious center and community meeting area. As the public took notice of indigenous peoples in the landfill, the group effectively managed television, newspapers, and social media to make their case. They attracted international assistance, including the construction of raised wooden houses to avoid the toxic effluent that drains through the region during heavy rains.

The more time I spent with Lali and her family, the more I appreciated the order and stability that they had garnered in the chaotic world they lived in. They earned some money, the kids went to school, and they had a roof over their heads and food on the fire. Lali was even getting government assistance to buy insulin for her diabetes. I came to understand their remarkable resilience in the face of environmental destruction, social injustice, and economic disadvantage. I saw how proud she was of her growing girls, how well dressed they were, and perhaps most importantly, how they were home rather than on the streets. The little group was making the best of a bad situation and marshaled what few resources they had to make a life for themselves.

The last picture I have in my collection of photos of Lali and her family is of her daughter Rosa, now a bit older than Lali was then and in jeans and a neat T-shirt, but with the same bright eyes and bashful grin. We are sitting outside their house at the edge of the garbage, but I realized that something of forest life had been carried by the Guaraní to the city. Although a refugee from environmental destruction, Lali had imparted something to her daughters that Ava-ka'é and Kunajeju had given her when she was growing up in the forest. In short, Lali and Cerro Potý stands as one example of the success that Guaraní have had in establishing a stable infrastructure in the urban arena. Although fraught with problems (sickness and pollution, to name the obvious), they draw on their rural experience to articulate effectively with the state and the Paraguayan nation, winning a modicum of stability in the urban system.

Notes

1. Within eastern Paraguay, there are significant differences among the range of Guaraní ethnic groups, generally divided into three closely related groups (Mbyá, Avá, and Paĩ-Tavytera) and a fourth (the Aché) with distinct social and physical characteristics. The first indigenous census carried out by the government, in 1981, identified 4,518 Avá, 4,986 Paĩ, and 2,460 Mbyá. A more complete survey in 2002, which incorporated considerable population growth, identified 13,340 Avá, 14,324 Paĩ, and 13,132 Mbyá (Murray-Smith et al. 2009, 151–63).

2. It is only fair to point out that the farmers and agroindustrialists who cleared these areas were often unaware of indigenous residents. As the large latifundios of eastern Paraguay were acquired by the government and sold to private developers, indigenous residents were caught between shifting attitudes about land use. Throughout the nineteenth and twentieth centuries, large landholders often allowed indigenous peoples to remain in small hamlets on large private holdings, provided they did not impede traditional extractive industries (in fact, they often worked in these industries). As land moved from extensive extraction to intensive agriculture, new landowners insisted on land titles that stipulated that the areas were unoccupied. The transfer legalized the displacement of the Native communities—with neither previous nor current landowner acknowledging responsibility.

3. This case has more thoroughly been analyzed by the author in a more comprehensive study of Guaraní urbanization (Reed 2015).

Bibliography

Allen, Julia C., and Douglas F. Barnes. 1985. "The Causes of Deforestation in Developing Countries." *Annals of the Association of American Geographers* 75, no. 2 (June): 163–84.

Bai, Zhanguo, David L. Dent, Lennart Olsson, and Michael E. Schaepman. 2008. *Global Assessment of Land Degradation and Improvement*. Vol. 1: *Identification by Remote Sensing*. Wageningen, the Netherlands: International Soil Reference and Information Centre.

Barros, Vicente, Ángel Menéndez, and Gustavo Nagy, eds. 2005. *El cambio climático en el Río de la Plata* [Climate change in the Plata River]. Buenos Aires: Centro de Investigaciones del Mar y la Atmosféra.

Huang, Chengquan, Sunghee Kim, Kuan Song, John R. G. Townshend, Paul Davis, Alice Altstatt, et al. 2009. "Assessment of Paraguay's Forest Cover Change Using Landsat Observations." *Global and Planetary Change* 67, nos. 1–2 (May): 1–12.

López, Por Paulo. 2015. "Fiscalía deja morir causa por fumigaciones ilegales en Campo Agua'e." *E'a*, January 7. Available at http://ea.com.py/fiscalia-deja-morir-causa-por-fumigaciones-ilegales-en-campo-aguae/.

Markley, Brooke. 2012. *Paraguay: Oil Seeds and Products Annual*. US Department of Agriculture. Washington, DC: Government Printing Office.

Murray-Smith, Charlotte, Neil A. Brummitt, Ary T. Oliveira-Filho, Steven Bachman, Justin Moat, Eimear M. Nic Lughadha, and Eve J. Lucas. 2009. "Plant Diversity Hotspots in the Atlantic Coastal Forests of Brazil." *Conservation Biology* 23, no. 1 (February): 151–63.

Reed, Richard K. 2015. "Environmental Destruction, Guaraní Refugees, and Indigenous Identity in Urban Paraguay." In *Climate Change, Culture, and Economics: Anthropological Investigations* (Research in Economic Anthropology, vol. 35), 263–92. Bingley, W. Yorks., England: Emerald Group Publishing.

United Nations Permanent Forum on Indigenous Issues (UNPFII). 2010. "Human Rights: Implementation of the United Nations Declaration on the Rights of Indigenous Peoples." E/C.19/2010/12/Add.2. Available at https://digitallibrary.un.org/record/677570?ln=en.

Paola Canova

three RETHINKING AYOREO URBANITY
LABOR RELATIONS AND LAND CLAIMS IN A MENNONITE COLONY OF THE CHACO[1]

Introduction

It is early morning in Casa Pasajera, an Ayoreo urban settlement of three hundred people in the Mennonite town of Filadelfia, the main urban center of Fernheim, a Mennonite colony in western Paraguay. An Ayoreo couple in their early fifties is dropped off by a Mennonite employer who has given them a ride to town. They will stay in the settlement for two days while visiting their son, who is at the local hospital. As they arrive, Ichajui is already on his way to an NGO, from where he communicates with his wife, who is back in the village, via VHF radio.[2] Like every other morning for the past eight months, Conami, one of the few people in the settlement with a permanent job in town, gets ready to leave for the carpentry shop. By midmorning, a large truck filled with bricks stops in front of Casa Pasajera. The driver leans his head out of the window and screams: "Diez!" ("Ten"). A handful of young men hurriedly scramble out of the piled-up plastic tents and jump into the back of the truck. They will offload the bricks at a local construction company and will be back a few hours later with some pocket money.

At the other end of Casa Pasajera, Pibai, a tall man in his mid-twenties, packs his belongings in a large, white plastic bag and gets ready to leave. He will be picked up by a Brazilian rancher who recently bought property on the Bolivian border and has hired him for three months to clear a patch of forest that will be turned into buffel grass. Meanwhile, Doria straps two empty twenty-liter containers around her bike and leaves to get water. After twenty minutes, she returns. This time, she brought the water from a nearby retention pond. She explains that ever since the

Mennonites decided to close all public faucets, she has been getting water from the house of her husband's employer, but he was not around that day. Later in the afternoon, a group of teenagers play a volleyball match against their neighbors, the Guaraní. The music is loud, and as the sun fades away the heat seems to dissipate. Five cheerful young Ayoreo girls make jokes and listen to music, as they prepare to go out for the night.

This was one of several temporary settlements in Filadelfia, where Ayoreo lived until 2015. For decades, they faced discrimination and evictions from Filadelfia, where the living conditions of this and previous settlements are iconic of the structural violence that the Ayoreo have historically experienced in the urban spaces of the Mennonite colonies. In this chapter, I trace the genealogy of Ayoreo urbanity specifically in Fernheim Colony, unveiling how it is closely intertwined with a history of labor relations with Mennonites and their fight for access to land in urban spaces and beyond. I show how early Ayoreo-Mennonite encounters triggered initial constructions of the Ayoreo as "out of place" in urban spaces. Later, Ayoreo refusal to conform and adapt to expected mobility patterns and economic roles fostered by the Mennonites further excluded them. And more recently, their land claims have remained invisible to local NGOs, as their urban living conditions challenge perceptions of "traditional" Ayoreo life. A priori, this situation would seem to fit well with Lucas Bessire's depictions of what he has termed Ayoreo "hypermarginality," that is, "a regime of social depersonalization and structural violence"; the condition of "those who do not fit the increasingly policed matrix of cultural life while also remaining at the very bottom of local socioeconomic class hierarchies" (Bessire 2014, 184). However, despite essentialized narratives and discriminatory practices that stigmatize Ayoreo as marginal in urban spaces, they have used their presence in the colonies not only as a strategy to access wage labor activities but as a bargaining tool to secure access to land. As I will show, Ayoreo urban incursions both challenge Mennonite and NGO expectations of them and resist theoretical categorizations such as hypermarginality. The Ayoreo case reveals how indigenous urbanity does not necessarily entail a process of deterritorialization (see Briones 2007; McSweeney and Jokisch 2015); rather, urban space and place are strategically reappropriated to create new social geographies (Soja 1989) that open up opportunities to advance land claims and strengthen the process of socioeconomic and political self-determination for indigenous people in a context marked by historical discrimination and ongoing rapid transformation.

Tracing Ayoreo Presence in the Mennonite Colonies

In 1930, a small group of Dutch–north German descent Mennonite refugees migrating from Russia settled to the west of the Paraguay River in the Chaco region, forming Fernheim Colony.[3] The Chaco is part of a vast ecoregion shared with Argentina, Bolivia, and Brazil and is considered the second-largest forested area after the Amazon in lowland South America. Initial encounters between Mennonites and Ayoreo did not take place until twenty years after the establishment of Fernheim Colony, at a time when the Ayoreo where still roaming the forests. Signs of their presence were noted in the northern edges of the colony, and over the next twelve years sporadic encounters resulted in the death of a handful of Mennonites.[4] These clashes fueled the settlers' constant state of panic and fostered popular beliefs among Paraguayans and other indigenous peoples about the Ayoreo as fearsome "Moros," as they were pejoratively called. This anxiety is evident in a correspondence from 1961 between the manager of the colony's experimental farm and the director of foreign relief and services from the Mennonite Central Committee (MCC)[5] in Pennsylvania, where the former described the reaction of the Mennonites to Ayoreo appearances:

> We, of course, cannot say for certain but to me it seems as if the Moros are not intending to make a hostile attack. The disturbing thing is that the Mennonites here are not doing anything to give them a chance to be friendly. Everyone, including the Ministers, tells me to have plenty of guns and ammunition at the farm and to do some shooting every day. (Graber 1964, 88)

Overall, Mennonite-Ayoreo encounters promoted a discursive construction of the Ayoreo as "wild" and "savage," thus belonging to the realm of wilderness. As this chapter shows, this collective imaginary about the Ayoreo has survived over time in the Mennonite colonies and has contributed to their exclusion from urban spaces.

In July 1962, an initial group of about twenty-seven Ayoreo of the Garaigosode subgroup emerged at the Fortín Teniente Martínez military post.[6] Salesian missionaries, who since 1957 had been trying to reach the Ayoreo, immediately formed a temporary camp at the site.[7] In December of that year, the Ayoreo started their sporadic visits to Filadelfia. Ayorei, a man in his late sixties, remembers: "I would make the trip with my friends. We were young back then and it took us two days by foot. We were curious about the white people." The initial Mennonite reaction was to provide shelter and work for the Ayoreo. Following an "orientation" session, men and women were taken to the MCC experimental farm to pick cotton, castor beans, peanuts, and corn (Graber 1964). According to David Hein, these visits began to overwhelm the Mennonites, because the Ayoreo preferred to spend their time "running around the *aldeas* [villages] rather than working" (1990, 129). By 1963, the visits abruptly stopped as the Salesians bought a property in Puerto María Auxiliadora in which to settle them.[8]

The presence of Ayoreo in Filadelfia triggered a renewed interest in reaching the still "uncontacted" Ayoreo. To do this, Fernheim Colony invited the New Tribes Mission (NTM) to collaborate with them.[9] The initial relationship between the two groups dates back to the mid-1950s, when the former were unsuccessfully trying to reach the Ayoreo and learned that the NTM had already settled Ayoreo on the Bolivian side of the border as early as 1948. At the time, Fernheim sent representatives with the aim of obtaining information that could facilitate contact with and settlement of the Ayoreo in Paraguay (Hein 1990). At the request of the Mennonites, by 1966 the NTM was ready to expand its work into Paraguay. Their missionaries received the support of Fernheim Colony to settle in Filadelfia, and from there they organized trips to search for the Ayoreo. That same year, contact was initiated with the Guidai-gosode subgroup of Ayoreo in the area of Cerro León.[10] This would become the site of their first mission station. In 1968 the mission moved farther south to Faro Moro, and in 1979 to Campo Loro, near the Mennonite colonies (Perasso 1987).

From the beginning, Mennonite-Ayoreo interactions would set the tone for their future relationship. The notion of the Ayoreo as primitive, and therefore "out of place," urged Mennonites to incorporate them into the social and spatial structure of Fernheim. However, the only cohabitation model that they could offer was based on Eurocentric ideas of work, faith, and progress. Such a model would later foster a politics of exclusion, and this became more evident as the Ayoreo established a more permanent presence in Filadelfia.

Indigenous Urbanity in Fernheim Colony: A Story of Labor Relations

The urbanity of indigenous peoples in the central Chaco region traces its beginnings to the history of labor relations with the Mennonite colonies. Since its formation, Fernheim saw an active flux of indigenous peoples to the area in search of work. Due to the economic expansion of the Chaco during the first half of the twentieth century, indigenous peoples, suffering land encroachment and with limited access to natural resources, became increasingly dependent on the regional market economy for their livelihood; as a result, they were drawn to the colonies, which would become one of the main poles of development in the region. The labor force was initially welcomed by Mennonites, who also assumed a civilizatory role toward the Native people. But the work relationship would soon come under scrutiny. In 1936, a researcher who visited Fernheim Colony speculated that the indigenous workers would develop into a "Chaco proletariat" that would provide "cheap labor to the colonists' farms" (Klassen 2002, 70). By 1955, increasing labor migrations to Fernheim obliged the Mennonites to establish agricultural settlements for them on the outskirts of Filadelfia to avoid having them settle in town (see Stahl 1982). It is estimated that the indigenous presence in Fernheim grew from three thousand individuals in 1951 to approximately ten thousand in 1976 (USAID 1977). This increase in the labor force was resultant of the expansion of the agricultural frontier in the region, a process mostly driven by Mennonites that had notably accelerated by the mid-1970s, attracting increasing amounts of capital to the region (Canova 2015). Access to freely moving labor that readily adapts to the shifting spaces of capital is critical for the development of an economic enclave (Harvey 2001). Living in close proximity and with temporary access to work, indigenous peoples formed a latent labor reserve, which could be conveniently drawn upon as needed. Over time, however, indigenous peoples put pressure on the colony's administration to also allow them to settle in Filadelfia.

Several scholars have noted the deplorable labor conditions of indigenous peoples in the colonies at the time (see Basso 1973, 1975; Hack 1977; for a rebuttal, see Redekop 1980). In 1971, Paraguayan anthropologist Miguel Chase Sardi denounced Mennonite employers at an international symposium.[11] He condemned the labor conditions, describing them as debt slavery. According to him, indigenous people were paid less than Mennonites for the same work. He also noted that most transactions with indigenous workers were not made in cash but in chits, fostering their dependency on the Mennonites for their livelihood. Marginal labor conditions continue to be a reality for most indigenous peoples in the Mennonite colonies and the region (see Bedoya Silva-Santisteban and Bedoya Garland 2005).

The Ayoreo were drawn into this labor pool at the beginning of the 1970s. According to John Renshaw, "they were so keen to find employment—or so desperate—that they offered to work for lower wages than other laborers. This caused tensions with other Indians ... but endeared the Ayoreo to the Mennonite farmers" (2002, 141). They were employed primarily clearing pastures, building fences, and cutting firewood on ranches. Initially, the NTM missionaries were opposed to Ayoreo migrations to the colonies because they considered this dispersion a hindrance to the successful expansion of their missionary enterprise. Missionary Henry Buschegger, who had previously worked among the Ayoreo in Bolivia and witnessed their process of proletarianization in that country, worried that the same would occur among the Ayoreo in Paraguay. He expressed this to Fernheim's leadership in the following terms: "Acaso yo, señores, arriesgue mi vida y la de mi familia para que al final los Ayoreo se conviertan en peones de ustedes?" ("Have I, gentlemen, risked my life and that of my family, only to have the Ayoreo become your peons in the end?") (Vysokolan 1988, 299).

Due to their close relationship with Mennonites, NTM missionaries lobbied for the restriction of Ayoreo access to jobs in the colonies. Since there was a massive pool of indigenous labor available at the time, Fernheim's administration responded positively to the missionaries' request, and in 1972 a decree was issued that prohibited all Mennonites from hiring Ayoreo (Vysokolan 1988). However, this measure was not strictly enforced, and Mennonites continued to hire them. And ironically, a few years later, with the prohibition of trapping (one of the main economic activities in the region and an important source of income for the Ayoreo) and the decline of work opportunities at the mission station in Faro Moro, NTM missionaries quickly made arrangements to have the earlier decree rescinded. The fact that the missionaries were promoting wage labor activities in the colonies among the Ayoreo not only clearly exposes the failure of their "economic programs" at the mission station but also unveils how their agendas changed in response to the vagaries of the economy.

By 1977, Ayoreo seasonal migration to Fernheim Colony had become constant. At times, only about one-third of the population at Faro Moro remained at the mission (NTM and ISB 1977). At the time, the Enhlet, Nivaclé, and Guaraní Occidental had already been granted communal lots to settle in Filadelfia after experiencing ongoing evictions from the town. But the Ayoreo were the only group not granted an urban settlement in Filadelfia. According to Mennonite anthropologist Wilmar Stahl, the administration of the colony restricted such settlement after 1969 because indigenous urban migration was then at its peak (personal communication, 2006). But Mennonites were taking a dual stance, as described in this document by the NTM:

> Mennonites are presently taking a dual stand: officially they are saying they cannot accept further massive Indian immigrations into their Colonies, but

unofficially, many Mennonite employers hire Ayoreo and make them feel that they are very much wanted in the Colonies. The Mennonite society, therefore, needs to be asked to make a decision on the issue of Ayoreo immigration and take a firm stand. (NTM and ISB 1977, 31)

In 1979, the NTM moved their mission from Faro Moro to Campo Loro, forty-eight kilometers north of Filadelfia. The Mennonites supported this decision and hoped that the action would bring a halt to Ayoreo urban migrations. It was hoped that Campo Loro would serve primarily as a bedroom community from where the Ayoreo would come into the colony to work and return when finished. Initially, it seemed to operate that way. During the early 1980s, NTM missionary Fred Sammons portrayed Campo Loro as "a place to spend the night, spend a few days or a couple of weeks, according to the amount of work the Ayoreo have among the Mennonite and Paraguayan employers" (Perasso 1987, 55). However, with time, Ayoreo kept returning to settle in Filadelfia.

In Campo Loro, they worked mostly as *hacheros* (woodcutters), which involved clearing forests and making firewood to supply the steam-powered plant that provided energy to the colonies. Their main employers included the NTM missionaries, who acted as intermediaries with the colony, and individual Mennonites, who also employed Ayoreo in the surrounding aldeas to clear their private lands. As Disi, an Ayoreo in his mid-sixties, put it: "We were the bulldozers of the Mennonites. We cut our forests for them with our own hands. Now they seem to have forgotten that." A Paraguayan truck driver who hauled firewood for the Colony's generator during the 1980s remembers doing up to four trips a day to Filadelfia from Campo Loro to transport the loads, each of which had around twelve thousand kilograms of firewood. Campo Loro soon became an organized labor camp, at the expense of its natural resources.

As they did toward indigenous peoples, the Mennonites took an inconsistent stance vis-à-vis the Ayoreo. On the one hand, they wanted Ayoreo labor, yet on the other hand they were unwilling to accept the social implications that this relationship entailed. This conflict is part of the process of capital accumulation within a specific space, which, according to William Roseberry (2002), creates a new set of economic and social relations, which in turn leads to particular power struggles. For the Ayoreo, the struggle would center around access to the urban spaces of the colonies.

The Fight for Access to Land in Urban Spaces

An important way in which the Ayoreo have responded to the labor regimes imposed by Mennonites has been through the social production and construction of space (Low 2000). Since the late 1960s, they have established temporary settlements in Filadelfia.[12] These settlements were an accommodation of the Ayoreo to the economic restructuring of labor in the region. Importantly, they also served as emergent fields of contestation of the unequal power relations fostered by the Mennonites.

From the beginning, Fernheim's administration was opposed to these settlements and constantly forced the Ayoreo to abandon them by resorting to overt violence. The modus operandi was to pick them up in trucks and send them back to Faro Moro. These evictions did not stop until 1981, when a group of Ayoreo successfully negotiated a permanent settlement in Filadelfia. Considering all the opposition that the Ayoreo faced to inhabit urban spaces, this settlement was a landmark in their fight for access to land (although it was never acknowledged by outsiders). It was the first "official" urban space the Ayoreo secured in the colonies. However, the living conditions in the settlement were precarious. The lot had been previously used as a garbage dump, it did not have access to basic services, and people squatted in plastic tents. Ironically, the place became known as Montecito (Little Forest). Conveniently located, Montecito was conceived of as a temporary space for the Ayoreo to settle while looking for jobs, while in between jobs, or while running errands in town. The people living there were from Campo Loro. The most common pattern of mobility in the settlement was to work for a couple of weeks away in a Mennonite aldea, then return to Montecito and stay there for a few days while in town buying food, supplies, and other commodities before going back to work. Some people also stayed there while trying to arrange jobs. During holidays, people would usually return to Campo Loro. Paraguayans and Mennonites alike recall Montecito as a squatter settlement where Ayoreo lived crowded together. The only infrastructure it had was a water retention area, two outhouses, and a chapel. Yet, the Ayoreo evoke their years there as a time with plenty of access to work and trustful labor relations with the Mennonites. According to some Ayoreo, the only reason why the Mennonites allowed them to stay there for so many consecutive years was because they spent most of their time working elsewhere, away from Filadelfia. Indeed, Ayoreo mobility was high during this time, as they had continuous access to wage labor because of the increasing agricultural and industrial development of the colony.

With time, as the population of Montecito grew, the lack of infrastructure caused living conditions to worsen. As a result, in 1995, instead of trying to improve the situation, Fernheim Colony decided to close down Montecito and send the Ayoreo back to Campo Loro. For a second time, the Ayoreo used their labor force as a bargaining strategy to negotiate access to land. They requested a meeting with Mennonite authorities and expressed their interest in a lot that was conveniently located near Filadelfia. The Mennonites supported this initiative, since they wanted the Ayoreo out of Filadelfia but still close enough to call on them as wage laborers. After declining the purchase of any property within the urban radius of the colony, the Mennonites finally agreed to buy a property (1,800 hectares) located forty-two kilometers north of Filadelfia, which the Ayoreo called Ebetogue. The Mennonites paid for the land and at the request of the Ayoreo agreed to provide food for six months until they were able to build their houses and prepare their gardens. And it was agreed that Mennonite employers would be responsible for picking up and dropping off their employees in Ebetogue rather than in Filadelfia.

As an alternative plan, the Mennonites introduced several economic programs in Ebetogue to prevent future waves of urban migration. But these activities were guided by an economic logic of accumulation that mainly supported the ongoing expansion of the Mennonite economy by exploiting Ayoreo resources and capacities. Activities such as firewood and charcoal production, even though they provided a marginal income for the Ayoreo while living in their village for several years, served mainly to fuel the Mennonite economy by taking advantage of the access to cheap labor. The social and ecological sustainability of these activities and the welfare of the people involved in them were continuously overlooked (Canova 2020).

The spatial dynamics that led to the establishment of Montecito and Ebetogue reveal the dual effect of colonial relations as also noted by scholars in other geographical contexts (see Comaroff and Comaroff 1997; Stoler 2002). Although Mennonites perceived the Ayoreo as "hard-working" people, apt to be deployed as a labor force, they were not considered socially "prepared" to inhabit the urban spaces of the colonies. As a result, Mennonites supported initiatives that would effectively drive the Ayoreo out of the city. The Ayoreo, in turn, audaciously responded by reappropriating the essentialized discourses toward them to their advantage, negotiating first the establishment of Montecito, which lasted thirteen years, and then Ebetogue. Moreover, they refused to follow the expected economic roles that the Mennonites had planned for them by prioritizing their own dynamics of work and spatial mobility, which would take them to Filadelfia again.

Casa Pasajera: A Site of Political Agency in the New Urban Landscape

In 1998, the local Mennonite governor opened a temporary shelter in Filadelfia where any indigenous individual could spend the night while running errands in town. As the Ayoreo were the only group without an urban neighborhood, they soon filled Casa Pasajera and refused to leave. In 2001, the colony's leadership decided to close the locale; in response, the Ayoreo did not return to their villages but rather decided to squat nearby. One group planted itself next to a strip of bushes on the side of the building and another on an empty plot located nearby. These places quickly became known as Casa Baje and Casa Pasajera by the Ayoreo. Casa Baje did not last long as it was soon cleared by bulldozers, but the Ayoreo fought to keep Casa Pasajera open. Their plight was autonomous, with no support from local NGOs, who at the time were invested in supporting "traditional" rather than urban land claims. Resorting to their temporary political alliances and local networks, and even managing to reverse a judicial decision to evict them, they finally secured their place in Casa Pasajera.

By 2013, the Ayoreo took advantage of elections and even received some infrastructure, despite not having legal access to the lot. As a result, three tin sheds, a well, and two outhouses were built in the one-hectare plot where three hundred individuals squatted. While Mennonite authorities dismissed the decision to reopen Casa Pasajera as a political move by some authorities to gain electoral support, for the Ayoreo living in Filadelfia, it was seen as yet another major victory. The reopening challenged the stance of Mennonite and Paraguayan local authorities who rejected an Ayoreo urban neighborhood by deploying a discourse that reinforced an image of the Ayoreo as "uncivilized" and "unprepared" for living with "the whites." During the negotiations to avoid eviction from Casa Pasajera, a local authority manifested this perspective: "[The Ayoreo] are not ready as a group of people to have a neighborhood in Filadelfia. First, they need to be trained on how to live in the white people's world within their communities; otherwise they become alcoholics and turn to prostitution here in the city."

Mennonite communal control over access to land in the colonies has also been a significant hindrance for the Ayoreo in their effort to establish themselves in Filadelfia, as such a decision depends on the colony's administration, which communally owns most of the land on which Filadelfia is built. By maintaining Casa Pasajera as a squatter settlement, Mennonites were able to restrict Ayoreo access to services, a policy that ultimately aimed at encouraging them to return to their rural villages. But this policy has been largely unsuccessful and indeed reinforced local perceptions of Casa Pasajera as a space of illegality and violence. Until the 2010s, local Paraguayans and Mennonites described it as a "dangerous" and "unsafe" place. This perception had a negative impact on the Ayoreo, as they were consequently portrayed as "violent" and often were the targets of accusations when problems arose in the colony.

Ultimately, the successful mobilizations of the Ayoreo to keep Casa Pasajera open reveal their drive to further their own political agency in an urban social space imbued with agendas that reveal racial discrimination. Casa Pasajera, like Montecito during the 1980s, became a major space of contestation toward Mennonites. From there, the Ayoreo have further challenged their historical exclusion from urban spaces and have crafted a new social space in which they can redefine themselves as an urban group of people with rights to inhabit the city, despite a politics of urban invisibility fostered by the state and civil society.

Urbanity as a Strategy for Rural Land Claims

The INDI is the government institution responsible for representing indigenous affairs in Paraguay; however, its presence in the Chaco region has been historically only marginal. Its highly bureaucratic and centralized administration lacks even a branch office in the Chaco, where 48 percent of Paraguay's indigenous population live (DGEEC 2012). The Ayoreo are highly aware of the limitations of this government agency to support their claims. Importantly, local NGOs are working alongside Ayoreo groups to secure access to land, although their strategy has been to put the Ayoreo in so-called voluntary isolation at the center of the claims. While this is an important and urgent task due to the rapid rates of deforestation that are endangering the survival of noncontacted Ayoreo (IWGIA 2010), such a strategy has had unintended negative consequences for urban Ayoreo. The precarious living conditions of Ayoreo in urban spaces and their long history of labor in the colonies drives outsiders to construct them as having lost their "culture" and "tradition" and therefore not worthy of receiving support—especially to further land claims. That is, urban Ayoreo do not fit the idealized image of the Indian as constructed by NGOs and government officials, an image that Alcida Rita Ramos has rightly referred to as the "hyperreal Indian"

(1992). Ayoreo living in Filadelfia, well aware of these constructions about them, have chosen to present their plight independent of NGOs. Over time, they have capitalized on temporary alliances with other local actors to advance their cause. Ironically, this has fostered a perception of them as being "easily manipulated" or "not being prepared yet to know what is best for them," as was stated by a local NGO officer in a patronizing tone. But the story of a group of Ayoreo living in Casa Pasajera furthering a rural land claim deeply challenges these stereotyped perceptions.

This story began with several groups of extended families a year after they moved to Casa Pasajera in 2003 from Ebetogue. The leader of the group, Chome Etacore, was already negotiating with local authorities in 2004 when the megaproject known in Paraguay as Corredor Vial Bioceánico—directed by the Ministry of Public Works and Communication—was announced to be implemented in the Chaco.[13] At the time, this project had funding for preliminary assessments and the execution of environmental and social mitigation plans for a total amount of US$14,544,610 (*ABC Color* 2005b). As soon as Chome learned about the project, he requested the support of the Gobernación de Boquerón to acquire 3,200 hectares, located 120 kilometers north of Filadelfia in the area of Estancia Tagua.

The request was welcomed by local authorities, as Casa Pasajera was at its peak of population and suffered from consequent social problems. Mennonite authorities even pressured the Paraguayan government to accelerate the paperwork for the land acquisition. In 2005, with the process still stalled, the Gobernación de Boquerón and the Mennonite nonprofit organization Esperanza Chaqueña, with the support of Fernheim's administration, came up with an alternative plan. A Mennonite rancher agreed to host Ayoreo families on his ranch for two years. In return, the families would clear 140 hectares of forest, and in exchange for their work they would produce and sell charcoal through Esperanza Chaqueña to the Mennonite Fernheim Cooperative. The groups of families from Ebetogue welcomed the project, since it would give them temporary work; thirty families moved to the Mennonite's ranch in early 2005, and the place came to be known as Chaidi 2. But simultaneously they continued to lobby the Ministry of Public Works and Communication, with the added support of the then nascent Ayoreo organization Union de Nativos Ayoreo del Paraguay (UNAP) to accelerate the process of land acquisition.[14]

The goal of local authorities was to decongest Casa Pasajera, which they successfully did by resettling this group in Chaidi 2. The Gobernación de Boquerón provided plastic tents and agreed to offer medical attention to the families at the ranch. The Ayoreo continued to come and go to Filadelfia to buy food provisions, visit family members, and conduct other business. However, their actual residence time in Casa Pasajera was minimal. As in previous, similar cases, the temporary solution to the overcrowding of Casa Pasajera was only partially solved, while simultaneously the charcoal production project allowed the Mennonites to continue to benefit from the Ayoreo labor force.

After a year and a half of the Ayoreo living in Chaidi 2, problems emerged with the owner of the ranch, as he did not keep his word about awarding each Ayoreo family a milking cow for each hectare of land that they cleared. As tensions arose, Chome Etacore demanded that the Gobernación accelerate the necessary paperwork so that they could move to their newly acquired land; otherwise, they threatened to return to Casa Pasajera. By then, the Gobernación already had the title to the land, but according to a staff member, they could not resettle the Ayoreo due to insufficient funds needed to provide basic infrastructure. Finally, in July 2006, they acquired the necessary funds for the resettlement project, and about half of the thirty families moved to the new village, Ijnapui.

This process of land acquisition reveals how the Ayoreo have tactically deployed essentialized perceptions of themselves as "a problem" in Casa Pasajera to put pressure on local authorities to further their land claim. This process also shows the colliding agendas of different actors, and how Ayoreo negotiators strengthened their political agency in an unequal field of power. Bureaucracy and lack of funds delayed the process of land acquisition for two years. Meanwhile, the Mennonites took this opportunity to engage the Ayoreo in their market-oriented "development" schema based on charcoal production. This not only proved to be environmentally unsustainable but also fostered Ayoreo dependency on them rather than nurturing their autonomy and self-sufficiency.

"The New Place": Urban Possibilities Reconsidered

By 2015, the Ayoreo were celebrating the establishment of Guidai Ichai (the New Community), their new and "official" urban neighborhood in Filadelfia. After decades of being denied an urban neighborhood, the Ayoreo were granted, like other indigenous groups in Filadelfia, an urban barrio. More than 110 families with a marked trajectory of urban residence and labor relations with Mennonites settled there. The formation of the neighborhood cannot be understood as an isolated project conceived exclusively by outsiders; rather, its establishment must be understood in the context of a long history of political mobilizations and contested negotiations furthered by the Ayoreo to inhabit the urban spaces of the Mennonite colonies as detailed in this chapter. The barrio was secured without the support of the INDI, the government institution in charge of indigenous affairs, which, to the present day, continues to be absent in the region. A group of progressive local authorities who envisioned a future for this project alongside the Ayoreo had the challenging role of convincing their fellow Mennonite community and the authorities of the Fernheim Colony to approve this initiative. Once the lot was granted, the Ayoreo and local authorities took the time to work together to establish a leadership style representative of the different groups of families living in the barrio. Despite the efforts put forward by local authorities toward this urban project, resistance to the Ayoreo urban presence remains. This is evidenced in the small size of the lot granted (less than three hectares for 110 families). In addition, basic services have not yet been fully installed, and the neighborhood is not yet legally recognized by the INDI, which prevents the Ayoreo from having legal autonomy over the affairs of the neighborhood. On the other hand, the Ayoreo families living there no longer experience the traumatic evictions of the past, a recurrent modus operandi of the colony that had intensified during the previous twenty years. Ultimately, the current legal status and environment of Guidai Ichai reveal the challenges still ahead for the Ayoreo as they continue to strengthen their political agency to secure land and dignified living conditions in urban spaces and beyond.

In recent years, while indigenous urbanity has gained renewed public and academic attention in Paraguay (see, e.g., Bogado, Portillo, and Villagra 2016; Conapi1 2017), the topic remains underexplored in the Paraguayan Chaco, receiving only minimal attention (e.g., Glauser and Patzi 2014; Schwarz et al. 2018a; Schwarz et al. 2018b). This chapter aims to contribute to the analysis of indigenous urbanity in this highly dynamic region, offering a renewed perspective to reflect on the complexities of this topic, which in the Ayoreo case reveals the intertwined connections between indigenous urbanity, labor relations, and political mobilizations for land claims.

An examination of the history of Ayoreo settlements in Filadelfia unveils the dual effects of colonialism as manifested through space. The contradiction of the colonial process of domination lies in the fact that, while it aims to incorporate a group of people, it simultaneously fosters their "Othering" (Sider 1987). From the beginning of the "contact" period, Mennonite perceptions of the Ayoreo were shaped by positivistic Eurocentric ideas about indigenous peoples as primitives, and so they relegated them to the realm of the wilderness (see Turner 1991; Ramos 1992). At the same time, by engaging in a "civilizing project," the Mennonites sought to incorporate the Ayoreo into their "natural" order of things—namely, their Western ideology shaped by ideas of individualism, hard work, and Christian faith. The Ayoreo, after being divested of their traditional livelihoods, were incorporated into a neocolonial system as laborers, who in order to adapt to new and changing conditions migrated to urban spaces. When this happened, the Mennonites reverted to their discursive construction of the Ayoreo as "Other," which rationalized their politics of exclusion, ultimately refusing that the Ayoreo establish themselves officially and permanently in Filadelfia.

Overall, the Ayoreo have responded by strategically reappropriating urban spaces to advance their demands. They have used their labor power and urban presence as a bargaining tool to fight for their rights to inhabit urban spaces. As a result, in the 1980s, they secured Montecito, an urban settlement, which despite its precarious conditions lasted thirteen years. A decade later, they fought to keep the urban settlement Casa Pasajera open despite constant threats of evictions, and by 2015 they were finally granted permission by the Mennonites to establish an urban barrio. In addition, the Ayoreo used their urban presence as a strategy to further rural land claims. From Filadelfia, they made their demands more visible to local authorities, sparking the latter to support their claims precisely because the Mennonites sought to facilitate Ayoreo efforts to leave Filadelfia. Through this, they secured rural land claims such as Ebetogue and Ijnapui. The challenges that the Ayoreo successfully negotiated in an independent manner—without the committed support of government institutions or NGOs—remain mostly invisible due to the persistent and prevalent construction of them as "marginal" in urban spaces and therefore lacking agency. These cases, however, reveal how Ayoreo urban production of space has been successfully reproduced despite the structural inequalities that result from economic transformations and a politics of exclusion, the primary forces that shape relations toward indigenous peoples in the region. At the same time, the changing configurations of Ayoreo social geographies in urban spaces are an expression of the ways in which indigenous peoples are creatively reconfiguring spaces for social participation and political recognition in today's Chaco.

Notes

1. Data presented in this paper were collected during long-term fieldwork conducted between 2004 and 2017 in Ayoreo villages and the Fernheim Mennonite Colony in Paraguay, partly funded with the kind support of the Wenner-Gren Foundation.

2. All the names in this chapter have been changed to protect the privacy of interviewed individuals.

3. This was one of the three *colonias*—as Mennonites call their communities—that were established in the central Chaco region between 1926 and 1947. The other two were Menno Colony and Neu-Halbstadt Colony. The Mennonites are a diasporic religious community who trace their origin to Huldrych Zwingli, the founder of an Anabaptist movement in Switzerland in 1525. They eventually migrated to Prussia, where they lived for approximately 250 years. When they were again obliged to migrate, Catherine II invited them to Russia, which received approximately thirteen thousand Mennonites from 1788 onward. From Russia, they started migrating again toward the end of 1800s (Urry 2006).

4. In one encounter, the Stahl family was suddenly attacked while at their home. The event resulted in the death of three of its members, while two others were injured (Hein 1990, 20–23). According to the Ayoreo, the man who led this attack was called Abuejane.

5. The Mennonite Central Committee was founded in 1920. It began as a response to the needs of fellow Mennonites in the former Soviet Union. However, it has expanded to support other Mennonite communities around the world (see www.mcc.org).

6. This post is located forty miles northwest of Filadelfia.

7. The Salesians, a Catholic order, were one of the religious groups interested in missionizing the Ayoreo. Their attempts to contact them started in 1957, a year after they had taken charge of an Ayoreo child, Ikevi Posorajai, who had been "hunted down" by Paraguayans in an area known as Ingavi. He was later used as a translator by Catholic missionaries as well as by New Tribes Mission (NTM) missionaries for contacting the Ayoreo. (For the history of Ikevi, see Amarilla 2004 and Vysokolan 1988.)

8. Puerto María Auxiliadora is located 240 kilometers north of Filadelfia, in the department of Alto Paraguay.

9. The New Tribes Mission—now known as Ethnos 360—is an evangelical missionary society composed of born-again Christians who are dedicated to the evangelization of "tribal groups." It was founded in 1942 by Paul Fleming and is based in Sanford, Florida. Currently, the society has more than three thousand missionaries working in twenty-five countries (see https://ethnos360.org/).

10. Today, Cerro León is located within the Parque Nacional Defensores del Chaco.

11. This was the Symposium on Inter-Ethnic Conflict in South America, organized by the Ethnology Department of the University of Bern (Switzerland) and the World Council of Churches and held in Bridgetown, Barbados. In the meeting, formal reports of indigenous situations in several Latin American countries were analyzed. Participants issued the Declaration of Barbados, in which several states, religious missions, and social scientists assumed responsibility for immediate action to halt aggressions and contribute significantly to the process of indigenous self-determination (see Dostal 1972).

12. In the late 1960s, some of these included the Pista de Aviación (which lasted approximately two years) and Oai Cachodi (two years). In the 1970s, they settled in Najunanie (one year), Ayoreode Chaidi (1972–1973), and later Pasigode (1974, again for one year).

13. This project is part of a larger transnational initiative started in 1997 by private companies and the governments of Argentina, Bolivia, Brazil, Chile, and Paraguay. The program, called Zona de Integración del Centro Oeste de América del Sur (ZICOSUR), aimed at fostering social and economic development in subregions of the participating countries by integrating asymmetric economies (through the construction of transportation networks, ports, etc.), with the larger goal of fostering interregional trade as a buttress against strengthening Asia Pacific markets. The component Corredor Vial Bioceánico involves the establishment of a communication net that crosses Brazil, Paraguay, Argentina, and Chile with the aim of connecting the Atlantic and Pacific coasts.

In Paraguay, the project crosses through the Chaco region, and in 2000, the Ministry of Public Works and Communication, with financial support from the Inter-American Development Bank, drew up a plan for seven road routes crossing the Paraguayan Chaco that would need to be asphalted and improved. Construction started in 2001 but was suspended due to lack of funding. The Brazilians in particular were interested in the completion of this project, since it would potentially allow them to market their beef products (ZICOSUR 2007). Construction has resumed only very recently, in 2019, with funding from various international and government institutions.

14. The total investment to buy the land was 500 million guaraníes (approximately US$100,000). The Ministry of Public Works and Communication was authorized by Congress in 2004 to utilize this amount; however, the land was not acquired until almost a year later due to bureaucratic paperwork (*ABC Color* 2005a).

Bibliography

ABC Color. 2005a. "Ayoreos reclaman compra de tierras." February 19.
——. 2005b. "Corredor Bioceánico es una trampa, afirman." October 17.
Amarilla, Deisy. 2004. *Captura del ayoreo Iquebi*. Asunción: Centro de Estudios Antropológicos de la Universidad Católica.
Basso, Ellen. 1973. Review of *The Situation of the Indian in South America: Contributions to the Study of Inter-Ethnic Conflict in the Non-Andean Regions of South America*, edited by Walter Dostal. *American Anthropologist* 75, no. 6 (December): 1865–68.
——. 1975. "Reply to Calvin Redekop." *American Anthropologist* 77, no. 1 (March): 83–84.
Bedoya Silva-Santisteban, Alvaro, and Eduardo Bedoya Garland. 2005. "Servidumbres por deudas y marginación en el Chaco de Paraguay." ILO Working Papers, International Labor Organization.
Bessire, Lucas. 2014. *Behold the Black Caiman: A Chronicle of Ayoreo Life*. Princeton, NJ: Princeton University Press.
Bogado, Marcelo, Rafael Portillo, and Rodrigo Villagra. 2016. "Alquiler de tierras y territorios indígenas en el Paraguay." *Cadernos do Lepaarq* 13, no. 26 (July–December): 106–23.
Briones, Claudia. 2007. "Our Struggle Has Just Begun: Experiences of Belonging and Mapuche Formations of Self." In *Indigenous Experience Today*, edited by Marisol de la Cadena and Orin Starn, 99–124. Oxford: Berg.

Comaroff, John L., and Jean Comaroff. 1997. *Of Revelation and Revolution*. Vol. 2, *The Dialectics of Modernity on a South African Frontier*. Chicago: University of Chicago Press.

Canova, Paola. 2015. "Los Ayoreo en las colonias menonitas: Un análisis de un enclave agroindustrial en el Chaco paraguayo." In *Capitalismo en las selvas: Enclaves industriales en el Chaco y Amazonía indígenas, 1850–1950*, edited by Lorena Córdoba, Federico Bossert, and Nicolás Richard, 271–86. San Pedro de Atacama, Chile: Ediciones del Desierto.

———. 2020. "Negotiating Environmental Subjectivities: Charcoal Production and Mennonite-Ayoreo Relations in the Paraguayan Chaco." *Journal of Mennonite Studies* 38: 61–84.

Conapi1. 2017. *Documental indígenas urbanos en Paraguay*. YouTube, March 4. https://www.youtube.com/watch?v=Sx1OnleC5Z8.

Dirección General de Encuestas, Estadísticas y Censo (DGEEC). 2012. *III Tercer Censo Nacional de poblacion y viviendas para pueblos indigenas: Pueblos indigenas en el Paraguay, resultados preliminares*. Asunción: DGEEC Publicaciones.

Dostal, Walter, ed. 1972. *The Situation of the Indian in South America: Contributions to the Study of Inter-Ethnic Conflict in the Non-Andean Regions of South America*. Geneva: World Council of Churches.

Glauser, Marcos, and Igor Patzi. 2014. *Indígenas en contextos urbanos de la región del Chaco Sudamericano*. Asunción: ICCO; La Paz: KiA.

Graber, Christian L. 1964. *The Coming of the Moros: From Spears to Pruning Hooks*. Scottdale, PA: Herald Press.

Hack, Henk. 1977. "Indianer und Mennoniten im Paraguayischen Chaco." Filadelfia, Paraguay: Asociación de Servicios de Cooperación Indigena-Menonita.

Harvey, David. 2001. *Spaces of Capital: Towards a Critical Geography*. Edinburgh: Edinburgh University Press.

Hein, David. 1990. *Los Ayoreos, nuestros vecinos: Comienzos de la misión al norte del Chaco*. Asunción: Imprenta Modelo.

International Work Group for Indigenous Affairs (IWGIA). 2010. "The Case of the Ayoreo." Report 4. Copenhagen: International Work Group for Indigenous Affairs.

Klassen, Peter. 2002. *Mennonites in Paraguay: Encounter with Indians and Paraguayans*. Vol. 2. Translated by Gunther H. Schmitt. 2nd ed. Kitchener, Ont., Canada: Pandora Press.

Low, Setha M. 2000. *On the Plaza: The Politics of Public Space and Culture*. Austin: University of Texas Press.

McSweeney, Kendra, and Brad Jokisch. 2015. "Native Amazonians' Strategic Urbanization: Shaping Territorial Possibilities through Cities." *Journal of Latin American and Caribbean Anthropology* 20, no. 1 (March): 13–33.

New Tribes Mission and Indian Settlement Board (NTM and ISB). 1977. "Proyecto Ayoreo: Economic Development at El Faro Moro; What Is Feasible?" Unpublished manuscript.

Perasso, José A. 1987. *Crónicas de cacerías humanas: La tragedia ayoreo*. Asunción: El Lector.

Ramos, Alcida Rita. 1992. *The Hyperreal Indian*. Série Antropologia 135. Brasília: Universidade de Brasília.

Redekop, Calvin. 1980. *Strangers Become Neighbors: Mennonites and Indigenous Relations in the Paraguayan Chaco*. Scottdale, PA: Herald Press.

Renshaw, John. 2002. *The Indians of the Paraguayan Chaco: Identity and Economy*. Lincoln: University of Nebraska Press.

Roseberry, William. 2002. "Understanding Capitalism: Historically, Structurally, Spatially." In *Locating Capitalism in Time and Space: Global Restructurings, Politics, and Identity*, edited by David Nugent, 61–79. Stanford, CA: Stanford University Press.

Schwarz, Burkhard Richard, et al. 2018a. *Colono colonización menonita y resistecia indígena: Indígenas urbanos y políticas públicas en el Chaco Central*. Filadelfia, Paraguay: Tierra Libre, Instituto Social y Ambiental.

———. 2018b. *Disidencia indígena urbana: Los nivaclé de cayin'o'clim*. Filadelfia, Paraguay: Tierra Libre, Instituto Social y Ambiental.

Sider, Gerald. 1987. "When Parrots Learn to Talk, and Why They Can't: Domination, Deception, and Self-Deception in Indian-White Relations." *Comparative Studies in Society and History* 29, no. 1 (January): 3–23.

Soja, Edward W. 1989. *Postmodern Geographies: The Reassertion of Space in Critical Social Theory*. London: Verso.

Stahl, Wilmar. 1982. *Escenario indígena chaqueño, pasado y presente*. Filadelfia, Paraguay: Asociación de Servicios de Cooperación Indígena-Menonita.

Stoler, Ann L. 2002. *Carnal Knowledge and Imperial Power: Race and the Intimate in Colonial Rule*. Berkeley: University of California Press.

Turner, Terence. 1991. "Representing, Resisting, Rethinking: Historical Transformations of Kayapo Culture and Anthropological Consciousness." In *Colonial Situations: Essays on the Contextualization of Ethnographic Knowledge*, edited by George W. Stocking Jr., 285–313. Madison: University of Wisconsin Press.

Urry, James. 2006. *Mennonites, Politics, and Peoplehood: Europe-Russia-Canada 1525 to 1980*. Winnipeg: University of Manitoba Press.

US Agency for International Development (USAID). 1977. "Mennonite Settlement Program for Indians in the Central Chaco." Unpublished manuscript.

Vysokolan, Oleg. 1988. "El regreso de Ikevi." In *Misión, etnocidio*, edited by Ticio Escobar, 287–306. Asunción: RP Ediciones.

Zona de Integración del Centro Oeste de América del Sur (ZICOSUR). 2007. "Objetivos." http://zicosur.co/objetivos/.

Sarah Patricia Cerna Villagra, Sara Mabel Villalba Portillo, Eduardo Tamayo Belda, and Roque Mereles Pintos

four **PARAGUAY'S POLITICAL SYSTEM FROM AUTHORITARIAN HEGEMONY TO MODERATE PLURALISM, 1954–2019**[1]

Introduction

President Horacio Cartes consolidated his position within the Colorado Party (ANR) in July 2015 when his favored candidate, Pedro Alliana, defeated dissident Mario Abdo Benítez in party leadership elections by a margin of more than one hundred thousand votes. With this triumph, the party's pro-Cartes faction, Honor Colorado (HC, replicating the initials of its leader), consolidated its control within the party but also exacerbated the party's fracturing following the establishment of the dissident group Colorado Añetete (Guaraní for "Authentic Colorado"), led by Abdo Benítez and mainly integrated by leading senators.

Despite this internal fracture, ANR territorial control at a national level was upheld in the 2015 municipal elections, in which it won 148 of 250 localities, or almost 60 percent of the country's municipalities. Although these results are positive for the ANR overall, as they confirm the party's power at a subnational level, the ANR suffered essential defeats in emblematic cities such as Asunción, where the Colorado candidate had the clear endorsement of President Cartes, and Encarnación, where the ANR had been continuously in power for the previous seventy-five years. Both cases demonstrate that the opposition can win when it joins forces around candidates with a strong level of popularity, as in the case of Mario Ferreiro in the capital and Luis Yd in the southeastern city of Encarnación.

The Partido Liberal Radical Auténtico (PLRA) won the mayor's office in seventy-five municipalities, the Unión Nacional de Ciudadanos Éticos (UNACE) in just three, the Frente Guasú only two, and the Revolutionary Febrerista Party no more than one, with twenty-one localities won by local electoral alliances. The general results of these elections showed Honor Colorado's strength at a subnational level. The current scattering of opposition forces, despite the ANR's internal factionalism, ensured the continuity of the Colorado Party's hegemony, reclaimed in 2013, in the presidential elections of 2018. This chapter aims to describe the evolution of the political system in Paraguay from the beginning of General Alfredo Stroessner's authoritarian regime in 1954, through the democratic transition and the new institutional rules of 1992, until the political change of 2008 and the most recent municipal elections of 2015.[2] The chapter underscores the principal characteristics of Paraguay's political system as well as the key features of the political organization and the party system in the country. Although burdened by the shadow of its authoritarian traditions, Paraguay continues to struggle to define itself as a new and emerging democracy in Latin America.

Principal Characteristics of Paraguay's Political System

The principal characteristics of Paraguay's political system are: (1) it is one of the most enduring political systems in the region, although not necessarily among the most stable; (2) it features two traditional parties with a minimum of ideological distance between them (Cerna and Solís 2014, 91); and it is marked by (3) a pernicious social-economic structure, (4) accentuated clientelism, (5) a systematic government agency problem (Barreda and Bou 2010), and (6) a political culture based on strong and charismatic leadership (Uharte Pozas 2012). This political system has its roots in the late nineteenth century, when the two traditional political parties were created. Since that time, these parties have been competing in diverse fields and have dichotomized Paraguayans' political preferences. These parties are the Asociación Nacional Republicana–Partido Colorado (ANR) and the historical Partido Liberal, now known as the Partido Liberal Radical Auténtico (PLRA) (Lewis 2016).

The political parties in Paraguay were established after the War of the Triple Alliance, or Paraguayan War (1864–1870). Around 1887, both the Democratic Center (later the Liberal Party) and the National Republican Party (later the National Republican Association, or Colorado Party) were created; these are the oldest parties in the country and among the longest-standing parties in Latin America (Alcántara 2004). The National Republican Party was established as a champion of republican and national values; the Democratic Center, after the economic, political, and social debacle of the Paraguayan War, instead supported economic liberalism and promoted foreign investment in Paraguay.

TABLE 4.1 Ideological Displacement of the Traditional Paraguayan Political Parties

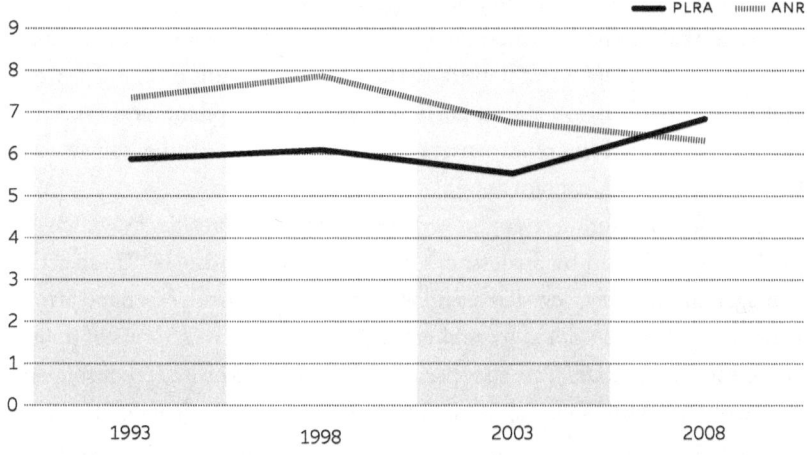

Source: The authors, based on data from PELA-USAL.

It is important to note that today, there is no significant ideological distance between the ANR and PLRA; both are clearly positioned at the right of the political spectrum, as evidenced by the Parliamentary Elites in Latin America Observatory (PELA) project at the University of Salamanca in Spain. According to tools developed by PELA, on a scale from 1 to 10 where 1 indicates the extreme left and 10 the extreme right, in 2008 ANR legislators were located, on average, at 6.33 and PLRA legislators at 6.78. However, it is interesting to observe how, from 1993 to 2008, the positions have been crossed; the ANR has experienced a little displacement toward the center whereas the PLRA has moved to the right.

Paraguay's socioeconomic structure is based on ranching and export agriculture. Just 2 percent of landowners hold more than 80 percent of rural property (MAG 2009). The economic and political elites enjoy strong bonds, and the political parties represent these elites' interests with respect to land, agricultural property, and tax policies. Paraguay's political system has been defined by certain patterns such as clientelism, corruption, and impunity and has obviously failed to establish the rule of law.

For most of the second half of the twentieth century, Paraguay was controlled by a single political party, the ANR. This hegemony in the political system was very significant for the country as it established the modern roots of the current political system and explains the following traits: (1) the presence of a state party without clear distinctions in functions, (2) a party with unlimited resources as a consequence of its extraction of the state's assets, (3) a majority loyal to the president that has transformed the legislative branch into a formal institution without real or independent powers, (4) formally democratic electoral processes that mask reality, as the official party was always triumphant, and (5) a party system that eroded the other parties' ability to function, to the benefit of the hegemonic party (Alcántara 2008).[3]

The 1940 constitution strengthened the powers of the presidency, which were further strengthened by Stroessner's reforms in 1967 and 1988. These actions damaged the country's legislative and judicial branches. Under General Stroessner, the ANR was co-opted by soldiers addicted to power. In terms of political culture and its practices, Paraguay has been distinguished by its: (1) consolidation of personality leadership, (2) patronage (*patronazgo*) as the principal structure to gain government employment, and (3) political control of the institutions of justice. These features are similar to those found in Mexico during the *priísta* regime that led the country for seventy years (Cerna 2017; Solís and Cerna 2017). In both settings, *caudillismo* leadership was solidified through perks given to those loyal to the regime, such as the reward of personal benefits or access to justice that was "hand-made" for their interests. Those most harmed by these practices have been the rule of law and society's majority, who do not benefit from privileged access to the hegemonic party (Cerna 2017).

PARAGUAY'S POLITICAL ORGANIZATION

Paraguay has adopted political decentralization in the context of a unitary system. The country is divided into seventeen departments and the capital, as established in the constitution of 1992. The distribution of central government functions provides for executive power to be held by the president of the republic, who is assisted by a vice president. Both have a five-year term and cannot be reelected. Members of the legislative power also serve a five-year term concurrent with that of the president, but they indeed can be reelected for the same post. Congress is bicameral. The Chamber of Deputies has eighty seats, and the Senate has forty-five. Election to corporate bodies like Congress is based on proportional representation, with seats assigned to parties through the D'Hondt formula.

PRINCIPAL FEATURES OF THE PARTY SYSTEM

The principal features of Paraguay's political system are: (1) the dominance (before 1989, the hegemony) of a single political party; and (2) a conservative stamp on political institutions. According to Giovanni Sartori's classification (1976), Paraguay discarded its authoritarian hegemonic party system and transformed into a two-party system during the democratic transition after 1989. In the late 1990s it became a moderately pluralistic system due to the estrangement of a Colorado Party faction led by General Lino César Oviedo. General Oviedo (who participated in the coup d'état against Stroessner in 1989) created a movement within the party called the Unión Nacional de Ciudadanos Éticos (UNACE, National Union of Ethical Citizens), which would later form a separate party of the same name.

The Effective Number of Parties formula measures the number of parties in a party system weighted by their electoral strength. It can weight parties by votes (Eff N_v) or by seats won (Eff N_s). This measure shows that Paraguay's party system has become more pluralistic since third forces have gained electoral relevance. Although these parties have won spaces of power and political representation, parties such as UNACE and the Partido Patria Querida (PPQ, Beloved Fatherland Party) do not seriously threaten the traditional parties (Colorados and Liberals), and they share the same space on the right of the political spectrum with the ANR and the PLRA. Paraguay's Left has faced deep adversity in breaking into a system dominated by conservative parties and actors.[4]

However, after holding power for more than six decades, the ANR became weaker, and its capacity to maintain the loyalty of its voters declined. Additionally, the country had suffered poor economic growth for several years and severe unemployment, coupled with political and social conflicts. In that political scenario, with a shortage of charismatic leaders in the traditional parties, Fernando Lugo emerged as a political force in 2006. According to Lorena Soler, Lugo "was above all, a president who couldn't be linked to the traditional political class," and from this status he "drew his principal legitimacy" (2012, 39).

As we can observe in table 4.3, 2008's elections were crucial for Paraguay's political system. The traditional parties confronted a critical situation in which power vacuums enabled new political movements to appear (Soler 2012, 40). For example, Lugo's Alianza Patriótica para el Cambio (APC, Patriotic Alliance for Change) became an unusual electoral tool as it took into account various proposals such as integral agricultural reform, economic recovery, combating corruption, judicial reform to increase the independence of the judiciary, the restoration of national sovereignty, and solutions to the most urgent social problems (Fretes 2012, 79). Given Paraguay's political climate, it is amusing to observe how it was possible that a movement such as the Alliance, and particularly Lugo, could

TABLE 4.2 Paraguay's Effective Number of Parties (Eff Ns, Chamber of Deputies)

Party[1]	Percentage of seats earned by party, Chamber of Deputies (n = 80 after 1993)						
	1989 (n = 72)	1993	1998	2003	2008	2013	2018
ANR	66.6	47.5	56.25	46.25	37.5	55.0	52.5
PLRA	29.1	41.25	32.5	26.25	33.75	33.75	21.25
PEN		11.25	11.25			2.5	2.5
PRF	2.7						
PLR	1.3						
PPQ				12.5	3.75	1.25	3.75
UNACE				12.5	18.75	2.5	
PPS				2.5			
MPT					1.25		
PDP					1.25		
APC					2.5	1.25	
ADB					1.25		
AP						2.5	
FG						1.25	
GANAR							16.25
PH							2.5
MCN							1.25
EFF Ns	1.89[2]	2.45	1.94	3.18	3.43	2.39	2.86

Source: Solís and Cerna 2019, 276.

1. ANR (Asociación Nacional Republicana–Partido Colorado), PLRA (Partido Liberal Radical Auténtico), PEN (Partido Encuentro Nacional), PRF (Partido Revolucionario Febrerista), PLR (Partido Liberal Radical), PPQ (Partido Patria Querida), UNACE (Unión Nacional de Ciudadanos Éticos), PPS (Partido País Solidario), MPT (Movimiento Popular Tekojoja), PDP (Partido Democrático Progresista), APC (Alianza Pasión Chaqueña), ADB (Alianza Departamental Boquerón), AP (Avanza País), FG (Frente Guasú), GANAR (Alianza GANAR, an electoral alliance including the PLRA, FG, PDP, PRF, and others), PH (Partido Hagamos), and MCN (Movimiento Cruzada Nacional).

2. See Gallagher 2019.

TABLE 4.3 The Evolution of Effective Numbers in Paraguay (1989–2018)

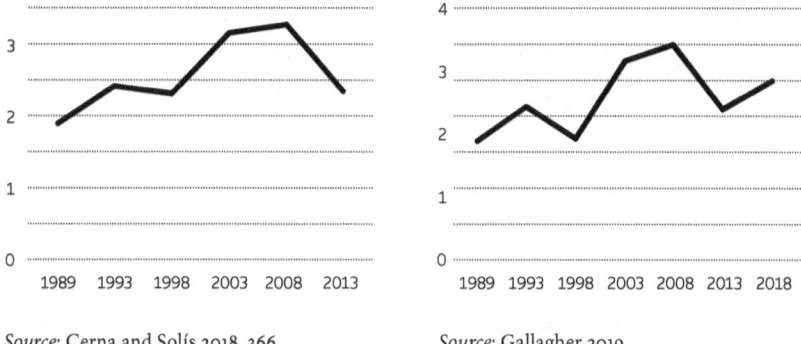

Source: Cerna and Solís 2018, 366.   Source: Gallagher 2019.

place the agricultural issue at the forefront of the national agenda and encourage its partners, especially the PLRA, as well as its opponents to share the same view.

Alfredo Stroessner's Regime (1954–1989)

General Alfredo Stroessner Matiauda's authoritarian regime began in 1954 after the coup d'état he led against President Federico Chaves, also from the ANR. Stroessner then stood for election as the only presidential candidate in the July 11, 1954, elections and took office constitutionally on August 15, 1954. Stroessner rose to power during an uncertain political period in the country. His arrival—which did not overturn the hegemonic party's regime, which had ruled since 1947 after the Civil War—"demolished constitutional mechanisms, glorifying the promise of stability with Executive Power under the rule of a soldier" (Gómez 2014, 88). Stronismo's political end was by way of another coup d'état generated from the regime's core. It was led by Stroessner's son's father-in-law, Andrés Rodríguez, who was trusted by Stroessner. Rodríguez was supported by a military group and a faction of Colorado Party leaders who were in confrontation with Stroessner.

THE REGIME'S PRINCIPAL FEATURES

The two principal features of the political development of the *stronista* regime are: (1) its *granitic unity* (strong alliance between the armed forces, the party, and the state); and (2) Paraguay's international cooperation with the national security doctrine of the United States.

Stroessner's regime rested on the tripartite alliance among the military, the Colorado Party, and the Paraguayan state, the three centers of power in the country. Stroessner's assumption of the presidency in 1954 was followed by a suspension of civil liberties and constitutional guarantees, and a series of political purges within the ruling ANR (Jara Goiris 2004, 192).

The party was subject to military domination, with Stroessner as the top military and party figure. Colorado Party leaders and military officers who did not agree with Stroessner were severely punished. These political purges and the "serious *stronista* repression" (Dalla-Corte 2012, 193) affected not only the Colorados and the armed forces but the whole of society and national politics throughout the almost thirty-five years the regime persisted (Pangrazio 2000, 193).

During the first years of Stroessner's government, the vast majority of opposition party leaders and union and student organization representatives were forced to leave the country (Jara Goiris 2004, 192), and hundreds of thousands of others departed the country fleeing oppression. The biggest stain on Stroessner's government was, without a doubt, the repression and systematic human rights violations across more than three decades that it imposed (Pangrazio 2000, 193).

Once dissent inside the armed forces and the party was crushed, Stroessner was strong enough to dismiss any social and political concerns that arose about his regime (Nickson 2014, 267). By 1960 he had acquired almost total control over the party and was able to put down any resistance, so that the presence of an "opposition" party could be allowed and tolerated by the regime insofar as it was needed to demonstrate a pretense of political plurality. *Et voilà*, the granitic unity (armed forces–party–state) was built, and Paraguay was cleared of any active defiance that could have confronted the regime and the interests of its supporters.

During the 1960s, a *fraudulent bourgeoisie* was forged,[5] a social group linked to the state bureaucracy and more closely related to the president than to the national bourgeoisie (which was mainly the cattle oligarchy). Proximity to the president allowed the fraudulent bourgeoisie to become enormously rich during this time through negotiations with the state, smuggling, clientelism, various other privileges reserved for the inner circle, and narcotrafficking of either local production or transshipment from neighboring countries to the United States. They also benefited from illegal grants of vast quantities of land supposedly allocated to the regime's agrarian reform. Colorado politicians and military officers became Paraguay's nouveau riche thanks to their access to such patronage (Fogel

1982). The Colorado Party transformed into a party-state, while the armed forces controlled and restrained society (Jara Goiris 2004, 193).

In a country that was mostly rural, that had little experience with democracy, and that had endured an authoritarian political culture, Stroessner found a way to be the vertex of the pyramid and to have the party, the state, and the military serve as supporting institutions (Jara Goiris 2004, 221–22). Even though the armed forces were strongly identified with the party-state, the regime was not fully a military regime but rather a personalistic dictatorship built around the figure of the caudillo. Stroessner reshaped the party so that soon it was no longer a traditional party of notable regional caudillos but rather a "political hierarchical machine that offered complete loyalty" to the autocrat (Nickson 2014, 278). At the peak of the party's structure was the Junta de Gobierno, which was responsible for securing support in regularly scheduled elections, enabling the regime to demonstrate a democratic facade.

The Paraguayan state, still governed under the 1940 constitution, was changed from a theoretically plural political system with certain democratic characteristics to an authoritarian, personalist, and nondemocratic regime. That constitution, which organized a strong state and gave superiority to the executive branch, established the president's power to declare a state of siege and to dictate law by decree should there be a legislative impasse. These powers were used by Stroessner for almost three lustrums to exercise de facto absolute power. The 1940 constitution limited the president to two five-year terms, which would have disqualified Stroessner from running in the 1968 elections. However, Stroessner had consolidated his personal power, so he was able to call a constitutional convention and promulgate a new constitution in 1967, which reset the clock on term limits, allowing Stroessner to run in 1968 and again in 1973. This constitution had authoritarian features that effectively subordinated legislative and judicial powers. A constitutional amendment in 1977 removed term limits altogether, permitting Stroessner to be indefinitely reelected. Overall, he was reelected seven times, each time through an exercise that was a simulacrum of democratic process (Nickson 2014, 280–81).

Stroessner maintained a democratic facade for his regime. He kept Congress open and functioning, and in spite of the absence of legitimate elections, multiple parties were represented in Congress. De jure, the state maintained a classic separation of powers and preserved the rule of law, providing legal legitimacy for the country's real political circumstances. The regime discursively claimed that it followed the constitutional order, but de facto power was arbitrarily exercised by the executive branch, and the legislative and judicial branches were just appendices. Stroessner was the chief of state, an authentic autocrat, and with the armed forces' and Colorado Party's support, he exercised an "army" hegemony in which the military and the bourgeoisie around him were the regime's biggest winners (Jara Goiris 2004, 193). The ANR was, during Stroessner's government, functional to him. It was marked as the party that supported Stroessner and that perpetuated these bad habits until the national democratization phase.

International Cooperation in the Context of the National Security Doctrine

US political and economic cooperation was vital for Stroessner. Most of his regime's political development was enabled by US connivance; according to Fatima Myriam Yore, the Paraguayan Communist Party denounced that the military coup of 1954 had been organized by the US Military Mission (1992, 83). Andrew Nickson supported this approach, pointing out that "in June 1953, at the height of the Cold War, Stroessner visited the USA for the first time at the invitation of the US army" (1988, 239), and, according to Carlos Gómez Florentín, "the Paraguayan Embassy in Washington summed up the hosts' views on General Stroessner on July 15, 1953 in a single sentence: 'a great boss'" (2014, 71). Less than a year later, "on 4 May 1954, he deposed the Colorado President, Federico Chávez, in a military coup" (Nickson 1988, 239).

According to a confidential dispatch from the US ambassador to Paraguay, George P. Shaw—text reproduced by Gómez Florentín (2014, 71)—the military was particularly sensitive to the aid granted by the government of the northern power in the Paraguayan political context: "The presence of a military mission of the United States gives prestige to Paraguay and, more particularly, to the Paraguayan military establishment. In the mind of each Paraguayan, what is shown to neighboring countries is that the United States supports the Government of Paraguay and the Party in power, which remain in power mainly due to military support" (Gómez Florentín 2014, 71).

According to Nickson, "the Pentagon helped Stroessner to power at the height of the Cold War in 1954 and ever since has regarded him as one of their staunchest allies in the fight against communism in Latin America" (1988, 251); released State Department documents of the period 1953–1954 from the US embassy in Asunción could give rare insight into the extent of US involvement in the events leading up to the overthrow of President Federico Chaves by Stroessner (Seiferheld

1987). As Nickson goes on to point out, "Asunción boasted one of the largest US embassies in the Americas, harboring a major CIA station and listening post for the Southern Cone and, for three decades, successive US governments have lent unswerving economic, military and diplomatic support to Stroessner" (1988, 251).

After the coup of 1954, Stroessner met with the chiefs of the US Strategic Command in Lima, where he agreed—in the context of the Cold War—to maintain a firm anticommunist position in return for gaining political and economic support from the United States. Paraguay was now the third-largest recipient of US aid in Latin America. A great portion of that aid was diverted as a result of the excessive corruption in the country, and despite Washington knowing about this, the aid continued to be provided. However, the greatest legacy of US political cooperation was the "fight against communism," establishing intelligence assistance against rebels in Paraguay. This assistance was focused on the national police corps, establishing an extensive network of informants for the police and creating a system of torture against political detainees. Many were killed, disappeared, or sent into exile. The prime torture center was La Técnica, organized by the Dirección Nacional de Asuntos Técnicos (National Directorate of Technical Affairs). This department was under the coordination of Colonel Robert Thierry, an American who had arrived in Paraguay as part of the USAID assistance program (Nickson 2014, 288).

The so-called National Security Doctrine was a repressive system developed by the United States and deployed throughout Latin America—including in Paraguay and other countries of the Southern Cone—beginning in 1960, mainly to halt the spread of communism (Mendonca 2009, 13–15). This doctrine utilized American influence to strengthen the armed forces and police of Paraguay and other countries by supplying technical and material aid. The CIA maintained close ties with the Paraguayan security forces and shared information with the military's Intelligence Division and the interior minister's political section (Mora and Cooney 2009, 195). The United States organized this system of repression among Southern Cone countries in a common project known as Operación Cóndor.[6] This operation enabled international collaboration in monitoring and controlling political repression in the region. US support was thus fundamental to the maintenance of the stronista regime, as it provided political support and technical assistance to the regime's internal mechanisms and its engagement in social repression.

Paradoxically, the fall of Stronismo was also marked by US intervention. In May 1985, President Ronald Reagan referred to Paraguay as a "dictatorship"

(Nickson 2014, 275). Progressively, the US government ended its protection of Stroessner and ultimately assisted General Andrés Rodríguez's coup in February 1989.[7] Even though Rodríguez had been barred from entering the United States for being the ringleader of drug trafficking commercialization in Paraguay in the 1970s, he was quickly acknowledged as Paraguay's president and the travel ban was abruptly lifted in November 1988. This close relationship between the United States and General Rodríguez's government delayed Paraguay's democratization progress (Nickson 2014, 289).

REGIME BREAKDOWN, COUP D'ÉTAT, AND THE END OF THE DICTATORSHIP

By the mid-1980s, the international political climate had visibly changed. As the crisis within the stronista regime arose in 1981 (Soler 2012, 138), the United States and other regional states started to look at Paraguayan authoritarianism in a different way. In the first half of that decade, the Southern Cone countries were turning to democracy. Although their circumstances were unique, Argentina, Brazil, and Uruguay all converged toward greater political openness (Paredes 2009, 176). Yet in Paraguay, the US desire to replace Stroessner stumbled into an unconquerable difficulty: "As the opposition had been so degraded and had such a lack of proposals and experience in government, [...] there was no alternative political force to run the country" (Paredes 2009, 177). The opposition, weakened by thirty-five years of repression, had no capacity to function in a position of power, although it did have the skill to discredit the existing government (Abente Brun 2014, 296). The absence of a viable alternative government arising from the opposition was one of the variables that accompanied Stroessner's displacement from his "own party-state core" (Paredes 2009, 177). There were two other fundamental variables: US intervention, and the ruling class's need to control the transition process to protect their political position and socioeconomic interests, within the discourse of protecting and guaranteeing liberties for the whole society.

The Colorado Party's *traditionalist*[8] group tried to set "a moderate pace in the process" so as to "freeze certain change aims" that could pose a threat to the status quo, particularly preventing the alternation in power (Paredes 2009, 194). The regime's final years were marked by a striking and increasingly bitter internal division in the party, striking because the party's strong unity had served as the political base of the authoritarian regime until this fissure. Between 1980 and 1987, the ANR's most characteristic feature was the permanent internal division in its core between the traditionalists and the *neocolorados* or *advenedizos* (Paredes 2011, 309). This irreconcilable gap between Colorado traditionalism and stronista militancy culminated in the coup d'état against Stroessner. At the same time, mechanisms of social control were becoming inadequate and opposition sectors had begun to rebuild their structures, undermining Stroessner's legitimacy and further weakening the regime (Paredes 2011, 309).

The internal divisions that emerged within the ANR marked a change in direction for Paraguay, introducing a new democratization phase. By 1985, the internal disagreements and "the imminent matter of having a post-stronista government" had shattered the party "into at least seven factions," and Stroessner answered dissent "with force" (Bouvier 2012, 59). The Colorado Party's internal crisis became particularly evident among young people (Bouvier 2012, 61).

The collapse's final phase was between January 1, 1987 (the day of the Colorado Party convention) and February 2, 1989 (the day of the coup d'état). At the party convention, the positions of the traditionalists (supporters of a supposedly eroded Colorado history and symbology) and the militants (determined loyalists of Stroessner and his rule) were clearly irreconcilable. The traditionalists were marginalized within the party; "therefore, they were doomed to attempted conspiracy" (Paredes 2011, 309). This opened a short opportunity for total control by the militants, resulting in the "breakdown of granitic unity in August 1987" (Coronel 2011, 243). This in-house division provoked the traditionalist Colorados to turn to democratic discourse as a tool to operate against the stronista regime. This would enable them to create, from within the Colorado Party, a discourse of political openness that could allow them to simultaneously break ties with Stroessner and place themselves at the forefront of the ultimate transformation of the state. In reality, after 1989 some traditionalist sectors were "almost as authoritarian as the stronista military," despite the fact that "they represented themselves as the new 'democrats' after the coup" (Coronel 2011, 243).

On the night of February 2, 1989, Paraguay experienced a coup d'état that inaugurated democratization in the country. The coup was done from the inside, as the new economic groups that had arisen thanks to the regime's development of new productive and financial structures came to consider the practices of the dictatorship to be obsolete (Soler 2012, 138).

The coup "that many people suspected, others announced, and many others dreamed of, was happening," but it had a "deep contradiction" (Abente Brun 2014, 295). A reconciliation was needed between a democratic system that now had to be implemented and the ANR, the same party that had supported the regime for more than three decades and that was to remain in power. The end of authoritarianism represented many things, but, according to Abente Brun (2014), in its most essential dimension it implied a break from a system of political domination based on the state's identification of its structures and goals with the Colorado Party and the military. But the coup leaders' proclamation was both "clear and vague; they argued that the coup had been orchestrated to defend democracy and to respect human rights, as well as to secure *coloradismo*'s values, unity, and continuity in power" (Abente Brun 2014, 295). The coup bannered by Andrés Rodríguez "was part of a project that would open the doors, in a democratic way, to a neoliberal era in Paraguay" (Coronel 2011, 243), but some sectors asserted that "the coup was a 'preventive' step against the suspected uncontrollable advance of the popular movement" (Coronel 2011, 243).

After the coup, Rodríguez called a snap presidential election in which he would be the winner, so "at the same time that General Rodríguez imposed the rules for a democratic transition, he had the distinction of having deposed General Stroessner" (Soler 2012, 143). In the coup against Stroessner, four class factions were allied: the financial class, which was led by Rodríguez and would benefit from the deregulation of the economy; the so-called Barons of Itaipú, who needed to overthrow Stroessner to establish themselves as the dominant class; the Colorado Party oligarchy, led by Luis María Argaña, who had collectively been relegated from power in the regime's final years; and finally, the agricultural export sector, which sought to liberalize the economy in the interest of speeding up and increasing its profitability (Ferreiro 1989). Some of the political actors involved in the transition—such as Lino Oviedo—"had amassed an enormous fortune, and they needed a good excuse for controlling power in order to continue their accumulation with impunity, and democratization provided one" (Coronel 2011, 244). It is for these reasons that, among the Paraguayan Left and the traditional opposition, the national transition aroused doubts (Ferreiro 1989, 58).

Paraguay's Democratic Transition (1989–2008)

The democratic transition, launched by coup d'état from inside the regime, can be considered what Manuel Alcántara Sáez and Flavia Freidenberg label a controlled transition directed "from above"[9] (2006, 3), whereby the military structures the democratization process while preserving the continuity of diverse authoritarian features. As Donald Share and Scott Mainwaring (1986) describe more generally for democratic transitions, the deep internal crisis in the ruling party undermined the regime's legitimacy and required an opening to allow civil liberties previously repressed, while the protagonists of the transition sought to ensure limits in order to avoid any prosecution of the old authoritarian elite or the armed forces for gross human rights violations.

As Benjamín Arditi (1992, 101) says, the Paraguayan democratic transition had a different meaning compared to other transitions in the region. Due to Paraguay's lack of past democratic experience, the country's "democratic transition" was the foundation for a democratic political regime rather than the reestablishment of a democracy displaced by the authoritarian regime from 1954 to 1989.

The transition period was principally characterized by Paraguay joining a regional platform, the Common Market of the South (Mercosur); the promulgation of the 1992 constitution and the establishment of new rules; and economic, social, and political turmoil in which financial crises, peasant marches, general strikes, and further coup attempts converged. In March 1991, the presidents of Argentina, Brazil, Uruguay, and Paraguay signed the Treaty of Asunción establishing Mercosur (Merlos 2014). In 1992, the new constitution established the structural basis and institutional rules for the creation of democracy. And a number of economic and social crises arose during the democratic transition, notably the 1994 peasant marches, the 1995 and 1997 financial crises, and the 1995 general strike provoked after the murder of peasant leader Pedro Giménez (Merlos 2014).

Another important feature of the Paraguayan transition was the political instability generated by repeated coup attempts by factions of the military. The most significant of these were connected to Lino Oviedo, who was one of the masterminds of Stroessner's overthrow. In 1996 and 2001, he showed willingness to break the new rules and undermine the country's embryonic democratic institutions. To these attempts can be added the impeachment threats to presidents Juan Carlos Wasmosy, Raúl Cubas Grau, Luis González Macchi, and Nicanor Duarte Frutos. The only successful vote to remove the president was against Cubas in March 1999.

New Institutional Rules: 1992 National Constitution

After Stroessner was deposed, the 1992 national constitution became the primary document for implementing institutional and legal changes in Paraguay, and it served as their central expression. The constitution was approved and promulgated three years after the coup d'état that brought authoritarianism to an end. The absolute majority of those elected in a direct popular election to serve in the constitutional convention were members of the Colorado Party, which had been in power continuously since 1954. Nevertheless, the convention delegates were largely heterogeneous, contributing to an environment for democratic innovation (Barreda and Costafreda 2002, 82).

The promulgation of the new Paraguayan constitution came during a time of constitutional reforms in Latin America, as a number of countries democratized after decades of authoritarian governments or constant crisis.[10] This was the period of the "new Latin American constitutionalism," beginning with the adoption of new constitutions in Brazil in 1988 and Colombia in 1991 (Uprimny 2011; Gargarella 2015). The transition toward democracy in Latin America involved the reorganization of power relations, and the tool used to achieve this was constitutional reform (Serna de la Garza 1998; Alcántara and Freidenberg 2006).

These reform processes resulted in a constitutional order marked by the defense of human rights. The new constitutions acknowledged a set of social, cultural, and environmental rights that had developed in international law principles and treaties. Likewise, new instruments for political participation and public control were established (Uprimny 2011, 110–14). One of the goals of these reforms was to increase citizen engagement and to address the crises of representation and governability that most countries were facing (Alcántara and Freidenberg 2006; Zovatto 2010, 94). The national constitution provided a new institutional design for the Paraguayan state based on the rule of law with separation of powers. New state institutions were created, and a set of guarantees and rights was included that corresponded to the international human rights regime.

Some of the 1992 national constitution's principal institutional changes are:

- Establishment of the social rule of law and democracy
- Acknowledgment of public power and the separation of powers
- Territorial decentralization
- Municipal and departmental elections
- Commitment to an international law regime
- Recognition of freedom of the press, association, and demonstration
- Acknowledgment of the rights of indigenous peoples
- Creation of mechanisms for direct democracy
- Establishment of new control bodies (Ombudsman's Office, Judicial Council, Jury for the Prosecution of Magistrates)

SOCIAL RULE OF LAW AND DEMOCRACY

The concept of "social rule of law" supposes a state that accepts and incorporates into the legal order fundamental social rights as well as classical political and civil rights. Social rights obligate certain state functions (Borda 2007, 82–83). The constitution establishes the right to work (Chapter VIII, Arts. 86–99), the right to housing (Art. 100), and the right to use and distribute land (Section II, Chapter IX, Arts. 114–16). Article 1 of the Paraguayan constitution, "Of the Form of the State and of the Government," declares that the Republic of Paraguay "constitutes itself as a social State of law, unitary, indivisible, and decentralized" and "adopts for its government the representative, participative, and pluralistic democracy."

ACKNOWLEDGMENT OF PUBLIC POWER AND THE SEPARATION OF POWERS

The constitution expresses that public power must be exercised by the people through voting (Art. 3). It also affirms that the government's legislative, executive, and judicial powers must be exercised "in a system of separation, balance, coordination, and reciprocal control." This arrangement reflects Montesquieu's ideas and is designed to avoid the concentration of power and the subsequent loss of citizens' rights. Among the modern state's basic features, the imposition of restrictions on state power is a consequence of the distribution of power in a system of checks and balances focused on limiting the state's monopoly over the use of force (Lindsay 1945, 168–69). All of these traits get finally translated as a system of mutual controls across the state's different powers.

Although the government's form is presidential, given past experience of authoritarianism and the concentration of power in the executive, the 1992 constitution grants prerogatives to Congress. The constitution notoriously increases the legislative power's representative and oversight functions as well as its capacity to nominate key officials in the state administration (Caballero 2003, 261). Although the executive branch has veto power, this power turns out to be weak, as it can be overridden by one chamber's absolute majority (Barreda and Costafreda 2002, 96). A cornerstone that indicates the difference between legislative and executive power is the prohibition on reelection for the republic's president and vice president. Article 229 states that both "will serve for a five-year term that cannot be extended," and that they "cannot be reelected under any circumstance." These words were included with the experience of stronismo authoritarianism in mind.[11] There is no prohibition on the reelection of legislators.

Furthermore, the constitution gives special importance to judicial power, ensuring in Article 248 its independence. The constitution articulates that "in no case may members of other powers, nor other government employees, arrogate judicial rights that are not specifically expressed in this Constitution," and that "those who make attempts against the Judicial Power's independence and its magistrates, will be unable to exercise any public function for five consecutive years, in addition to penalties prescribed by the law." The constitution provides the remedy of impeachment as a response to "improper performance of [an officeholder's] functions, crimes committed during the exercise of their functions, or ordinary crimes" (Art. 225). This measure may affect the president and vice president of the republic, executive branch ministers, members of Supreme Court of Justice and Superior Court of Electoral Justice, the attorney general, the head of the Ombudsman's Office, the comptroller general, and the sub-comptroller.

TERRITORIAL DECENTRALIZATION

Another of the important changes to the Paraguayan state has been territorial decentralization, with the creation of subnational governments for the departments and districts (municipalities).[12] These territorial units possess their own governments and political, administrative, and normative autonomy in order to manage their interests, collect taxes, and manage the investment of their resources. All these matters are addressed in Chapter IV of the constitution, which describes the creation and operation of national services in municipal and departmental jurisdictions.

Additionally, the constitution determines the election procedure and length of term for municipal and departmental authorities along with the requirements that must be met to take office, and the institutional resources, competencies, attributions, and origin that are available to them. It conveys that departments can form multidepartmental regions to improve their communities' development, and that municipalities can associate to work together to implement common policies.

MUNICIPAL AND DEPARTMENTAL ELECTIONS

The principles of territorial decentralization led to provision for the election of municipal and departmental authorities being for the first time addressed in a national constitution. The guidelines for electing governors and department councils by means of citizens' direct votes in elections concurrent with general elections are considered in Article 167; mayors and municipal councils are also elected by direct suffrage, in elections nonconcurrent with general elections.

Municipal elections in 1991 were the first to permit direct election to the office of mayor, and in more than forty municipalities the opposition took office (Flecha and Martini 1994, 15–16).[13] National and subnational elections are fundamental to the right to vote, which "constitutes the foundation of a democratic and representative regime" (Art. 118). Likewise, the principles of direct and secret suffrage are applied to internal elections of intermediate, political, union, and social organizations (Art. 119).

COMMITMENT TO AN INTERNATIONAL LAW REGIME

The transition toward democracy also hastened Paraguay's reintegration into the international community. In August 1989, the first national legislative act under the new regime was to approve Law 1/89, which ratified the American Convention on Human Rights, and progressively other general and particular agreements of a similar nature were concluded and ratified. The constitution stated that international treaties "concerning human rights cannot be renounced but by the procedures for the amendment of this Constitution" (Art. 142). Article 143 establishes the Paraguayan state's acceptance of international law, conditioned by the principles of national independence, people's self-determination, legal equality among states, international solidarity and cooperation, international protection of human rights, free navigation on international rivers, nonintervention, and condemnation of every form of dictatorship, colonialism, and imperialism. The foundational text states that Paraguay accepts the legal supranational order for the purpose of "ensuring the exercise of human rights, peace, justice, cooperation, and development in political, economic, social, and cultural aspects" (Art. 145).

RECOGNITION OF FUNDAMENTAL FREEDOMS

The 1992 constitution explicitly ensures freedom of expression and of the press (Art. 26), stated as the right to disseminate "thoughts and opinions, without censorship, with no limitations other than those imposed by this Constitution." Another freedom recognized is that of religion, worship, and ideology. Article 24 says that "no [religious] confession will have official status." This proclaims the secularization of the Paraguayan state, as the previous constitution had declared the Catholic religion to be official. Article 24 does say that "all relations between the State and the Catholic Church are based on independence, cooperation, and autonomy."

Within the framework of citizens' liberties, a meaningful inclusion in the constitution is freedom of association and demonstration (Art. 132). Similarly, Article 125 addresses freedom of association for political parties and movements and establishes that all citizens have the right to freely associate in groups such as these to participate, by democratic methods, in the election of constitutional authorities.

ACKNOWLEDGMENT OF THE RIGHTS OF INDIGENOUS PEOPLES

The 1992 constitution, in line with international tools for the protection of indigenous people, officially acknowledges indigenous peoples' existence for the first time in Paraguayan history. Chapter V, Articles 62–67, stipulate the express recognition of indigenous peoples, defined as "cultural groups [that existed] prior to the formation and organization of the Paraguayan state." The articles also recognize the rights of indigenous peoples to preserve their ethnic identity; political, social, economic, cultural, and religious systems; communal ownership of land; customary law; participation in national life; and exemption from military, social, and civil service.

The inclusion of this chapter was a response to the pressure mounted by indigenous people and allied social organizations. Approximately 134 representatives of sixty-four indigenous communities from both regions of the country demanded their participation in the 1992 National Constituent Convention. After being refused by the executive and the legislature, representatives of fourteen communities submitted the request directly to those elected to the convention. Finally, four indigenous representatives were allowed—two representatives from the Oriental Region and two from the Occidental Region—as observers and consultants (Kowalski 1993, 102–3).[14]

With the inclusion of specific rights for indigenous peoples, Paraguay's Magna Carta acquired a multicultural nature, in step with other Latin American countries that have explicitly incorporated certain indigenous and cultural groups' rights in their own respective constitutions. Latin American countries have incorporated different degrees of multiculturalism in their constitutions (Van Cott 2002; Bengoa 2003; Martí i Puig and Villalba 2012).

THE INVOLVEMENT OF DIRECT DEMOCRACY MECHANISMS

Direct democracy mechanisms such as initiative and referendum appeared for the first time in Paraguay in the 1992 constitution. The inclusion of these instruments had been proposed by diverse draft bills before the 1992 National

Constituent Convention. Articles 121, 122, and 123 briefly state their modalities and methods of implementation. Article 40 provides for the right to petition authorities in a personal or collective way.

Despite the innovation that initiative and referendum represent, their scope is fairly narrow, and they exclude direct democracy from matters such as international relations; international treaties, conventions, and agreements; limitations on or expropriation of real estate; national defense; taxation; monetary and banking systems; the acquisition of loans; the national budget; and national, departmental, and municipal elections. Additionally, many normative and procedural filters obstruct the effective implementation of the constitution's direct democracy provisions (Villalba 2017).

ESTABLISHMENT OF NEW CONTROL BODIES

As a way to establish the new control mechanisms of public administration, some "outside power organs" were created, called this as they do not fit within the three classical powers of the state but are related to them (Flecha and Martini 1994, 217). Included among these organs are the Judicial Council and the Ombudsman's Office. The key function of the Judicial Council (Consejo de la Magistratura) is to nominate slates of candidates to the Supreme Court of Justice and lower court posts, as well as judges and tax officials, "based on appropriate suitability, taking into account merits and capabilities."

The Ombudsman's Office (Defensoría del Pueblo) is tasked with defending human rights, handling complaints from the general public, and protecting community interests (Art. 276).

Economic Development

In the prelude to the elections of April 2008, Paraguay was enduring difficulties brought on by slow economic growth, despite the rebound experienced in the previous year when the GDP grew at a rate of 6.8 percent. In general terms, the country suffered at least a decade of low and even recessive economic performance (see table 4.4), with inflation rates, if not very high—except in 2002 and 2003—nevertheless disturbing enough for a country whose population works mainly in the primary sector or the informal economy (i.e., in low-paying tasks), or in occupations with unstable incomes (Solís and Cerna 2016, 127–28).

To the above, it should be added that Paraguay has one of the lowest tax burdens in the region; although the IRP tax (*impuesto a la renta personal*, or personal income tax) has been part of the Paraguayan legal code since 2004, it was not until the 2010s that it began to be applied in practice, and therefore the national fiscal system did not tax personal income until then. Accordingly, the primary income to the public coffers came, and still comes today, from consumption taxes (VAT) and royalties from the Itaipú and Yacyretá binational hydroelectric plants shared with Brazil and Argentina, respectively (Solís and Cerna 2016, 128).

Political Alternation and the ANR's Return to Power (2008–2015)

Electoral history was made in 2008 with the first transfer of power from one party to another of the country's democratic era, when the Colorado Party peacefully turned over the presidency of the republic to a different party's candidate. In the elections of April 20, 2008, the candidate of the Patriotic Alliance for Change (APC), Fernando Lugo, vanquished the Colorado candidate, Blanca Ovelar, by a margin of almost two hundred thousand votes. In August of the same year, Lugo inaugurated a government that generated great expectations for change, but in the end failed as Lugo was removed from office through impeachment.

Fernando Lugo's Rise to Power

Fernando Lugo, former bishop of the diocese of San Pedro (one of the country's poorest departments), emerged as an outstanding figure in Paraguay's political arena after leading a citizens' march in March 2006 against the reelection pretentions of president Nicanor Duarte Frutos, whose term would expire two years later, in 2008 (presidential reelection is not allowed in the Paraguayan constitution of 1992). Although Lugo's activism with peasant organizations in San Pedro Department had begun several years earlier, it was not until these marches that, in addition to denouncing Duarte's attempted violation of the constitution, Paraguayan citizens expressed their dissatisfaction with the Colorado Party's way of exercising power. In the marches, Lugo became a national political figure and was seen as a potential presidential candidate, able to capitalize on this dissatisfaction.

After officially quitting the priesthood, Lugo announced his candidacy for the presidency in December 2006. In July 2007, an agreement was reached between Lugo and the Partido Liberal Radical Auténtico (the most popular of the opposition parties) to form the APC. Several parties and left-wing movements joined the Alliance, while other groups and social movements gave their support to the

TABLE 4.4 Performance of the Paraguayan Economy (1999–2008)

	1999	2000	2001	2002	2003	2004	2005	2006	2007	2008
GDP Growth	-1.5	-3.3	2.1	0.0	3.8	4.1	2.9	4.3	6.8	5.8
Inflation	6.8	9.0	7.3	10.5	14.2	4.3	6.8	9.6	8.1	8.3
Tax revenue (% of GDP)	9.9	9.9	10.8	10	10.3	11.9	11.8	12	11.6	n. d.

Source: the authors, based on World Bank data.

Frente Social y Popular (Social and Popular Front), which also backed Lugo. The agreement between Lugo and the PLRA provoked the alienation of the Partido Patria Querida (Beloved Fatherland Party), as it expected to have a place in the presidential coalition.

Lugo was joined on the ticket by Federico Franco of the PLRA. They were elected as president and vice president on April 20, 2008, having received more than 40 percent of the votes, thus ending sixty-one continuous years of Colorado Party governance. Diego Abente Brun (2008, 332) asserts that many factors helped the winning ticket: (1) "republican institutional deterioration," (2) internal fractures in the Colorado Party and the loss of votes to other candidates, (3) the extraordinary concentration of opposition forces by the APC, and (4) widespread social unrest in response to deteriorating living conditions among broad sectors of the Paraguayan population. According to Abente Brun, institutional deterioration in the final years of Duarte Frutos's presidency resulted from Duarte's "rearrangement of hegemonic power in partisan and self-oriented terms" to make himself the *tendotá* (Guaraní for caudillo or strongman) (2008, 332). These actions encouraged the tendency toward authoritarianism and corruption in the government. In fact, in concentrating power, Duarte Frutos treated significant state administrative functions as if they were his own personal assets. For a short period of time, he assumed his party's presidency, in clear contravention of the constitution's limitations on the president's public functions.

Another factor in the APC's 2008 victory was the intense factionalism within the Colorado Party, which was expressed in the 2007 party primary elections. Duarte Frutos's preferred candidate, Blanca Ovelar, defeated dissident faction candidate Luis Castiglioni in a process marred by accusations of fraud. The Colorados did not resolve their divisions with the traditional "republican embrace," and the party's candidate failed to mobilize a large enough number of Castiglioni supporters to prevail in the general election. Moreover, the unprecedented agreement among opposition forces within and in support of the APC, in which nine parties and a great number of national, departmental, and district-level movements came together, created unusual uncertainty about the Colorado Party's chances. The popular approval and high expectations of change motivated by the APC's candidate were crucial in strengthening the Alliance's coalition of diverse parties and movements, which had to face the Colorado machinery, still formidable even while experiencing profound internal clashes.

Among social factors that played a role in the election results, one can point to widespread social unrest in response to the deterioration of living conditions for numerous segments of the population. One of the most important signs of this deterioration was Paraguayans' mass emigration looking for better living conditions in other countries of the region and in Europe, particularly Spain, where 116,000 people went between 2001 and 2006 (Carrón 2007). This situation provoked the slogan "Make Them Go," an allusion to the ANR's elected officials. The chant turned into a roaring message against the ANR during the electoral campaign. The sum of these factors led to the APC's historic victory.

Lugo's Presidency: A Government without Real Power

Fernando Lugo's government (2008–2012) was characterized by chronic fragility caused by: (1) the absence of a favorable majority in Congress, (2) internal competition within the APC for political space, (3) early desertions by some parties and movements from the Alliance, (4) Lugo's and his cabinet's general inexperience administering the state, (5) the progressive demobilization of related social organizations that could have provided popular support, and (6) reticence from the conservative segment of Paraguay's population toward the new government's proposed reforms (López 2010, 104; 2014a, 99; 2014b, 179).

In spite of having accumulated sufficient votes for its presidential candidate, the APC did not submit a unified list for seats in Congress. Not doing so allowed the Colorado Party to win 509,907 votes for senators, with the PLRA winning 507,413 votes, the UNACE 336,763 votes, and the PPQ 151,991, according to official electoral data from the Tribunal Superior de Justicia Electoral (Superior Electoral Tribunal; TSJE 2008, 245). Similar results for the Chamber of Deputies elections left the APC with just one seat; thus, the governing alliance did not have a majority in either the Chamber of Deputies or the Senate.

The relationship between the executive and the legislature became troublesome due to the lack of a parliamentary majority in favor of the government. This lack of legislative support impeded the implementation of the executive's plans that required legislative approval and affected the administration's capacity, as it was constantly questioned about its actions and decisions.

The APC also showed early signs of fissure due to conflicts over the distribution of posts in the government, which led to a profound degree of fragmentation between the social movements and political groups that were in the Alliance. A critical cleavage was caused when Lugo and some associates created the Frente Guasú (Broad Front), leaving out their biggest ally, the PLRA.

Along with the challenges of distributing political positions in such a way as to ensure continuing loyalty among members of the governing alliance, the general inexperience of the new public administrators in managing the state bureaucracy due to decades of Colorado Party dominance (based on a bureaucracy with strong party ties), plus the inclusion of activists from nongovernmental organizations in government posts, led to declining support from the Alliance's member parties.

The greatest obstacles to the stability and continuity of Lugo's government were various conservative social, corporate, and political entities. Seeing their interests and privileges at risk, conservatives felt the urgency to stop the new government from enacting its programs. According to Tomás Palau Viladesau, the sectors opposed to modifying the status quo in Paraguay are the ranching oligarchy, businesspeople, drug traffickers, and transnational corporations. Through their economic power and political influence, these actors sought to eliminate the risk that Lugo's government posed to their privileges (Palau 2010, 140).

Despite this context, the Lugo government attained certain social achievements and policies, making palpable some of the changes it had proposed. Some of the most significant goals accomplished were to provide public, universal, and free health-care service; to increase social investment through cash-transfer programs targeted at the country's most disadvantaged segments; to ratify energy sovereignty, especially in relations with Brazil, where compensation fees were tripled for energy ceded to Eletrobras by Itaipú Binacional; and to seek agrarian reform through stronger regulation of the sale of public land in the border areas and attempt to recover lands illegally obtained by Stroessner's cronies (Duré et al. 2012, 294).

All these policies generated unprecedented political debate, tinted with strong ideological traces, "bringing to the discussion matters that divided and that imposed on each political and social actor the need to adopt a position and assume an identity" (Lachi 2009, 39). The dominant media (essentially *ABC Color*) played a key role in channeling ideologically motivated critics to speak against Lugo's government. The media's discursive role in the matter was significant, as media powers endorsed the majority of legislators who approved the articles of impeachment against Lugo and also gave "public visibility" to the events that, allegedly, demonstrated Lugo's "poor performance of duties" (Libelo Acusatorio 2012).

Lugo's Removal and the End of Alternance in Office

The immediate antecedent to the impeachment and removal of Fernando Lugo was the murder of eleven peasants and six police officers during an attempt to serve a search warrant and eviction notice to occupants of a parcel of land known as Marina Cue in Curuguaty.[15] The "Curuguaty massacre" of June 15, 2012, created an environment conducive to the impeachment of the president, which was effected just a week after the massacre.[16]

The articles of impeachment (*libelo acusatorio*) enumerated Lugo's poor performance of duties, such as the government's endorsement of a political meeting in 2009 of left-wing youth organizations at the Armed Forces Engineering Command; the Ñacunday case, for which Lugo was indicated as "solely responsible for being instigator and facilitator of the recent encroachments on land"; the "increasing insecurity" and Lugo's inability to develop a policy or programs to enhance public safety; responsibility for acceding to the Ushuaia II Protocol, which, according to the allegation, threatened Paraguay's sovereignty; and the Curuguaty case, for which the president was considered the carperos' accomplice. All of these accusations were, as stated in the articles, of public notoriety; "thus, in agreement with our current legal system, they do not need to be proved" (Libelo Acusatorio 2012). The impeachment was carried out in just two days, with seventy-six of eighty deputies and thirty-nine of forty-five senators voting in favor of removal. This process was the last of more than twenty-three earlier attempts to remove Lugo from office, finally succeeding merely nine months before the end of Lugo's constitutional mandate.

Lugo's removal and the abrupt termination of his alternative policies also was a defeat for the peasant and social movements that had been pushing for the fulfillment of promises made during the APC campaign, specifically for agrarian reform and social programs. After Lugo's dismissal and Federico Franco's installment as president, these sectors almost immediately became the targets of state repression, resulting in an increasing number of social movement leaders and peasants murdered, charged with crimes, or imprisoned (CODEHUPY 2012, 116).

The impeachment also demobilized a growing urban sector that had been raising claims against the National Congress; just a few weeks before, demonstrators had surrounded the Congress building protesting the postponement of implementation of a law to unblock party lists, forcing senators to flee. At a regional level, Lugo's removal prompted Paraguay's suspension from regional bodies such as Mercosur and the Union of South American Nations (UNASUR), which considered the incident a "parliamentary coup d'état" against a government that had been lawfully elected, leading to Paraguay's diplomatic isolation. Paraguay would have to wait until new elections to earn recognition for having returned to the democratic path. These elections were held in April 2013.

Internally, the postimpeachment scenario was marked by the evident social polarization between supporters and opponents of the impeachment. On one side were social and political groups that clustered around "resistance to the coup," and on the other side the "sovereigns" argued for the legality of the trial and declared themselves against intrusion by regional states in Paraguay's internal affairs. Lugo accepted his removal and stated that he was leaving "through the big door of the hearts" of his compatriots (*ABC Color* 2012). Franco's government, while brief in duration, engaged in numerous corrupt acts and constant nepotism, and made executive decisions favorable to the business and multinational sectors. Although the PLRA had sufficient public funds to improve its electoral campaign in 2013, the Liberal Party could not keep itself in power. In August of the same year, it handed the government once again to the ANR, thus concluding the period of political alternance in the democratic era.

The Outsider Horacio Cartes and the Return of the Colorado Party

Horacio Cartes, who at age fifty-nine had never voted in general elections and had been enrolled in the voting rolls only in 2009, burst onto the political scene when the Colorado Party was out of power.[17] His political debut provided an important source of funding needed by the ANR at that juncture. Cartes's political image was built upon his entrepreneurial success and financial capital. The Colorado Party lacked leadership, and as Cartes did not meet the party's requirement to have been a member of the party for at least five years in order to be eligible for nomination, the ANR modified its statutes to permit his nomination as the party's presidential candidate in the 2013 elections.

As reported by Sarah Patricia Cerna Villagra and Juan Mario Solís Delgadillo

(2014, 201), "Cartes had been building his presidential candidacy since 2009, an approach that became his permanent campaign strategy," positioning himself as an effective mobilizer of Colorado voters for the municipal elections in 2010 and for the Colorado's party leadership elections in 2011, in which his favored candidate, Lilian Samaniego, was elected. With his discourse of giving "a new direction" to Paraguay, away from the "Castro-Chavista" path that had supposedly been Lugo's direction, Cartes won popularity in spite of questions about the origin of his fortune, linked apparently with money laundering, tax evasion, smuggling, and drug trafficking.

In the 2013 presidential elections, the ANR candidate received an unprecedented 1,104,169 votes, 45.8 percent of the total, while his closest rival, from the PLRA, received just 36.9 percent of the votes. The Colorado Party again captured the republic's presidency and moreover obtained an absolute majority of seats in the Chamber of Deputies while bolstering its seats in the Senate to twenty out of forty-five (Solís and Cerna 2013, 421). Additionally, the ANR won twelve of the seventeen departmental governorships.

The ANR's big victory was made easier by the shattering of the Left, the failed alliance between the PLRA and UNACE (after UNACE candidate Lino Oviedo's death in a helicopter crash), and the reunification of Colorado forces; in other words, by virtue of having a political configuration completely different from that of 2008. As Cerna and Solís (2014, 215) point out, the return of the ANR to the presidency, after having lost it for just one term, demonstrates that the ANR is the one party with a truly national presence in Paraguay; despite its removal from power in 2008, it never lost its territorial control.

The run-up to the 2018 presidential elections nonetheless was contentious. While the Paraguayan constitution does not permit presidential reelection, the Cartes faction of the Colorado Party and a collection of opposition parties, including the Frente Guasú and the PLRA, tried unsuccessfully to introduce a procedural change in Senate rules that would allow the incumbent to run for reelection. Public disapproval of this maneuver was evident from widespread demonstrations in the streets of Asunción. During one of these, in March 2017, a fire was started in the National Congress, the offices of the PLRA were broken into, and a young protester was killed in an incident that is still under investigation.

In the end, the Colorado Party primaries pitted a young technocrat, Santiago Peña, against a seasoned politician, Mario Abdo Benítez. Peña had served as finance minister in the Cartes administration and was apparently supported by the Honor Colorado faction of the party; his campaign was likely bankrolled by Cartes. Like Cartes, Peña's association with the Colorado Party was recent; he and his family previously had been active in the Liberal Party. Peña's opponent, Mario Abdo Benítez, came from a well-known Colorado family with long-standing ties to the party; his father had been Stroessner's private secretary. Abdo Benítez first became active in party politics after a short stint in the air force and had served as Colorado Party vice president in 2005 before being elected to the Paraguayan Senate in 2015. In the end, Abdo Benítez won the Colorado primary with almost 51 percent of the vote.

The opposition candidate in the 2018 presidential elections was Efraín Alegre. A career politician, Alegre had served as president of the Paraguayan Chamber of Deputies during 1999–2000. A lawyer by training, he had been minister of public works during the Lugo administration and the PLRA candidate for president in 2013, losing to Cartes with 39 percent of the popular vote. In the 2018 elections, Alegre led the Gran Alianza Nacional Renovada (GANAR), a coalition ticket that included the PLRA, Lugo's Frente Guasú, the UNACE, and three other parties or movements.

The 2018 elections for national, local, and Mercosur positions took place during a period of economic growth but marked by political uncertainty. Paraguay's economy was growing faster than those of its neighbors at a healthy 4 percent. The Colorado Party was expected to win overwhelmingly, but, in the end, turnout was low and the vote was relatively close. Abdo Benítez won just shy of 51 percent of the vote, while Alegre claimed some 45 percent. Participation among young voters was lower than expected. Women lost two seats in the Paraguayan Senate in the 2018 elections. According to reports on the election, "[t]he new composition of the Senate will be the following: 17 seats for the Colorado Party, 13 seats for the PLRA, six seats for the Frente Guasu, three seats for the Patria Querida Party, two seats for the National Union of Ethical Citizens (UNACE), two seats for the Progressive Democratic Party, one seat for the Movimiento Hagamos, and one seat for the National Crusade movement, with a total of 37 men and eight women" (Gómez Romero 2018).

In August 2018, Mario Abdo Benítez was inaugurated as president, becoming one of Paraguay's youngest presidents since the fall of the Stroessner regime. He was a conservative, Catholic leader who ran on a pro-business, anticorruption platform. He promised not to raise the tax rate on individuals or corporations and not to expand taxes on soybean exports. Voters, however, expressed concern about security, health, and education. In response, Abdo Benítez pledged to modernize policing, improve access to health care in rural areas, and upgrade educational infrastructure.

After a year in office, the new president faced substantial opposition. His very modest tax reform proposal was strongly disputed but eventually approved. Paraguay still has one of the lowest tax rates for corporations in Latin America. The new administration's spending on expanding public health services has been applauded, but spending on education has fallen short of expectations; needed improvements have exceeded planned spending significantly (Horwitz 2019). Internationally, Abdo Benítez reversed his predecessor's decision to move the Paraguayan embassy in Israel to Jerusalem, keeping the embassy in Tel Aviv. In response, the Israelis broke off diplomatic relations with Paraguay. In January 2019, Paraguay broke off diplomatic relations with Venezuela and recognized Juan Guaidó as president of that country.

Despite continuing the policies of previous Colorado administrations, Abdo Benítez is not a popular figure in Paraguayan politics. After a year in office, his approval rating was just over 30 percent, whereas at the same time in their administrations, Horacio Cartes enjoyed a 50 percent approval rating and Fernando Lugo 54 percent (Horwitz 2019). In mid-2019, Abdo Benítez faced the possibility of impeachment over a secret agreement signed with Brazilian president Jair Bolsonaro regarding the cessation of rights to electric power from the Itaipú Dam. Abdo Benítez was forced to rescind the agreement, which, when it became public, was widely regarded as very unfavorable to Paraguayan national interests.

While the 2018 election results extended the hold of the Colorado Party over national politics in Paraguay for another five years, it was clear that Abdo Benítez's administration would be different from previous Colorado administrations. He had won with a narrower margin than previous Colorado candidates and faced a Senate without a Colorado majority. At the same time, after nearly a decade of solid economic expansion, Paraguayans anticipated more widespread evidence of economic and social well-being. Achieving the reforms necessary to achieve those goals would not be easy. Almost two years into his term, President Mario Abdo Benítez seemed unlikely to be able to forge the sort of alliances that might make such reforms possible.

Notes

1. The authors would like to thank Erika López Amaro for translating this chapter from the Spanish, and Brian Turner for his invaluable assistance in finalizing the text.

2. The municipal elections scheduled for 2020 have been rescheduled to 2021 due to declaration of a public health emergency for COVID-19. Ley 6547/20.

3. These features match those described by Manuel Alcántara Sáez (2008) about the Mexican political regime, which shares many similarities with the Paraguayan political regime, such as the presence of a hegemonic party in government during most of the twentieth century.

4. Since the democratic transition, the Left has not been able to recover from the physical dismantling it suffered in the 1947 Civil War and throughout the Stroessner regime, as leftist leaders were persecuted and the main left-wing parties banished. This long period of political persecution, as well as other factors such as the country's historical tendency toward fragmentation, ANR populism, and the rural nature of Paraguayan society (which discouraged the establishment of strong labor unions), explain why the Left's political force has been weak.

5. The term "fraudulent bureaucracy" was coined by the Paraguayan economic historian Juan Carlos Herken to refer to the small group of millionaires who shaped the national economic elite during Stroessner's time. They were members of the ANR and the military elite. Due to their loyalty to the regime, these families amassed great fortunes through privileged access to state contracts, corruption with national companies, and illegal activities linked to their business and public functions.

6. Operation Condor was an international network that enabled police and military cooperation in the Southern Cone. It involved the creation, organization, training, and development of the personal, material, and technical requirements for the repressive institutions of the dictatorial governments of Paraguay, Argentina, Uruguay, Chile, Brazil, and Bolivia in the 1970s and 1980s. Operation Condor was launched within the context of the Inter-American Treaty of Reciprocal Assistance; the United States, through the CIA and other institutions and organizations, was the operation's head and coordinator, and Henry Kissinger, who served as US secretary of state from 1973 to 1977, was the project's main mentor. The aim was to build a comprehensive database and common repressive mechanisms against subversive agents, to organize and coordinate the fight against communism in the Southern Cone.

7. The Jimmy Carter administration (1977–1981) turned away from the policies of Carter's predecessors, who had systematically emphasized the containment of the Soviet Union, and developed a foreign policy raising the importance of human rights at the international level. The Carter administration withdrew US support from some governments the United States had historically backed, such as Anastasio Somoza's regime in Nicaragua. Although Paraguay and Chile sent representatives to the signing of the Panama Canal Treaty in 1977, Carter personally criticized those countries' respective dictators, Stroessner and Augusto Pinochet.

8. This traditionalist group was formed of ANR leaders who held political, military, and economic weight in the country.

9. Transitions effected by internal factors are associated with controlled transitions from above, as in Peru, Ecuador, Uruguay, Brazil, Chile, and Paraguay. Transitions effected by external factors are associated with regulated transitions from outside, as in Nicaragua, Panama, the Dominican Republic, and Haiti; and negotiated transitions, as in El Salvador and Panama.

10. This process was acknowledged in fifteen Latin American countries during 1978–1990, in the context of the so-called Third Democratic Wave described by Samuel Huntington (1991). The exceptions to this "wave" were Mexico, Costa Rica, Cuba, Colombia, and Venezuela.

11. The transitional provisions of the 1992 constitution state that the new constitution's constraints on reelection to electoral positions of the three state powers apply to the then-current holders of those offices, including President Andrés Rodríguez, who had led the coup d'état of 1989.

12. Due to the historical situation of a persistent exterior threat to its sovereignty, Paraguay had been since its national independence in 1811 a centralized state (Flecha 2003, 297).

13. In February 1990, more than two years before the National Constituent Convention, Congress reformed the electoral code. This allowed for the registration of political organizations that had been prohibited in the previous regime (Flecha and Martini 1994, 16, 71).

14. Indigenous people had support from the Grupo de Apoyo, formed by the National Team of Missions of the Catholic Church, the Friendship Mission, and the Catholic University of Asunción. In 1991, the Grupo de Apoyo held its first general meeting, in which leaders and community members considered those rights that should be included in the constitution. The meeting's discussions were recorded and the material distributed to indigenous communities (Kowalski 1993, 99, 101).

15. This property of almost two thousand hectares had been occupied by peasants for their own use. The land was claimed by Campos Morombí, an enterprise owned by Colorado politician Blas N. Riquelme.

16. The massacre at Curuguaty was the culmination of increasing tensions in the countryside, due to pressure from landless peasants (*carperos*) who wanted to recuperate state-owned lands that were in the hands of private enterprises, generally linked to agribusiness or illegally awarded to Stroessner's cronies who were not eligible to receive land under agrarian reform laws. A similar conflict took place in Ñacunday, where a group of carperos demanded lands that had been exploited by a Brazilian agribusinessman, Tranquilo Favero. These conflicts were the central arguments for Lugo's dismissal, as well as accusations about public insecurity and the failure to defend national sovereignty.

17. Lugo claimed that Cartes, a tobacco businessman and sports club owner, was the financier of his impeachment and removal from office.

Bibliography

ABC Color. 2012. "'Salgo por la puerta grande,' dijo el exjefe de Estado en su último discurso." June 23. Available at http://www.abc.com.py/edicion-impresa/politica/salgo-por-la-puerta-grande-dijo-el-exjefe-de-estado-en-su-ultimo-discurso-417753.html.

Abente Brun, Diego. 2008. "Paraguay: ¿Jaque Mate?" *Revista de Ciencia Política* 28, no. 1: 329–45.

———. 2014. "Después de la dictadura." In *Historia del Paraguay*, edited by Ignacio Telesca, 295–313. Asunción: Taurus.

Alcántara Sáez, Manuel. 2004. *¿Instituciones o máquinas ideológicas? Origen, programa y organización de los partidos políticos latinoamericanos*. Barcelona: Institut de Ciències Polítiques i Socials.

———. 2008. *Sistemas políticos de América Latina*. Madrid: Editorial Tecnos.

Alcántara Sáez, Manuel, and Flavia Freidenberg. 2006. "El proceso político en perspectiva comparada." In *Historia contemporánea de América Latina*. Vol. 6, *1980–2006: Reformas económicas y consolidación democrática*, edited by Manuel Alcántara Sáez, Ludolfo Paramio, Flavia Freidenberg, and José Déniz, 85–150. Madrid: Editorial Síntesis.

Arditi, Benjamín. 1992. *Del granito al archipiélago: El Partido Colorado sin Stroessner*. Asunción: Centro de Documentación y Estudios.

Barreda, Mikel, and Marc Bou. 2010. "La calidad de la democracia paraguaya: Un avance sobre caminos toruosos." *América Latina Hoy* 56: 133–61.

Barreda, Mikel, and Andrea Costafreda. 2002. "La transición democrática y el sistema político institucional." In *Diagnóstico institucional de la República del Paraguay*, edited by Joan Prats i Català, 71–126. Barcelona: Institut Internacional de Governabilitat.

Bengoa, José. 2003. *Relaciones y arreglos políticos y jurídicos entre los estados y los pueblos indígenas en América Latina en la última década*. Santiago: United Nations Economic Commission for Latin America and the Caribbean.

Borda, Luis Villar. 2007. "Estado de derecho y estado social de derecho." *Revista Derecho del Estado*, no. 20: 73–96.

Bouvier, Virginia Marie. 2012. *El ocaso de un sistema: Encrucijada en Paraguay*. Asunción: Intercontinental.

Caballero, Esteban. 2003. "Partidos políticos y sistema electoral." In *Cultura política, sociedad civil y participación ciudadana: El caso paraguayo*, edited by Alejandro Vial, 255–83. Asunción: Centro de Información y Recursos para el Desarrollo.

Carrón, Juan M. 2007. "La emigración paraguaya en el contexto de la globalización." Paper presented at the third Congreso Paraguayo de Población, Cambio Sociodemográfico, Urbanización y Pobreza, Asunción, November 21–23.

Cerna Villagra, Sarah Patricia. 2017. "La representación sustantiva de las mujeres: Un análisis de la legislación sensible al género en México y Paraguay." PhD thesis, Universidad Nacional Autónoma de México.

Cerna Villagra, Sarah Patricia, and Juan Mario Solís Delgadillo. 2014. "La reinvención del dinosaurio: Entre la nostalgia y el pragmatismo del Partido Colorado en Paraguay." *Revista Debates*, January–April.

———. 2018. "Paraguay: Entre el pluralismo moderado y el predominio de los actores tradicionales." In *Elecciones y partidos en América Latina en el cambio de ciclo*, edited by Manuel Alcántara et al., 353–76. Madrid: Centro de Investigaciones Sociológicas.

Coordinadora de Derechos Humanos del Paraguay (CODEHUPY). 2012. *Derechos Humanos en Paraguay 2012*, Asunción.

Coronel, Bernardo. 2011. *Breve interpretación marxista de la historia paraguaya (1537–2011)*. Asunción: Arandurã Editorial; Base Investigaciones Sociales.

Dalla-Corte Caballero, Gabriela, ed. 2012. *Estado, nación e historia en el bicentenario de la independencia del Paraguay*. Asunción: Intercontinental.

Duré, Elizabeth, Guillermo Ortega, Marielle Palau, and Luis Rojas Villagra. 2012. *Golpe a la democracia: Antecedentes y perspectivas*. Asunción: Base Investigaciones Sociales.

Ferreiro, Adolfo. 1989. "Perspectivas de la transición en Paraguay." *Revista Nueva Sociedad*, no. 102 (July–August): 58–60.

Flecha, Víctor. 2003. "La descentralización como reforma del estado." In *Cultura política, sociedad civil y participación ciudadana: El caso paraguayo*, edited by Alejandro Vial, 285–328. Asunción: Centro de Información y Recursos para el Desarrollo.

Flecha, Víctor, and Carlos Martini. 1994. *Historia de la transición: Pasado y futuro de la democracia en Paraguay*. Asunción: Última Hora.

Fogel, Ramón. 1982. *Estado, campesinos y modernización agrícola*. Asunción: Centro Paraguayo de Estudios Sociológicos.

Fretes, Luis Antonio. 2012. "La consolidación democrática en Paraguay." *América Latina Hoy* 60: 67–82.

Gallagher, Michael. 2019. "Electoral Systems." Department of Political Science, Trinity College Dublin. Available at http://www.tcd.ie/Political_Science/people/michael_gallagher/ElSystems/index.php.

Gargarella, Roberto. 2015. *La sala de máquinas de la constitución 200 años de constitucionalismo en América Latina (1810–2010)*. Buenos Aires: Katz Editores.

Gómez Florentín, Carlos. 2014. *1954: El contexto histórico*. Asunción: El Lector.

Gómez Romero, Celeste. 2018. "2018 General Election in Paraguay." Institute for Democracy and Electoral Assistance, May 22. Available at https://www.idea.int/news-media/news/2018-general-elections-paraguay.

Horwitz, Luisa. 2019. "Paraguay: Mario Abdo Benítez's First Year in Office." Americas Society/Council of the Americas, August 29. Available at https://www.as-coa.org/articles/paraguay-mario-abdo-benitezs-first-year-office.

Huntington, Samuel P. 1991. *The Third Wave: Democratization in the Late Twentieth Century*. Norman: University of Oklahoma Press.

Jara Goiris, Fabio Aníbal. 2004. *Paraguay: Ciclos adversos y cultura política*. Asunción: Servilibro.

Kowalski, Alejandro. 1993. "Indígenas e indigenistas en la Convención Constituyente del Paraguay: Entrevista a la Dra. Mirna Vázquez." In *Después de la piel: 500 años de confusión entre desigualdad y diferencia*, edited by Alejandro Kowalski, 99–104. Posadas, Argentina: Departamento de Antropología Social, Universidad Nacional de Misiones.

Lachi, Marcello. 2009. "El debate ideológico en la era Lugo." In *Ciudadanía y partidos políticos: Protagonistas del proceso electoral 2008*, 39–67. Asunción: Decidamos, Campaña por la Expresión Ciudadana.

Lewis, Paul. 2016. *Partidos políticos y generaciones en Paraguay, 1869–1940*. Asunción: Editorial Tiempo de Historia.

Libelo Acusatorio. 2012. Available at https://ladiaria.com.uy/media/attachments/Documento_acusatorio_Lugo.pdf.

Lindsay, Alexander Dunlop. 1945. *El estado democrático moderno*. Mexico City: Fondo de Cultura Económica.

López, Magdalena. 2010. "La democracia en Paraguay: Un breve repaso sobre los partidos políticos tradicionales, el sistema electoral y el triunfo de Fernando Lugo Méndez." *Revista Enfoques* 8, no. 13: 89–106.

———. 2014a. "Democracia en Paraguay: La interrupción del 'proceso de cambio' con la destitución de Fernando Lugo Méndez (2012)." *Cuadernos de Cendes* 31, no. 85 (January–April): 95–119.

———. 2014b. "Elecciones generales y votos en el Paraguay de 1989–2013: Develando algunos mitos." *Diálogos de Saberes*, no. 40 (January–June): 159–82.

Martí i Puig, Salvador, and Sara Mabel Villalba. 2012. "¿Pocos pero guerreros? Multiculturalismo constitucional en cinco países con población indígena minoritaria." *Revista Uruguaya de Ciencia Política* 21, no. 2 (December): 77–96.

Mendonca, Daniel. 2009. *Tortura, represión y constitución*. Asunción: Intercontinental.

Merlos, Claudia. 2014. "Los momentos de la transición." *ABC Color*, February 2, 2014. Available at http://www.abc.com.py/especiales/25-aniversario-del-golpe-de-1989/los-momentos-de-la-transicion-1204417.html.

Ministerio de Agricultura y Ganadería (MAG). 2009. "Resultados preliminares del Censo Agropecuario Nacional 2008." Available at http://www.mag.gov.py/Censo/Book%201.pdf.

Mora, Frank O., and Jerry W. Cooney. 2009. *El Paraguay y los Estados Unidos*. Asunción: Intercontinental.

Nickson, R. Andrew. 1988. "Tyranny and Longevity: Stroessner's Paraguay." *Third World Quarterly* 10, no. 1 (January): 237–59.

———. 2014. *La Guerra Fría y el Paraguay*. Asunción: El Lector and *ABC Color*.

Palau Viladesau, Tomás. 2010. "La política y su trasfondo: El poder real en Paraguay." *Nueva Sociedad*, no. 229 (September–October): 134–50.

Pangrazio, Miguel Ángel. 2000. *Historia política del Paraguay*. Vol. 2. Asunción: Intercontinental.

Paredes, Roberto. 2009. *Operación 33: La versión de los protagonistas*. Asunción: Servilibro.

———. 2011. *Stroessner y el stronismo*. Asunción: Servilibro.

Sartori, Giovanni. 1976. *Parties and Party Systems: A Framework for Analysis*. Cambridge: Cambridge University Press.

Seiferheld, Alfredo M., ed. 1987. *La caída de Federico Chaves: Una visión documental norteamericana*. Asunción: Editorial Histórica.

Serna de la Garza, José. 1998. *La reforma del estado en América Latina: Los casos de Brasil, Argentina y México*. Mexico City: Universidad Nacional Autónoma de México.

Share, Donald, and Scott Mainwaring. 1986. "Transiciones vía transacción: La democratización en Brasil y España." *Revista de Estudios Políticos*, no. 49 (January–February): 87–135.

Soler, Lorena. 2012. *Paraguay: La larga invención del golpe; El stronismo y el orden político paraguayo*. Buenos Aires: Imago Mundi.

Solís Delgadillo, Juan Mario, and Sarah Patricia Cerna Villagra. 2013. "De la llanura al palacio: La reinstauración de la pax colorada en Paraguay." In *Procesos políticos y electorales en América Latina (2010–2013)*, edited by Manuel Alcántara Sáez and María Laura Tagina, 401–30. Buenos Aires: Eudeba.

———. 2016. "Las elecciones en Paraguay en 2008." In *Elecciones en Latinoamérica 1985–2015: 30 años de transformación democrática*, edited by Leandro Querido and Fernando Domínguez Sardou, 120–29. Buenos Aires: Editorial Dunken.

———. 2017. "Paraguay: El cuestionable giro a la izquierda." In *¿Fin del giro a la izquierda en América Latina: Gobiernos y políticas públicas?*, edited by Mario Torrico, 123–49. Mexico City: Facultad Latinoamericana de Ciencias Sociales.

———. 2019. "Fricción, (re)concentración y afianzamiento conservador tras las elecciones de 2018 en Paraguay." *Estudios Políticos* 54: 259–85.

Tribunal Superior de Justicia Electoral (TSJE). 2008. "Memoria y estadísticas electorales: Elecciones generales y departamentales 2008." Available at https://www.tsje.gov.py/e2008/pdf/2008.pdf.

Uharte Pozas, Luis Miguel. 2012. "El proceso de democratización paraguayo: Avances y resistencias." *América Latina Hoy* 60: 17–42.

Uprimny, Rodrigo. 2011. "Las transformaciones constitucionales recientes en América Latina: Tendencias y desafíos." *Revista Pensamiento Penal*, no. 122: 1–22.

Van Cott, Donna Lee. 2002. "Movimientos indígenas y transformación constitucional en los Andes: Venezuela en perspectiva comparativa." *Revista Venezolana de Economía y Ciencias Sociales* 8, no. 3: 41–60.

Villalba, Sara. 2017. "Límites de los mecanismos de democracia directa a la participación en Paraguay." Paper presented at the ninth Congreso Latinoamericano de Ciencia Política, ¿Democracias en Recesión?, Montevideo, July 26–28.

Yore, Fatima Myriam. 1992. *La dominación stronista: Orígenes y consolidación, "seguridad nacional y represión."* Asunción: Base Investigaciones Sociales.

Zovatto, Daniel. 2010. "Las instituciones de la democracia directa a nivel nacional en América Latina: Balance comparado: 1978–2010." *Revista de Sociología* 24 (January): 87–124.

Brian Turner

five GENDER QUOTAS AND WOMEN'S POLITICAL IDENTITIES IN PARAGUAY[1]

Introduction

In July 2015, the Paraguayan news media breathlessly reported the words of Pope Francis, who during his visit to the country lauded "the women, wives and mothers of Paraguay, who at great cost and sacrifice were able to lift up a country defeated, devastated and laid low by an abominable war," referring to the Paraguayan War (1864–1870) and its aftermath. The pope went on to say: "God bless the women of Paraguay, the most glorious women of America" (Holy See 2015). In a 2017 interview with *El País*, Pope Francis explained his admiration for the women of Paraguay for having, in addition to contributed their energy to the war effort, defended their nation's faith, culture, and language and for repopulating the country (*El País* 2017). The pope, an Argentine no less, touched a powerful, and powerfully gendered, strain of Paraguayan nationalism with these remarks (Potthast 2004). However, contemporary historians have concluded that the contribution of women to the war effort "did not lead to a significant alteration in women's status in Paraguayan society" (Ganson 1990, 371). Indeed, Paraguay would be the last country in Latin America to grant women the right to vote, in 1961.

As of September 1, 2019, Paraguay ranked 134th in the world (tied with Bahrain and Brazil) for the percentage of women elected to the lower house of the national legislature, at 15 percent (IPU 2019). On the same measure, Paraguay ranked last out of the nineteen republics of Latin America. The percentage of women in the Paraguayan national legislature was below the global average of 24.6 percent and the average in the Americas of 30.6 percent. Furthermore, Paraguay's rank declined from 2011, when it ranked 96th in the world and 15th in Latin America.

This is in spite of the fact that Paraguay has an electoral gender quota that requires the "promotion of women to at least 20 percent of elected offices in legislative bodies." The law states that "in internal elections, candidate lists should have one woman candidate for every five spots on the list, appearing in whatever place on the list but with one woman for every five spots. Every party, movement, or alliance presenting lists is free to set the order." The law states that parties, movements, or alliances that do not comply with this requirement in their internal elections will not be permitted to contest the relevant election.[2] This law was approved in 1996, making Paraguay the second country in the region to adopt a gender quota for its national legislature, after only Argentina (IDEA 2020).

Also, several major parties have internal party statutes setting higher quotas for women. These include the two largest and oldest parties, the Asociación Nacional Republicana–Partido Colorado (ANR) and the Partido Liberal Radical Auténtico (PLRA), with a 30 percent and a one-third quota, respectively.

Since the gender quota law was passed, Paraguay has shown gains in the number of women elected to office, but only in the three most recent municipal council elections, the 2013 Senate election, and the 2018 departmental junta election have women been elected to at least 20 percent of seats.

This chapter charts the relative progress of women elected to office in Paraguay and explains what factors have kept the number of women elected to under 20 percent in most cases. It explores the challenges activists have faced in attempting to increase the quota itself. Finally, it raises the question of whether the number of women in office (in Paraguay's case fewer than in many other Latin American countries) affects the status of women in society and the ability of women to promote state policies that serve their interests. In sum, does the election of women to public office matter?

Some context for these questions is provided by the World Economic Forum's (WEF) "Global Gender Gap Report 2017." This report ranks Paraguay 96th in the world on its gender equality index. In Latin America, Paraguay is only ahead of Guatemala on this index. The report rates countries on four sets of criteria. The variation across the globe in the gender gap in educational attainment and health and survival is quite limited, so Paraguay's relatively low rankings in these criteria (61st and 97th, respectively) are not particularly meaningful. There is much greater variation in the gender gap in economic participation and opportunity, and in political empowerment. Paraguay ranks 90th in economic participation and opportunity (9th among the nineteen Latin American countries) and 113th in political empowerment (last in Latin America). The report notes a correlation between these two criteria, but it does not suggest the causal link between them (WEF 2017, 29).

In 2006, Paraguay was ranked 38th by the WEF in political empowerment and had a slightly higher score on the index; its decline in rank is largely due to many other countries greatly improving their scores in women's political power, especially in Latin America. Nicaragua, for example, ranked second in the world for women's political empowerment and sixth overall for gender equity. Bolivia, Argentina, Ecuador, and Mexico have all improved on this specific measure over the past decade. The political empowerment index is based on the percentage of women legislators and women cabinet ministers, and the number of years that country has had a female head of state. The 2017 WEF report states that in Paraguay, women held 15.4 percent of ministerial positions and just 13.8 percent of legislative seats, and of course Paraguay has yet to have a woman serve as president.

Representation of Women in Politics

Studies of political representation of specific identity groups have identified distinct types of representation (Schwindt-Bayer 2010, 6–32). Descriptive representation is the concept that legislative bodies reflect politically significant demographic characteristics of society. Since gender is widely understood to be of political significance, a legislature should include men and women, ideally in proportion to their presence in society. Substantive representation is the concept that women in political office will enhance the representation of women's political concerns. Identifying the political concerns of a segment of the population as numerous and diverse as women raises conceptual challenges, as does identifying whether a particular woman legislator substantively represents women's interests. Symbolic representation is the concept that the presence of some number of "people who look like me" in political office influences a voter's perceptions and opinions about politics and about regime legitimacy (Franceschet, Krook, and Piscopo 2012).

Gender Quotas and Descriptive Representation

Concern for improving the representation of women and ethnic minorities in newly established democratic regimes in the period after 1989 led to the adoption of various measures to enhance regime legitimacy. Many countries adopted legalistic and institutional mechanisms, such as a cabinet-level "secretariat of women"[3] and gender quotas for election to legislative bodies. Gender quotas can be established through reserved seats, legislated candidate quotas, and voluntary political party quotas. Ballots for election to reserved seats include only women candidates. Twenty-three countries reserve seats for women, mostly in Africa and Asia, but only in Haiti in the Americas. Legislated candidate quotas are the most common approach in Latin America, employed by fifteen countries.[4] Voluntary party quotas without a legislated minimum are found in two Latin American countries.[5]

While gender quotas may be adopted in order to empower women and enhance women's participation broadly in formal, state-organized political processes,[6] the first and obvious measure of quota laws' success is the growth in the number of women elected to office. Given the relative ease of measurement, a considerable literature has developed analyzing the impact of these laws on the election of women.

Even with legislated candidate quotas, various cultural and institutional characteristics may limit growth in the number of women elected to office. Patriarchal political cultures may cause party leaders to deploy a minimalist interpretation of the law and limit female political participation. Gendered concepts of political power can operate on those who select candidates, whether candidates are chosen by party leaders or by voters (Archenti and Tula 2007, 188).

Institutional characteristics such as the design of the electoral system also affect whether women are successful in political competition. Nélida Archenti and María Inés Tula (2007) identify district magnitude and ballot structure as having the most important impact on electoral outcomes for women.

District magnitude is simply the number of seats available in each district. Larger district magnitudes allow for more precise proportional representation of political parties based on the proportion of votes earned. While larger district magnitudes alone do not guarantee seats for any constituency not directly represented by a political party, Archenti and Tula argue that women, even if placed disproportionately below the top of the party list, are more likely to be elected when district magnitude is high. Following Dieter Nohlen (1994), Archenti and Tula classify multimember districts that elect five or fewer members as low magnitude, those that elect between six and ten members as medium magnitude, and those electing eleven or more as high magnitude.

Ballot structure for multimember districts refers to the possibility of voters casting a preferential vote. In closed-list systems (*listas cerradas y bloqueadas*), voters must select a party list, with no opportunity to affect the order of candidates on the list. In open-list systems (*listas cerradas y desbloqueadas*), voters may cast their vote for a particular candidate. The vote counts for the party and for the preferred candidate's position on the list. Archenti and Tula analyze the impact of open and closed lists in consecutive elections in Tierra del Fuego Province, Argentina, finding that women are less likely to earn preferential votes when voters have the opportunity to alter the order on a party's list.

Another important determinant of the effectiveness of a gender quota law is the interpretation of that law. Archenti and Tula note that the Cámara Nacional Electoral of Argentina contributed to the effectiveness of that nation's gender quota law when it ruled that the one-third quota for women also meant that women should occupy at least every third seat on a list—that the lists should be intercalated as demanded by the set quota. Indeed, in Argentina as of late 2017, women held 38.1 percent of the seats in the national Chamber of Deputies and 41.7 percent of the national Senate. Whether sanctions are imposed for violations of the gender quota law is also a consideration in the law's effectiveness.

Drawing from Archenti and Tula's analysis, one would predict that the most favorable environment for an effective quota law is one where district magnitudes are high, the voting system is closed list, lists must be intercalated, and parties suffer meaningful sanctions for failure to comply with the law.

The Electoral System in Paraguay

Under the national constitution of 1992 (CN92), Paraguay holds national elections and nonconcurrent municipal elections every five years. National elections are for the offices of president and vice president, the forty-five member Senate, and the eighty-member Chamber of Deputies. Also elected are the governors and councils (*juntas departamentales*) of the seventeen subnational governments, called departments. Municipal elections had been held three and a half years after the national election until 2010, when they were moved up one year so as to hold them near the midterm of the nationally elected offices.[7] For the 2015 elections, there were 250 municipalities (the number continues to grow), each with a mayor (*intendente*) and council (*junta municipal*) of between nine and twelve members, depending on the size of the municipality.[8] Asunción's junta municipal has twenty-four members.

Seats to all legislative bodies (Senate, Chamber of Deputies, departmental juntas, and municipal juntas) are determined by proportional representation through the D'Hondt highest averages method for allocating seats. The Senate and all of the juntas are single, multimember districts. Thus, the forty-five senators are elected from a single national district from party lists. Likewise, the nine or twelve members of the municipal junta are elected from a single, multimember district. The Chamber of Deputies is elected from departmental districts (including an electoral district for the capital, as Asunción is not part of any department). Thus, district magnitudes vary greatly for the Chamber, with the populous Central Department (the area surrounding Asunción) electing nineteen deputies, and two sparsely populated departments in the Chaco (Alto Paraguay and Boquerón) electing just one deputy each.

All elections are by closed-list ballot. This has been a target of reformers, who bemoan the closed list as system of protection for powerful party insiders who are widely seen as "hiding" on the closed list to gain election and the benefit of the protection of *fueros* that protect legislators from prosecution for corruption or other crimes while in office. Early in 2012, Congress passed legislation that would have allowed open-list ballots for the 2013 election. However, the measure has repeatedly been postponed and is still not in place.

Open lists would likely have a negative impact on the number of women elected to office. The adoption of the preferential vote is anticipated by advocates of women's participation to reduce the number of women elected in the national elections. In 2012, the Secretariat of Women and the Gender Office of the Superior Electoral Tribunal were holding training sessions for women candidates to encourage their more active participation in campaigns that would require personal vote seeking. The sponsor of preferential vote legislation agreed that a negative effect on women candidates would be likely, and he said that he and his party (Patria Querida) had always supported a 50 percent quota.[9]

A key feature of Paraguayan elections is the constitutional requirement of primary ("internal") elections. Article 118 of CN92 guarantees the right to "universal, free, direct, equal, and secret" suffrage, and Article 119 extends an individual's voting rights to intermediary organizations such as political parties, unions, and social organizations. This requirement dates to the adoption of a new electoral code in 1990 (superseded by the electoral code of 1996), and as far as I can determine is the only requirement of its kind in the world to apply to intermediary organizations (Barboza 1993, 567–69; Dendia 2001). This feature has an important impact on the operation of the gender quota requirement.

Methodology

The Tribunal Superior de Justicia Electoral, which oversees all elections in the country, created a Gender Office (Unidad de Género) in 2009, which publishes data on the numbers of women candidates and elected officials. In compliance with the electoral code, parties must submit lists sorted by candidates' gender. Data sorted by gender were available on the Gender Office's website for elections beginning with the municipal elections of 2001, but I could not locate these data for the municipal elections of 2015. Data on candidates in the national elections of 1998 and the municipal elections of 2015 were compiled through my review of the published candidate lists, identifying candidates' gender by names. Very few names used by ethnic Paraguayans are androgynous, but still there are a few, and in some parts of the country there are candidates from the Brazilian and Asian immigrant communities whose naming practices are less familiar to me. In these cases, absent other indicators of female gender (such as last names indicating marital status), candidates were coded as male. Undoubtedly, I made a small number of errors in this review. A similar procedure was used for the lists of elected mayors and members of the municipal juntas in the 1996 election, and for all those elected in the national and departmental elections of 1993.

I also reviewed candidate lists from all legislative elections to determine the percentage of lists that were headed by women. Especially in multiparty elections in jurisdictions with low district magnitude, heading the list of a competitive party may be the only way to gain election. Gender quotas can be met by concentrating women at the bottom of the list, with no hope of election, so growth in the number of lists headed by women would be an indication of progress being made toward the goal of actually electing women to office. Gender quotas can in some countries be met by concentrating women in the list of replacements (*suplentes*), those who would take the place of the elected *titular* should that person vacate their seat (Archenti and Tula 2007), although this is not the practice in Paraguay. I reviewed candidates' genders from the lists for suplentes in municipal council elections from 1996 to 2010.

I also calculated candidate success rates by gender for elections since 1998. If women candidates are less likely to win election than men, that is an indicator that women may be disproportionately placed at the lower ranks on the candidate lists, or are recruited more readily by marginal political parties unlikely to elect candidates to office. The success rates should only be compared across gender, but not across elections, as the rates are vulnerable to variation in the number of lists competing in any given election. I calculated an index for comparative success rates by dividing the male success rate (the number of men elected divided by the number of male candidates) by the female success rate. Lower numbers on this index suggest greater gender equity.

Finally, I identified the number of legislative bodies that were all male, and those in which gender equity or a female majority had been achieved. At the level of Congress (Senate and Chamber), neither condition has held since the adoption of the gender quota law. Data for the 2010 municipal elections come from the Gender Office; for all other elections, data come from my review of lists of elected officers.

Findings

Unfortunately, data for elections before passage of the 1996 gender quota law are incomplete and would apply to just two democratic elections, the 1991 municipal elections and the 1993 national elections.[10] Therefore, we lack a clear baseline from before the law's adoption to measure its impact. However, with the exceptions of the Senate and the departmental juntas, women have won more seats in every election since 1996 than they had won in the previous election.

CONGRESS

With a district magnitude of forty-five, women are more likely to win seats in the Senate than in the Chamber of Deputies. Within the Chamber of Deputies, women are more likely to win seats from the higher district magnitude electoral districts.

With the exception of 2003, a larger proportion of seats in the Senate have been held by women than in the Chamber of Deputies. Between 1993 and 1998, the presence of women increased in the Senate from five senators to eight, but there was no growth in the number of women elected to the Chamber of Deputies, with just two women elected each year. In 1998, there were thirty women candidates for the Chamber of Deputies, eighteen of whom were candidates from Asunción. These eighteen were concentrated on the lists of marginal political parties that failed to elect anyone to Congress. In most of the departments, only two lists contested the election, thus women's failure to gain election is a result of their uncompetitive placement on the lists. Both women elected in 1998 were from the top of their party's list, in one case from the Colorado Party list in Central Department (district magnitude at that time = 18), and in the other from the united opposition Alianza list in Presidente Hayes Department (district magnitude = 2). The highest-placed woman otherwise was second on the list of the Alianza in Misiones Department, but with a district magnitude of just 2, the Alianza would have had to have won over two-thirds of the votes for her to gain election. She was unsuccessful. All other women candidates in this election were placed in the bottom half of their list.

Combining the results from the four national elections since 2003, forty-two women candidates have won election to the Chamber of Deputies. Twelve of these were elected from Central Department (15.6 percent of seats available across four elections in this department), the only large-magnitude district. Eleven were elected from Asunción (33.3 percent of the seats available), a medium-magnitude district but with a relatively diverse political culture and a larger number of viable political parties. Eight women were elected from the other medium-magnitude districts (Caaguazú, Itapúa, and Alto Paraná; 9.8 percent of seats available). The thirteen low-magnitude districts elected a total of ten women in these four elections (7.6 percent of seats available). Clearly, high district magnitude and the capital city's more diverse political culture make election more likely for women.

In the 1990s, the Senate was the legislative body with the highest proportion of women, but in the 2000s other legislative bodies have surpassed the Senate. No party submitted a list headed by a woman in Senate contests until the 2013 elections.

PARTISANSHIP AND WOMEN'S ELECTION

The Paraguayan party system continues to be dominated by the two conservative traditional parties founded in the nineteenth century, the Asociación Nacional Republicana–Partido Colorado (ANR) and the Partido Liberal Radical Auténtico (PLRA). In the period since 1991, other parties have contested for the "third space" in this system. In the 1990s, the centrist Partido Encuentro Nacional (PEN) held this third space, and in the early 2000s the Unión Nacional de Ciudadanos Éticos (UNACE), a personalist excision from the Colorado Party, and the center-right Partido Patria Querida (PPQ) contested this space. In 2008 and 2013, parties from the center-left and left collectively were for the first time able to together occupy the "third space."

Nine of the ten women elected to the Chamber of Deputies from low district magnitude departments since 2003 were members of the Colorado or Liberal Parties, with one woman from Patria Querida elected in Presidente Hayes in the Chaco. The three Chaco departments have developed a somewhat distinct party

TABLE 5.1 Senate and Chamber of Deputies Elections in Paraguay, 1993–2018

SENATE ELECTIONS

	Women elected	% lists headed by women	% candidates women	% elected women	Gender success index
1993	5	0.0		11.11	
1998	8	0.0	30.22	17.77	2.00
2003	4	0.0	35.71	8.88	5.71
2008	7	0.0	36.16	15.55	3.08
2013	9	18.18	40.30	20.00	2.25
2018	8	17.24	39.95	17.78	3.08

CHAMBER OF DEPUTIES ELECTIONS

	Women elected	% lists headed by women	% candidates women	% elected women	Gender success index
1993	2	2.85		2.56	
1998	2	5.88	19.67	2.56	9.55
2003	8	12.50	30.03	10.00	3.86
2008	10	10.63	31.17	12.50	3.17
2013	12	20.27	32.52	15.00	2.83
2018	12	16.85	33.74	15.00	2.89

TABLE 5.2 Party Distribution of Seats Held by Women in Congress

	2003		2008		2013		2018	
	Senate	Deputies	Senate	Deputies	Senate	Deputies	Senate	Deputies
ANR	1	1	2	2	3	6	2	6
PLRA	1	4	3	3	4	3	3	3
UNACE	1		1	2				
PEN								2
PPQ	1	3	1	1		1	1	1
Left				2	2	2	2	

system in which the PLRA tends to form coalitions with other non-Colorado movements. Notable is the increase of Colorado Party women legislators in 2013, earning 50 percent of the seats won by women from all parties in the Chamber of Deputies that year and again in 2018. In both 2013 and 2018, the Colorados elected six women with only ten women candidates across the country. This was the smallest number of candidates of any party or movement that contested more than four of the eighteen electoral districts.

Women are more likely to be elected from third parties in the medium and high district magnitude departments, with thirteen out of thirty-two women from those jurisdictions coming from parties other than the ANR and PLRA.

JUNTAS DEPARTAMENTALES

Departmental governments were created by the CN92. Departments previously had been administrative units headed by a delegate (*delegado*) who was appointed by the President of the Republic and was responsible for the supervision of the police and the management of the president's political interests (Nickson 1995). In the constitutional convention of 1992, representatives from the interior of the country united across party lines to insist on political decentralization to create popularly elected governors and departmental councils (Turner 1998).

Women were increasingly successful in winning seats in the departmental juntas up to 2008. In 1993, just nine women were elected to the 167 seats, but by 2008 forty women occupied what had grown to 214 seats. The percentage of female candidacies grew through the 2013 elections, and women have headed at least 10 percent of the lists in the past five elections. While women have yet to achieve parity in number of seats on any departmental junta, all-male departmental juntas had disappeared by 2008. The number of women elected to the 228 seats available in 2013 actually declined to thirty-eight, but increased to fifty women elected to the 246 seats available in 2018.

District magnitude for all juntas is either medium or high. Combining results from the 2003, 2008, 2013, and 2018 elections, 155 women won seats on the departmental juntas. Forty-three were elected from medium-magnitude districts and 110 from high-magnitude districts. The medium magnitude districts elected a total of 239 members to the juntas across the four elections; thus, women won 17.99 percent of the seats available. In the high-magnitude districts, women won 110 of the 640 seats available in the four elections, or 17.19 percent. District magnitude does not seem to have been a significant factor in determining women's success, but then the variance in magnitudes is not great for these elections.

TABLE 5.3 Junta Departmental Elections

	Women elected	% lists headed by women	% candidates women	% elected women	Gender success index
1993	9			5.38	
1998	16	11.76	17.81	9.30	2.11
2003	27	17.24	28.61	14.13	2.43
2008	40	10.90	32.87	18.69	2.12
2013	38	18.80	36.96	16.67	2.93
2018	49	12.37	36.39	19.92	2.30

In the 2013 departmental junta elections, the Colorados presented lists with women representing just 23.25 percent of the total, again the lowest proportion of women candidates among the broadly national parties or movements and well below the party's own 30 percent threshold. In 2018, women made up 21.54 percent of the Colorado Party candidates. In 2013, the PLRA fielded lists with women representing 29.61 percent of the candidacies, still below the party's quota of one-third. Of the thirty-eight women elected in 2013, twenty-one were from the Colorado Party, fourteen from the PLRA, two from the Frente Guasú, and one from Avanza País (the latter two being left-leaning parties). Notable in the 2013 election were the results from the northern department of San Pedro (district magnitude = 18). The Colorado Party ran five women on its list, who occupied the twelfth, fourteenth, fifteenth, sixteenth, and seventeenth positions. None were elected, and only one women, from the PLRA, was elected to this departmental junta. In San Pedro in 2018 (district magnitude increased to 21), only three women ran on the Colorado list, and the only woman elected was once again a candidate of the PLRA.

JUNTAS MUNICIPALES

The 1996 municipal elections were the first to be regulated by the gender quota laws. In that year, women won 14.33 percent of the seats available on the municipal juntas. In subsequent elections, women won a higher percentage of seats, reaching 21.86 percent in 2010, but in 2015 women won 20.97 percent of the seats. Parties are not permitted to rely on the suplente lists to achieve their gender quotas, and the percentage of female titular candidates has been greater in each election than the percentage of female suplente candidates. The gender

TABLE 5.4 Junta Municipal Elections and Gender (Im)balances in Juntas Municipales

MUNICIPAL ELECTIONS

	Women elected	% lists headed by women	% suplente candidates women	% titular candidates women	% elected (titulares) women	Gender success index
1996	311	8.76	14.92		14.33	
2001	412	14.42	20.57	26.46	18.50	2.10
2006	523	14.76	23.91	28.37	20.95	1.51
2010	553	16.68	26.09	36.85	21.86	2.08
2015	552	17.47		30.46	20.97	1.65

GENDER (IM)BALANCES

	All male JM elected	Equal or majority female JM
1996	43	0
2001	22	3
2006	17	2
2010	17	5
2015	18	4

success index has been the lowest (meaning greater gender equity) for municipal elections, although male candidates are still between one and one-half to twice as likely to win election as female candidates.

Women have achieved either parity or a majority of seats on a municipal junta fourteen times. In 2003, the districts of General Artigas (Itapúa), Sapucaí (Paraguarí), and Pilar (capital of Ñeembucú) became the first in which women won a majority or parity. On the other hand, even in 2015 there were still eighteen all-male municipal juntas.[11] The district of Yasy Cañy (Canindeyú) has yet to elect a woman in its first three municipal contests. Four districts have elected all-male juntas at least three times in the five municipal elections considered.[12]

District magnitude for municipal elections varies little, so no analysis of the impact of district magnitude is appropriate.

Gender Quotas and Women's Political Identities

EXECUTIVE POSITIONS

Of course, gender quotas do not apply to executive offices that can be held by just one individual. Still, there has been modest growth in the number of women elected as mayor (*intendenta*), including the election of María Evangelista "Evanhy" Troche de Gallegos as mayor of Asunción for the 2006–2010 term and Sandra McLeod de Zacarias in Ciudad del Este for the 2010–2015 and 2015–2020 terms. Thirteen women have won reelection, and one woman, Eusebia María del Carmen Benítez Díaz, has been elected three consecutive times to the intendencia of Ybycuí. So far, forty-nine different municipalities have elected a woman mayor. Since 2001, women representing the Colorado Party have won forty-four mayoral contests, PLRA women have won twenty, the Frente Guasú has won one, and a local list has won twice in the same municipality. In 2015, women candidates were equally likely to win election as men (gender success index = 0.98).

Only three women have won one of the 102 gubernatorial races so far: Mirta Ramona Mendoza Díaz (PLRA) in Concepción in 2003, María Cristina Villalba (ANR) in Canindeyú in 2008, and Marlene Ocampos in Alto Paraguay in 2013. And in 2008, Blanca Ovelar was the Colorado Party candidate for president, after winning a bitter primary contest. Ovelar lost the presidency to Fernando Lugo of the Alianza Patriótica para el Cambio. Two other women have run for president representing small parties: Teresa Notario of the Humanist Party in 2003, and Lilian Soto of the feminist electoral movement Kuña Pyrenda in 2013.

Reporting on the 2013 elections, the European Union Electoral Observer Mission found that women were "well represented in administrative categories of lower responsibility" in the bodies responsible for managing elections, but only two of sixteen electoral judges and only seven of the thirty members of the electoral tribunals were women. The EU noted that only Kuña Pyrenda highlighted gender issues in the 2013 election campaign. The other parties did not use campaign messages specifically targeted at winning the votes of women (Misión de Observación Electoral 2013, 31). The EU recommended increasing the quota from 20 percent and requiring that women be assigned candidate positions with the real possibility of election (2013, 45).

The EU's analysis of the media coverage of the 2013 elections shows that women were even more poorly represented in the media than they were on the ballots. Only 4–8 percent of "political actors" appearing on Paraguay's four television stations and in the three major national newspapers were women.

TABLE 5.5 Mayoral Elections

	Women elected	% candidates women	% elected mayors women	Gender success index
1996	6		2.72	
2001	10	8.58	4.38	1.77
2006	13	9.07	5.77	1.66
2010	18	10.13	7.56	1.37
2015	26	10.30	10.44	0.98

TABLE 5.6 Gubernatorial Elections

	Women elected	% candidates women	% elected governors women	Gender success index
1993	0			
1998	0	2.50	0.0	∞
2003	1	8.73	5.88	1.53
2008	1	11.65	5.88	2.11
2013	1	13.22	5.88	2.44
2018	0	9.02	0.0	∞

TABLE 5.7 Legislative Production by Women Members of the Chamber of Deputies

Session	# of diputadas	Total proposals	Gender-sensitive proposals
2003–2008	8	131	3
2008–2013	11	875	25
2013–2015	9	1132	19

Source: Adapted from Cerna Villagra 2015.

Women did somewhat better on radio, representing 16 percent and 13 percent of political actors appearing on Radio Nacional and Radio Ñandutí, respectively (Misión de Observación Electoral 2013, 72–73).

Factors Limiting the Election of Women

The trend lines suggested by the data show that women are increasingly contesting and winning seats to Paraguay's legislative bodies, but to date gains have been modest and rarely have achieved the goal of 20 percent. Further, Paraguay has fallen short when compared to most of its neighbors in the rates of election of women.

The first and most obvious reason for Paraguay's relatively poor performance is that its gender quota, at 20 percent, is the lowest of any Latin American country that has adopted this norm. Brazil, Peru, and the Dominican Republic all adopted 25 percent quotas for their lower houses (at least) in 1997, and in each case subsequently increased the quota to at least 30 percent.

Second, there is no mandate to place women any higher than fifth, tenth, fifteenth, and so on, on the candidate lists. My review of internal (primary) election lists for the ANR and PLRA in 2002–2003 show that most lists at minimum placed one woman in every fifth spot, and this practice is standard. However, when there are fewer than five spots available, as in the many low-magnitude districts for the Chamber of Deputies, there is no requirement that any women must be included on the list, and in many cases in 2002–2003 women were omitted by party factions in low-magnitude districts. For example, none of the five Colorado Party factions that successfully elected senators named a woman to the four-person list for the Chamber of Deputies from the department of San Pedro. Two of the four deputies elected from San Pedro were Colorados, and obviously neither was a woman (nor were the two elected from other parties).

Third, Paraguay's primary election requirement, and the gender quota law's focus on primary electoral slates, allow for party lists presented in general elections to fall short of the 20 percent threshold. Panama, now with a 50 percent quota, is the only other country in Latin America that limits the quota to internal primary elections. The impact of this can be illustrated by the 2003 Senate election. Here, the two largest parties, the ANR and PLRA, together won twenty-eight Senate seats, sixteen and twelve, respectively. One might then expect that at least five women would be elected by these two parties. But just two were elected (although see endnote 13).

For example, in the Colorado Party primaries held in late 2002 for the 2003 general elections, twelve lists competed for the party's Senate nominations.[13] Remember, seats are awarded based on proportional representation, and the order of the party list is set by the results of the internal primary election. The most-voted list, Reconciliación Colorada (whose presidential candidate in the primary was Nicanor Duarte Frutos), won nine of the top sixteen spots. Reconciliación Colorada placed women on its internal list in the fifth, tenth, fifteenth, and twentieth spots. The woman occupying the fifth spot, Ada Fatima Solalinde de Romero, ended up in the eighth spot on the party list, good enough to win election to the Senate in 2003. The woman occupying the tenth spot on her faction's list, María Digna Roa Rojas, ended up no better than the eighteenth spot on the party list and thus missed out on a Senate seat, since the Colorados only won sixteen seats.

The second-place list in the Colorado primary was Coordinadora Colorada Campesina, which eventually elected three senators.[14] This list included women in the fourth, fifth, ninth, and eleventh spots, but none of them were elected senator.[15] Three other lists were successful enough in the primary to get at least one of their number elected to the Senate, but in all three cases the top women were placed in the fifth and tenth spots, with no chance of ultimately occupying a Senate seat.

Of the remaining seven lists, three were headed by women. This pattern is repeated throughout the election process. Marginal factions or marginal parties more readily recruit women, thus swelling (relatively) the number of female candidates but with little impact on the ultimate election of women to public office. On the other hand, one list, Comunitario Colorado, was headed by María Evangelista "Evanhy" Troche de Gallegos, who won the Asunción mayoral race in 2006 after having served as minister of tourism in the administration of President Nicanor Duarte Frutos. In 2010, Troche was elected to the Asunción municipal junta.

In the case of the PLRA primary for the 2003 Senate elections, the most successful list was Proyecto Liberal de Renovación y Abertura, earning seven of the top fifteen spots on the party list for the general elections. Women occupied the fifth and seventh spots. No other faction earned as many as five spots, or included women in the top faction spots, and thus only two women, not three, occupied the top fifteen PLRA spots. As the PLRA won twelve Senate seats in 2003, only one woman, Mirtha Vergara de Franco (wife of the PLRA presidential candidate Yoyito Franco), was elected to represent the party in the Senate.

The Colorado Party Senate list for the 2018 general election repeats this pattern, with women occupying the fourth, eleventh, nineteenth, and twenty-third positions on the ballot (ANR 2018). The party faction lists in 2018 also show that the voluntary party quotas are largely meaningless to the increased descriptive representation of women, as the factions assigned just 20 percent of ballot places to women in the top tiers of the ballot, well below the Colorado Party's 30 percent voluntary quota.

Why are women routinely placed on the lower rungs of the party lists of the two most competitive parties? The formation of candidate lists by the factions within the major parties depends on criteria other than appealing to issue or identity voters, to the kinds of concerns that would argue for identifying women for higher-profile candidacies. One criterion is referred to in Paraguay as the "commercialization" of spots on the lists. Candidates are expected to contribute financially to their list's campaign. Spots high on the list are valuable to some candidates for the fueros that accompany election to office. Female politicians are not immune to corruption and crime and thus might be interested in a fuero, but many fewer women than men have been in politics, and for considerably less time, so one can expect that there are more men who are wary of giving way to a political newcomer when it puts their election, and legal protection, in doubt. Spots low on the list may still be valuable to the interests of candidates, who can hope for access to state resources from their faction's elected officials in exchange for the unelected candidate's contributions to the campaign. The lack of meaningful campaign finance regulations facilitates these relationships (Nickson 2010, 296). As Liliana Rocío Duarte-Recalde (2017, 77) concludes, these arrangements "bind electoral competition to economic power." The identification of candidates by these criteria also serves established economic and political interests (Cerna Villagra 2015, 118).

Eight countries in Latin America have increased the quota originally adopted. So, despite being an early adopter of this mechanism, Paraguay has fallen behind in the percentage of women elected to the national legislature. Activists have made efforts to increase the legal quota to 50 percent.[16] In 2004, the congressional Commission on Social and Gender Equity in the Chamber of Deputies held public hearings on possible legislation to increase the quota and require alternate placement of men and women on the lists (USAID 2005). Legislation was introduced in March 2008 to this effect by three women deputies joined by a male colleague. The bill was approved by the Commission on Social and Gender Equity in November 2008 (five of its eight members were women), but in August 2011 two other, all-male, commissions revised the proposal to a 33 percent quota. No further action has been taken on this bill.

Mona Lena Krook (2007) says that there are four "stories" about the adoption (or in this case, the reform) of quotas. These "stories" are that women mobilize for quota adoption, that political elites recognize strategic advantages to supporting quota adoption, and that quotas support normative development regarding representation, both domestically and internationally. Paraguayan women activists certainly mobilized for the original quota law and have continued to do so for parity (Soto and Schvartzman 2014), but the domestic norms have been slow to change, and political elites do not see strategic advantages in any electoral reform.

Substantive Representation: Women, Participation, and Public Policy

Will more women in office influence the adoption of public policy priorities that reflect the concerns of women in the electorate? Clearly, this is a question that is difficult to answer. Certainly not all women desire a feminist political agenda, so identifying "women's" issues requires some imposition. Women legislators are also representatives of some portion of the electorate not identified by gender, such as corporate interests, class interests, and local constituencies. Women legislators are likely as interested as men in building their political power, and a strong focus on "women's issues" may lead to committee assignments and a legislative agenda that does not advance careers inside the legislative body.

Sarah Patricia Cerna Villagra (2015, 100) defines "gender-sensitive legislation" as legislative proposals that promote affirmative action, policies of specific interest to women, policies with a gender perspective, and policies that seek to introduce gender-sensitive policies into other issues ("*tranversalización*"). Using these categories, she identifies the gender-sensitive legislative proposals of all women members of the Chamber of Deputies from 2003 to 2015.

The eight women deputies serving in 2003–2008 were not particularly active legislators, filing 131 bills, only 3 of which were gender sensitive. The eleven women deputies serving in 2008–2013 were much more active, filing 875 bills, of which 25 were gender sensitive. In the first two years of the 2013–2018 period, several women legislators were extremely active proponents of bills, with 19 gender-sensitive bills identified by Cerna Villagra. The growing legislative activity of women legislators in areas not related to gender demonstrates their growing role in the representation of multiple constituencies.

TABLE 5.8 Gender-Sensitive Legislative Proposals
by Political Party of the Proponent

	2003–2008	2008–2013	2013–2015
ANR–P. Colorado		3	4
P. Liberal Radical Auténtico	1	5	3
P. Patria Querida	1	4	
Independent (ex–Patria Querida)			2
P. UNACE		7	
P. Demócratico Progresista		3	
Movimiento Para Todos		3	
Avanza País			10

Source: Adapted from Cerna Villagra 2015.

Political party does influence legislative activity. In general, Colorado Party women deputies filed fewer proposals overall, and few gender-sensitive pieces of legislation, considering their greater numbers in the legislature. The nineteen women from the two traditional parties (Colorado and Liberal) across all three legislative sessions in Cerna Villagra's dataset filed less than half of the number of bills than the ten women from smaller parties (721 compared to 1,447) and barely half of the gender-sensitive legislation (16 compared to 30). Legislators from smaller parties are likely to feel the need to push their party's total legislative agenda, while those from larger parties do not need to do so alone. For instance, three women legislators have proposed more than 200 bills in a session: Olga Ferreira of Patria Querida in 2003–2008 and again as an independent (elected on the PPQ list) in 2008–2013, and the two legislators from Avanza País, Rocío Casco and Karina Rodríguez, in 2013–2015. Casco and Rodríguez each filed 5 gender sensitive bills in 2013–2015. In 2008–2013, Fabiola Oviedo of Partido UNACE filed 107 bills, 5 of which were gender sensitive, but in 2013–2015 Oviedo, now a Colorado Party legislator, filed 55 bills and just 1 that was gender sensitive.

Filing bills is a form of substantive representation, but getting bills passed into law is a political art. Cerna Villagra reports that just four gender-sensitive bills passed into law between 2003 and 2015, only one of which, the integral law against human trafficking, being of major significance. Cerna Villagra notes that successful gender-sensitive legislation tends to focus on traditional roles for women as mothers, "leaving aside matters . . . of sexual and reproductive rights" (2015, 119). She contrasts this with the roadblocks that proposed legislation dealing with sexual, reproductive, and maternal health has repeatedly encountered due to opposition from social conservatives. This particular initiative has been sponsored by Senator Carlos Filizzola from the leftist Frente Guasú. In 2015, legislation to protect the labor rights of domestic workers became law, formalizing their right to pensions, eight-hour workdays, days off, and overtime pay (Duarte-Recalde 2017, 79). In 2016, Deputy Rocío Casco's legislation for the protection of women against all forms of violence, dubbed by the legislator as the #PorEllas law, was promulgated. Casco organized a successful social media campaign in support of this legislation.

Symbolic Representation

Whether the election of women helps address the often identified "crisis of representation" in Latin America is a difficult question to assess, and in Paraguay's case the low (but growing) number of women actually elected seems to obviate the question. Measures of symbolic representation are at best indirect. Leslie Schwindt-Bayer (2011) tested the hypothesis that gender quotas would enhance women's political participation and political interest by comparing quota and nonquota Latin American countries' results from surveys conducted by the research project AmericasBarometer. She found little measurable impact of quotas on women's self-reported political interest and participation. Her case study of Uruguay, the most recent country to adopt a gender quota in Latin America, further confirms her null findings.

Duarte-Recalde (2017) argues that there have been declining levels of voter turnout in Paraguay, although turnout did rebound to 68.02 percent in 2013, from 60.3 percent in 2008. She notes that there are only weak connections between civil society organizations on the one hand and the political parties and electoral process on the other (2017, 84). Paraguayans' confidence in institutions, especially Congress, has not improved consistently since 2006; in 2014, just 33 percent reported confidence in Congress (Boidi and Zechmeister 2015, 194–95). Of course, anger at Congress exploded on March 31, 2017, after the Senate approved a constitutional amendment allowing presidential reelection in a highly irregular procedure. Protesters damaged the congressional building by setting fires. While this was not an incident related to gender, it does show popular dissatisfaction with political institutions, and that extra-institutional means are more effective than engaging with the legislative process. The presidential reelection bid was defeated by popular protests.

Conclusions

That women are gaining more candidacies at the top of the party lists suggests both that women are increasingly building successful party careers, and that at least for some parties in some jurisdictions, a woman at the top of the list is not seen as an electoral liability. It is certain that more women are building careers in politics, although gains have been modest given the institutional limits on the application of the gender quota, and the modest nature of the quota itself.

As an abstract expression of representation in democratic politics, these data point to a modest improvement in the election of women and in the promotion of women's political careers. However, it is not at all clear whether gender quotas have had much impact on women's participation in politics more broadly, or to what degree more women in office has had an impact on policy.

On the other hand, there has been observable growth in women's role inside legislative bodies, and at least some women have taken leadership on presenting and advocating for gender-sensitive legislation. The ability to gain allies across political parties demonstrates that legislators from small parties can achieve success on progressive legislation, establishing at least normative principles on which to build future legislative and judicial action on behalf of women's interests.

Notes

1. Support provided by the Walter Williams Craigie Teaching Endowment, Randolph-Macon College.
2. Ley 834/96, Código Electoral Paraguayo, Título I, Capítulo V, Art. 32 r).
3. Paraguay established the Secretaría de la Mujer in 1992.
4. Argentina, Bolivia, Brazil, Colombia, Costa Rica, the Dominican Republic, Ecuador, El Salvador, Honduras, Mexico, Nicaragua, Panama, Paraguay, Peru, and Uruguay.
5. Chile and Guatemala.
6. See Mona Lena Krook 2007 for an analysis of the politics of the adoption and implementation of quota laws.
7. Ley 2460/2004. The municipal elections scheduled for 2020 have been rescheduled to 2021 due to declaration of a public health emergency for COVID-19. Ley 6547/20.
8. Paraguay is divided into *departamentos* and *distritos*. Each distrito includes an urban center and, in most cases, the surrounding rural areas. No part of the country lies outside of a distrito. The governments of the distritos are called *municipalidades*.

9. Interview, Deputy Sebastián Acha, May 7, 2012. In a "preprimary" held August 26, 2012, Patria Querida became the first party to use open-list ballots. Tellingly, the top-ranked woman, incumbent senator Ana María Mendoza de Acha, finished only seventh for the party's Senate list (*ABC Digital*, August 31, 2012).

10. The first two women to serve in the Paraguayan Congress were elected in 1963. One of these women, Dolores de Miño, was the first woman to serve in the Senate (1968–1973), once a bicameral legislature was reestablished in 1967. Three women were elected to the Chamber of Deputies for the 1973–1978 term, the only time more than two women served in a single chamber before 1989. In the last legislature elected under the dictatorship of Alfredo Stroessner, in 1988, two women senators (out of thirty-six) and two women deputies (out of seventy-two) served (Honorable Congreso de la Nación 2000).

11. In the 2015 elections, all-male municipal juntas were elected in Sargento José Felix López (first municipal election), Choré, Lima, Tacuatí, Yataity del Norte, Juan de Mena, Coronel Martínez, Paso Yobai, Maciel, Juan E. O'Leary, San Cristóbal, Santa Rita, Yguazú, Areguá, Mariano Roque Alonso, Villa Ygatimí, Yasy Cañy, and Nanawa. Equal or majority female municipal juntas were elected in San Pedro de Ycuamandyyú, Quyquyhó, General José María Bruguez, and Teniente Primero Manuel Irala Fernández.

12. These are: Yataity del Norte (San Pedro), Juan de Mena (Cordillera), Villa Ygatimí (Canindeyú), and Yasy Cañy.

13. These lists were obtained from ANR party headquarters. They make up the only complete list of all internal party candidates for a national election that I have. Lists published by the Tribunal Superior de Justicia Electoral only include successful primary candidates.

14. There is nothing "peasant" about this internal faction. It claims to represent party leaders from the interior who relied on their ability to mobilize peasants during the Stroessner era.

15. The woman in the fourth spot, Ana María Figueredo Amaro, was the seventeenth Colorado on the party list for Senate. The Tribunal Superior de Justicia Electoral subsequently invalidated the election of José Luis Alder Ibáñez, who happened to have been second on the same list as Figueredo in the primary, and declared Figueredo elected to the Senate as the next Colorado on the list.

16. The QuotaProject (IDEA 2020) reports that five countries have a parity rule: Bolivia, Costa Rica, Ecuador, Nicaragua, and Panama, although Panama's rule governs internal (primary) contests, and it is not clear that there is a rule for alternation in positions on the ballot. I consulted the project's website for this information on July 15, 2017.

Bibliography

Archenti, Nélida, and María Inés Tula. 2007. "Cuotas de género y tipo de lista en América Latina." *Opinião Pública* 13, no. 1: 185–218.

Asociación Nacional Republicana–Partido Colorado (ANR). 2018. Tribunal Electoral Partidario, "Informe Final." Available at http://www.anr.org.py/pdftep/informe-final-17-12-2017-y-com plementaria-07-01-2018.pdf.

Barboza, Ramiro. 1993. *Constitución de la República del Paraguay 1992.* Vol. 1. Asunción: Centro Interdisciplinario de Derecho Social y Economía Política de la Universidad Católica; US Agency for International Development.

Boidi, María Fernanda, and Elizabeth J. Zechmeister. 2015. "Cultural política de la democracia en Paraguay y las Américas, 2014: Gobernabilidad democrática a través de 10 años del Barómetro de las Américas." Centro de Información y Recursos para el Desarrollo, the Latin American Public Opinion Project, AmericasBarometer, and the US Agency for International Development. Available at https://www.vanderbilt.edu/lapop/paraguay/AB2014_Paraguay_Country_Report_V5_W_082115.pdf.

Cerna Villagra, Sarah Patricia. 2015. "Decidirse a decidir: ¿Cómo se promueva la legislación sensible al género en Paraguay?" *Estudios Paraguayos* 33, nos. 1–2: 95–122.

Dendia, Rafael. 2001. *Organizaciones intermedias: Principios y normas del sufragio; Alcances del mandato constitucional*. Asunción: Intercontinental.

Duarte-Recalde, Liliana Rocío. 2017. "Democracy and Representation in Paraguay." *Partecipazione e Conflitto* 10, no. 1: 65–88.

Duarte-Recalde, Liliana Rocío, and Cynthia González Ríos. 2016. "Paraguay: Entre las movilizaciones sociales y el reordinamiento electoral." *Revista de Ciencia Política* 36, no. 1: 287–312.

El País Internacional. 2017. "Papa Francisco: 'El peligro en tiempos de crisis es buscar un salvador que nos devuelva la identidad y nos defienda con muros.'" January 21. https://elpais.com/internacional/2017/01/21/actualidad/1485022162_846725.html.

Franceschet, Susan, Mona Lena Krook, and Jennifer M. Piscopo. 2012. Introduction to *The Impact of Gender Quotas*, edited by Susan Franceschet, Mona Lena Krook, and Jennifer M. Piscopo, 3–24. Oxford: Oxford University Press.

Ganson, Barbara A. 1990. "Following Their Children into Battle: Women at War in Paraguay, 1864–1870." *The Americas* 46, no. 3 (January): 335–71.

Holy See. 2015. "Homily of the Holy Father: Esplanade in Front of the Marian Shrine of Caacupé, Paraguay." English text, July 11. Available at http://w2.vatican.va/content/francesco/en/homilies/2015/documents/papa-francesco_20150711_paraguay-omelia-caacupe.html.

Honorable Congreso de la Nación. 2000. *Revisión Histórica*. Asunción: Congreso de la Nación.

International Institute for Democracy and Electoral Assistance (IDEA). 2020. "Gender Quotas Database: Paraguay." Available at https://www.idea.int/data-tools/data/gender-quotas/country-view/249/35.

Inter-Parliamentary Union (IPU). 2019. "Monthly Ranking of Women in National Parliaments: September 2019." Available at https://data.ipu.org/women-ranking?month=9&year=2019.

Krook, Mona Lena. 2007. "Candidate Gender Quotas: A Framework for Analysis." *European Journal of Political Research* 46, no. 3: 367–94.

Misión de Observación Electoral de la Unión Europea. 2013. "Paraguay: Informe Final; Elecciones generales de 21 de abril 2013." Available at https://eeas.europa.eu/sites/eeas/files/informe_final_moe_ue_paraguay_2013_-_final.pdf.

Nickson, Andrew. 1995. *Local Government in Latin America*. Boulder, CO: Lynne Rienner.

———. 2010. "Political Economy of Policymaking in Paraguay." In *Losing Ground in the Employment Challenge: The Case of Paraguay*, edited by Albert Berry, 265–94. New Brunswick, NJ: Transaction Publishers.

Nohlen, Dieter. 1994. *Sistemas electorales y partidos políticos*. Mexico City: Fondo de Cultura Económica.

Potthast, Barbara. 2004. "Protagonists, Victims, and Heroes: Paraguayan Women during the 'Great War.'" In *I Die with My Country: Perspectives on the Paraguayan War, 1864–1870*, edited by Hendrik Kraay and Thomas L. Whigham, 44–60. Lincoln: University of Nebraska Press.

Schwindt-Bayer, Leslie A. 2010. *Political Power and Women's Representation in Latin America*. New York: Oxford University Press.

———. 2011. "Gender Quotas and Women's Political Participation in Latin America." Paper presented at the Marginalization in the Americas: A View from the AmericasBarometer conference, Miami, October 27. Available at http://www.vanderbilt.edu/lapop/papers-ab-smallgrants.php.

Soto, Lilian, and Gabriela Schvartzman. 2014. *Las mujeres y la política en Paraguay: ¿Qué mueven las mujeres en la política y qué mueve la política en las mujeres?* Asunción: Centro de Documentación y Estudios.

Turner, Brian. 1998. "Descentralización en el Paraguay." Working paper no. 97, Base Investigaciones Sociales, Asunción, April.

US Agency for International Development (USAID). 2005. USAID/Paraguay "Gender Assessment," March 2005, 14.

World Economic Forum (WEF). 2017. "The Global Gender Gap Report 2017." Available at https://www.weforum.org/reports/the-global-gender-gap-report-2017.

Melissa H. Birch

six PARAGUAY AND MERCOSUR
UNLOCKING GLOBAL POTENTIAL IN A REGIONAL TRADE AGREEMENT?

Introduction

Isolated by both geography and politics, Paraguay has been something of an outlier among Latin American countries. Located in the "heart of South America," with a single riverine outlet to the sea, Paraguay was early to independence and quick to dictatorship. José Gaspar Rodríguez de Francia served as independent Paraguay's first ruler, governing with an iron hand for more than a quarter of a century and isolating the country from foreign influence. Almost a century and a half later, Alfredo Stroessner would rule Paraguay for thirty-five years, South America's longest dictatorship in modern history. His government rejected most of the economic policy patterns of the period in favor of a local kleptocracy that he called "the price of peace."

The upsurge of interest in regional integration agreements that characterized much of Latin America in the wake of the debt crisis of the 1980s seemed to offer Latin American countries the opportunity to reinforce the transition to democracy and establish new pathways to growth. These multilateral agreements reached by neighboring countries created mechanisms that enhanced trade and economic cooperation. The North American Free Trade Agreement (NAFTA) is perhaps the best-known such agreement in the United States, but the European Union is a regional trade agreement that aims for a much deeper integration of European economies.

The Common Market of the South, Mercosur, was created in 1991 by four countries in Latin America's Southern Cone with the aim of creating something more like the EU than NAFTA. For Paraguay, Mercosur offered the opportunity to leave behind the political isolation of the past and embrace a democratic future characterized by more and deeper ties to it larger neighbors. A development strategy not without its challenges and risks, Mercosur would challenge many of Paraguay's economic patterns and practices. The chapter will focus on Paraguay's participation in Mercosur and its impact on the country's economic growth and development. After reviewing the economic policies of the Stroessner regime and the challenges faced by the democratic governments that immediately followed, we will examine the impact of Mercosur on Paraguay's economic performance and explore the ways that Mercosur will shape the country's economic future. This chapter reviews economic policy-making under the dictatorship of Alfredo Stroessner and during the transition to democracy, and the impact that Mercosur has had in shaping the Paraguayan economy in the twenty-first century.

Mercosur is the largest trading bloc in Latin America, and Paraguay is its poorest member. A landlocked country with one of the most open economies in the region, Paraguay has enjoyed the price stability that has eluded so many of its Latin American neighbors, but it has not been able to develop a robust economy that provides adequate income and employment for its small population. The creation of Mercosur, the Common Market of the South, changed the dynamic of regional relationships and created the potential for Paraguay to transform its economy and set a course toward more sustainable development.

Paraguay under Stroessner: The Economic Record[1]

The Stroessner regime perhaps will be best remembered for its emphasis on the development of Paraguay's physical infrastructure. The Stroessner government proved very astute at attracting foreign assistance for development projects by playing Paraguay's rival neighbors, Argentina and Brazil, against each other, a strategy sometimes referred to as "pendulum politics" (Birch 2000). Conspicuous displays of the government's anticommunist convictions in the days of the Cold War won it economic and military support from the United States. Aid from Argentina, Brazil, the United States, and the Inter-American Development Bank paid for major infrastructure projects including roads, schools, airports, and dams. The combined effect of economic and political stability was to more than triple investment as a share of gross national product (GNP) from less than 10 percent in 1957 to almost 35 percent in 1981 (Baer and Birch 1984).

Unlike the rest of Latin America, Paraguay never seriously followed an import-substitution industrialization (ISI) strategy. Instead, it served as an entrepôt, selling electronics and luxury goods to Argentina and Brazil, countries that were following the ISI development strategy that was prevalent at the time. For almost a decade beginning in the early 1970s, rapid economic growth was achieved as the result of a combination of increasing production of agricultural commodities during a period of high international prices and the construction of the Itaipú Dam, what would be the world's largest hydroelectric dam (Baer and Birch 1984). When construction ended and commodity prices dropped, the Paraguayan economy entered into a period of sharp contraction and stagnation, which lasted from 1981 until 1989. Again, unlike other countries in the region, Paraguay's economic stagnation in the 1980s was brought on by internal policy mistakes and was only tangentially related to the hemisphere's international debt crisis.

Population settlement patterns began to change significantly beginning in the mid-1960s. A government program established in the 1930s to relocate peasants to Paraguay's less-populated eastern region accelerated that region's activities, and informal migration increased, facilitated by the construction of roads into the area. At the same time, Brazilian peasants, forced off their land in that country's westward expansion, began moving into the border region and eventually into Paraguay.[2] An old border dispute that dated from the War of the Triple Alliance flared in the mid-1960s. The negotiations that followed led to the signing of the Itaipú Treaty between the governments of Brazil and Paraguay in 1973. The treaty created a binational entity that would undertake the construction and operation of the world's largest hydroelectric project, flooding the disputed boundary and providing ample electricity for both countries.

Itaipú was clearly the crown jewel in the Stroessner regime's infrastructure program. At a time when many Latin American countries were accumulating substantial amounts of foreign debt to finance continued growth in the wake of the oil shocks, Paraguay's persistent current account deficit was financed by capital inflows for the Itaipú project. Relative to the size of the Paraguayan economy, these capital inflows were massive and financed a five-year spending spree. Later, income from the sale of electric power from Itaipú to Brazil would continue to provide a steady stream of foreign exchange.

Rising incomes derived from construction activities associated with the Itaipú project generated a second wave of spending. Demand for everything from wage goods to luxury imports increased. Land for small farms as well as for large agribusiness operations was quickly spoken for all along the eastern border.

The influx of Brazilian farmers accelerated, often displacing small Paraguayan farmers and indigenous communities (Nickson 1981). In the capital, Asunción, small homes for urban workers and mansions for the nouveau riche were built. Whole new towns sprang up in Paraguay's eastern region. The arrival of so much cash also generated inflation and, as working-class salaries failed to keep pace, an increasingly unequal distribution of income evolved in Paraguay.

Between 1974 and 1981, the years of the Itaipú boom, the Paraguayan economy was the fastest growing in the hemisphere. It grew at an average annual real rate of 9.2 percent, reaching a high of 12.8 percent in 1977. Construction and agricultural exports drove the economic growth of the 1970s. The construction sector grew at annual rates of about 23 percent between 1974 and 1981. Agricultural production was also strong during this period, which coincided with the international commodity boom of the late 1970s. Export revenues doubled between 1976 and 1979. Significantly, industrial production as a share of GDP stagnated.

Almost inevitably, after the boom came the bust. Massive construction projects and export agriculture had been the twin engines of rapid economic growth in Paraguay in the 1970s. In their absence, economic growth stopped. According to government plans, another binational hydroelectric project, this time with Argentina, would pick up the slack as the Itaipú project wound down.[3] Unfortunately, political changes in Argentina, disputes over financing, and charges of corruption delayed the project significantly. To complicate matters, floods and droughts in the early 1980s diminished agricultural production, and recessions in Argentina and Brazil (accompanied by sharp devaluations of their currencies) reduced the demand for Paraguayan exports. After growing by nearly 6 percent per year during the 1970s, Paraguay entered a period of slow and more variable annual growth that would last for nearly two decades.

The Stroessner government responded, quite typically, by trying to secure additional foreign aid for new projects. The international environment, however, had changed. Brazil and Argentina were suffering from the effects of the debt crisis and were in no position to undertake new ventures. The United States was only interested in supporting anticommunists in Central America and was considerably more critical of human rights abuses and the absence of democratic institutions in Paraguay than it had been in the past. A few small and ill-conceived investment projects can be seen as the last gasps of a failing development model that hinged on foreign assistance and domestic patronage to guarantee economic growth and political stability.

The experience of decades of rather effortless economic growth, a stable rate of exchange, and low levels of inflation seemed to have left the government unprepared to take the bold steps needed to address the changing international context and Paraguay's increasingly urgent economic problems. Unlike most of its Southern Cone neighbors, Paraguay had only briefly flirted with import-substitution industrialization in the 1960s before swinging toward market-driven, primary product exports subject to the cyclicality characteristic of such commodity markets. Democratic governments that followed would inherit little in the way of institutions that could formulate or execute economic policy. Paraguay under Stroessner had become the exporter of mostly unprocessed commodities to global markets and hydroelectric power to the industrial sectors of Argentina and Brazil. As a result of its low tariffs and a stable exchange rate, it was also the Southern Cone's source for imported products from Europe, the United States, and, increasingly, Asian markets (Baer and Birch 1987; Arce 2010). The combination of legal and illegal operations along the border region, what Stroessner termed "the price of peace," would become the focus of increasing attention and ultimately alarm.

Economic Policy and the Transition to Democracy[4]

Paraguay may be one of Latin America's most consistent followers of an open-economy strategy for economic growth. Donald G. Richards (2009) has characterized Paraguay's persistent dependence on commodity products as "export-led stagnation." Little attention was paid to domestic manufacturing, and, consistent with the open-economy strategy, imported consumer goods served the small domestic market as well as a thriving border trade in cities close to Argentina and Brazil. While both the composition and destination of the country's primary products has shifted over the years, the reliance on these products for both employment and income has left Paraguay subject to the whims of the climate and global markets. In recent years, the Paraguayan economy has been characterized by long periods of stagnation, punctuated by booms and busts often triggered by climatic conditions (Borda 2011).

A military coup in 1989 ended the thirty-five-year rule of General Alfredo Stroessner, but it did not end the rule of the Colorado Party. Somewhat surprisingly, during the first decade of transition to democracy, much weaker but still Colorado governments provided some continuity amid dramatic changes. In the space of three years, from 1989 to 1991, Paraguay experienced the end of the Stroessner dictatorship but also the end of the Cold War and the introduction of new regional trading arrangements with the advent of Mercosur. These three events dramatically changed the political and economic landscape for policy makers who tried with varying degrees of success to formulate economic policy in this unfamiliar political and economic context (Birch 1993). The first and most immediate challenge was the rise of Mercosur. It also represented, arguably, the best opportunity to reorient the Paraguayan economy toward a more sustainable and equitable path to development.

Regional integration initiatives in Latin America were in some ways part and parcel of the import-substitution industrialization strategy so widely adopted in Latin America in the 1950s and 1960s. As industrialization advanced, it was understood that larger markets would be needed to enable firms to gain economies of scale and achieve greater competitiveness. Even countries like Paraguay that were not following the ISI strategy participated in numerous bilateral and multilateral discussions. Paraguay was a founding member of both the Latin American Free Trade Area (LAFTA) and the Latin American Association for Integration (Asociación Latinoamericana de Integración, ALADI), which established basic principles and mechanisms that would lay the foundation for the future of intra–Latin American trade.[5]

In the wake of the 1980s debt crisis, and with many countries in the region led by new, democratic governments, a new interest in regional integration emerged. Often termed "open regionalism," this idea sought to balance the neoliberal pressure toward the global trading system embodied in the World Trade Organization with a more managed process of trade expansion based on preferential trade arrangements between countries in Latin America and often built around strategically important industries. The goal was to deregulate gradually and build competitive regional industries as stepping stones to effective participation in the global marketplace (United Nations 1994).

Emblematic of this shift in regional thinking was Argentine president Raúl Alfonsín's 1985 proposal for an economic cooperation agreement with Brazil. Signaling significant geopolitical change, the proposal was accepted by Brazil's new civilian president, José Sarney, leading to the signing of the Act of Argentine-Brazilian Integration in 1986. In 1988, the Treaty for Integration, Cooperation, and Development established a roadmap for the creation of an Argentine-Brazilian common market within ten years, starting with twelve sectoral plans that would be expanded to twenty-four during later summits. The deadline for achieving a common market was shortened to four years by the Act of Buenos Aires in 1990, which also opened the door to the possibility of additional regional members.

Paraguay and Uruguay were both likely targets, but each country viewed the prospect with a mixture of hope and fear. In the end, they would join their larger neighbors in signing the Treaty of Asunción in March 1991.

Paraguay had been watching on the sidelines as the former rivals, Argentina and Brazil, forged stronger economic ties with each succeeding cooperation agreement. With democratic elections completed in Paraguay shortly after the coup, the opportunity to join the regional integration project that had been heralded as a partnership of democratic governments became a real policy choice. Mercosur threatened to end the effectiveness of the pendulum politics strategy that had been used so successfully for more than fifty years, and it would seem to require the identification of a new approach to economic development in Paraguay (Masi 2011; World Bank 1992).

Unlike Argentina and Brazil, Paraguay had not experienced high inflation, a large state sector, or a protected domestic market in the years prior to 1991. Paraguay's tariffs were lower than the Mercosur average, and the exchange rate had been stable, even if unrealistic, for long periods under the Stroessner regime. With the country's transition to democracy, Mercosur became an immediate political issue in Paraguay. The economic policy orientation of the first two democratic administrations in Paraguay fit well with the prevailing economic wisdom that had been coming from Washington in the 1980s: free trade and less government intervention in the economy. It also represented (economic) policy continuity amid so much political change. Membership in Mercosur, however, represented a fundamental change in development strategy and regional economic relations.

The business community was divided on the merits of joining Mercosur. Manufacturing accounted for only a small portion of the Paraguayan economy, so despite the potential threat of cheaper imports from other Mercosur countries, manufacturers did not represent a powerful political opposition. Campesinos, workers, and labor unions generally opposed Mercosur, but they were a small and fractured group. Another, more politically well-connected part of the private sector, however, would theoretically face extinction if Paraguay joined Mercosur. This was the prosperous group of merchants who made their living selling US, European, and Asian imports to tourists from neighboring Argentina and Brazil, where taxes and regulations made it hard to acquire such products, a result of the import-substitution development strategy pursued by these countries for decades. Paraguay's economy was well known for open borders and high levels of unregistered trade (Beittel 2010). Mercosur was a threat to the entrenched political and economic elites associated with these activities.

The most salient political opposition to Mercosur came from a fiercely nationalistic wing of the Colorado Party that emphasized the sanctity of borders and feared being overtaken by the victors of the War of the Triple Alliance. Since the nineteenth century, Paraguayan foreign policy had been wary of domination by Argentina and then Brazil. For some Paraguayans, one interpretation of Mercosur was that it represented the ultimate endgame: Paraguay absorbed—at least economically—by the combination of Argentina and Brazil (Rodríguez 2001). While this perspective lost political visibility with the assassination in 1999 of its most avid proponent, it remained not far below the surface among a small but influential set of Paraguayan politicians.[6]

Paraguay's Ministry of Foreign Relations urged the government to devise a new, proactive strategy to defend the nation's interests in the upcoming Mercosur negotiations (Rachid and Ramírez 2008). The ministry found little interest from other parts of the government, whose apparent apathy likely reflected less an ideological commitment to laissez faire than an inability to reach consensus regarding a policy direction. To reap the benefits of Mercosur membership, policy makers needed to design and implement of a set of policies that would encourage the competitiveness of the private sector in this new regional context, one that offered Paraguay preferential access to large, neighboring countries but more limited ties to global markets.

Suffering from economic stagnation and a fragile democratic transition, and lacking a tradition of proactive development management, Paraguay seems to have been incapable of designing a constructive policy response (Rodríguez 2001; Kaltenthaler and Mora 2002). Instead, Paraguay was apparently paralyzed by the uncertainty. Would the advantages offered by greater market access be sufficient to compensate for the social dislocation that greater competition would likely cause? Economic integration with Argentina and Brazil would likely put an end to the highly lucrative commercial reexport activities in the tri-border region. How could Paraguay hope to find a competitive niche given its weak industrial sector? Still, being excluded from three neighboring markets as they grew stronger through integration was not an attractive option, either. In the end, the head of Paraguay's trade delegation, Hugo Saguier Caballero, said: "There was no other alternative than to jump right into the process. We were willing to absorb some of the economic costs of integration for the political and international benefits Paraguay was to obtain" (qtd. in Kaltenthaler and Mora 2002, 89).

TABLE 6.1 Growth of Paraguayan Exports to Mercosur, 1980–2018

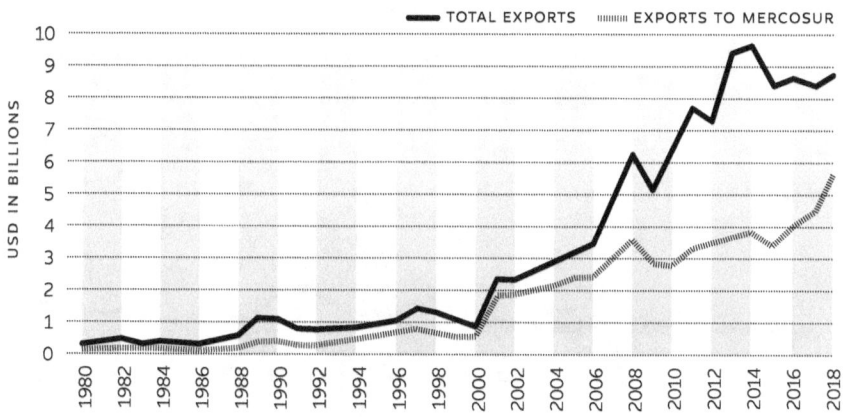

Source: IMF, Directions of Trade Statistics.

Impact on the Paraguayan Economy[7]

When the Treaty of Asunción was signed, Paraguay's leaders hoped that the country's comparative advantage in terms of cheaper land and labor might lead to its integration into the supply chain of major industrial sectors in Argentina and Brazil, fostering the formation of globally competitive clusters in the Southern Cone that would serve the world market. Industries as diverse as automobiles and processed meat were often mentioned. Given the relatively small scale and landlocked location of Paraguayan producers, many believed that their best chance for reaching global markets competitively lay in becoming part of the production process of larger Argentine or Brazilian industries that were already selling to both domestic and global customers. Were this to happen, Paraguay's pattern of production and trade would shift, investment would rise, and incomes would grow, providing a higher standard of living for Paraguayans.

Trade

Immediately after the formation of Mercosur, Paraguay's exports to its Mercosur neighbors grew faster than exports to other markets, but by 2001 that trend had ended (see table 6.1). Exports to Mercosur have continued to grow but so, too, have exports to the rest of the world, and the latter more quickly.

TABLE 6.2 Paraguayan Exports to Mercosur by Country, 1980–2018

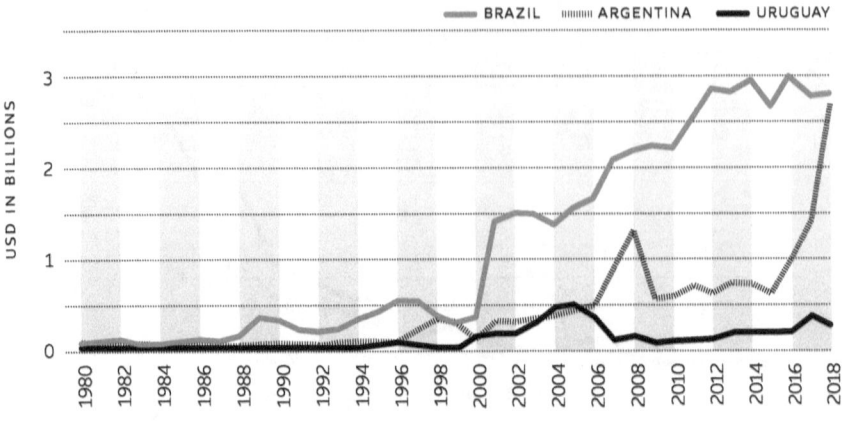

Source: IMF, Directions of Trade Statistics.

And while Paraguayan exports to Brazil have always made up the largest share of Paraguayan exports to Mercosur countries, around the turn of the century Paraguayan exports to Brazil expanded dramatically. By 2016, Paraguayan exports to Argentina and Uruguay combined amounted to less than one-third of the value of exports to Brazil (see table 6.2). Climatic conditions changed that, and by 2018 Paraguayan exports to Argentina, mostly soybeans, were almost equal to those of Brazil.

The interpretation of these phenomena is complicated. First, beginning in the 1980s but accelerating rapidly by the early 2000s, large-scale agriculture took root in eastern Paraguay, and by 2014 Paraguay was the fourth-largest exporter of soybeans in the world. While the ultimate destination of this crop was world markets, much of it was transshipped through neighboring countries (particularly Brazil and Uruguay) and is identified in Paraguayan export data as shipments to those countries. As a result, data for exports to Mercosur may give an unrealistic picture of the true destination of Paraguayan products. Second, while reexport trade seems to have been declining since around 2010, it has persisted despite the creation of Mercosur. While some of these transactions are registered and legal, many are not (Beittel 2010). As a result, the reliability of Paraguayan trade statistics is always suspect. Efforts are underway to improve the way exports are recorded, and a more accurate picture may emerge.[8] Stella Guillén (2012) has reconstructed trade data for the period 1995–2011. By her estimates, for example,

TABLE 6.3 Growth of Paraguayan Imports from Mercosur, 1980–2018

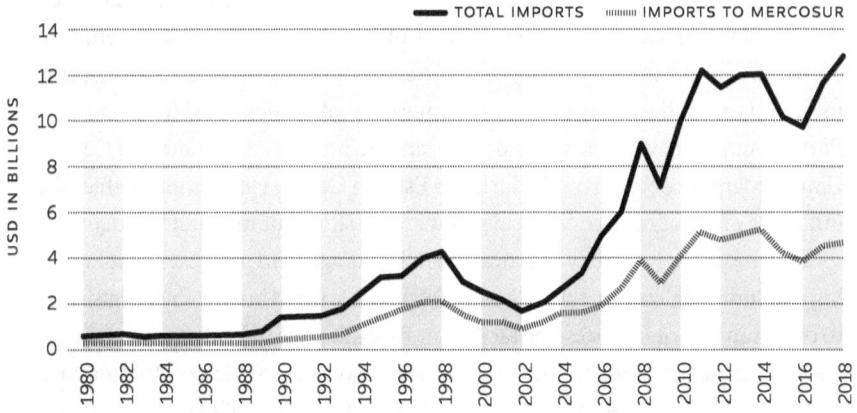

Source: IMF, Directions of Trade Statistics.

Brazil, Chile, and Russia were Paraguay's top three export markets in 2011 rather than Uruguay, Argentina, and Brazil.

A similar pattern is observed for Paraguayan imports from Mercosur countries. Like exports, imports from the trading bloc rose immediately after the Treaty of Asuncion was signed but stalled by the end of the decade (table 6.3). Imports from Mercosur would resume growth beginning in 2002. By then, however, imports from the rest of the world were growing faster. We might expect first to see a change in the composition of items imported to include more intermediate goods and equipment rather than finished consumer goods, as firms invest in manufacturing plants and associated equipment. Five product categories generally account for almost 75 percent of Paraguayan imports, all manufactured products. They include chemicals and plastics, petroleum, automobiles and auto parts, electronics, and machinery and equipment. Products in the first category are widely used in agriculture, and those in the last are closely connected to manufacturing. About 40 percent of all imports come from Mercosur, while China provides about half of the remainder. This distribution of products and markets has been fairly constant since 2015, although a slight increase in the relative share of industrial goods seems to be taking place and will be discussed below. It suggests a growing connection with world markets and perhaps the creation of additional industrial linkages.

In the years immediately following the Treaty of Asunción, concerns about trade diversion were widespread. A highly influential World Bank report suggested that much of the "new" trade taking place among Mercosur members had been diverted from trade that had been taking place with potentially more efficient extraregional partners (Yeats 1998). But even the conservative Cato Institute took issue with the study along with a number of academics (Hudgins 1997). Further studies have dismissed this idea, and in a recent study, Eduardo Cuenca García, Margarita Navarro Pabsdorf, and Estrella Gómez Herrera found that "the influence of the agreement on trade has been positive but moderate" (2013, 336).

The one proactive policy initiative taken by Paraguay to promote manufacturing and industrialization, the Law of the Maquila, is timid but notable. Legislation to create an in-bond processing facility, or maquila, was passed in 1997 and took effect in 2000. Designed to encourage foreign investors to think of Paraguay as a lower-cost location within Mercosur, the law permits foreign investors to import raw materials and equipment tax-free and locate assembly operations anywhere in the country, unlike the Mexican maquila operations, which were initially limited to the border region. Products created in a Paraguayan maquila can be sold to Mercosur customers (including in Paraguay itself) paying a single, very low tax rate of 1 percent on the value added in Paraguay.

By 2018, Paraguayan exports hovered close to $9 billion annually, including reexports and the export of hydroelectric power. The value of goods actually produced in Paraguay (excluding energy) hovered around $6 billion, of which 42 percent were commodities and 46 percent were agro-related products such as soybean oil and frozen beef, leaving a mere 13 percent of Paraguayan exports consisting of manufactured or industrial products. These proportions were relatively constant between 2013 and 2016, but the participation of maquila production in manufactured exports showed notable growth during that time. By 2016, maquila exports accounted for more than one-third of all non-agro-industrial manufactured exports (Masi 2017, 17). By 2018, some fifteen thousand workers found employment at maquila plants, but slowing economic growth in Brazil, the source of more than 80 percent of the investment in maquilas, suggested that the growth of maquilas in Paraguay might slow in the immediate future (IMF, 2019:19).

In the first ten years of maquila operation, only fifty companies participated. Food, motorcycles, plastics, and apparel were manufactured for export under the maquila and usually exported to Brazil (Masi 2011). By 2017, the bulk of maquila manufacturing consisted of auto parts, textiles, and plastics with employment in auto parts and textiles accounting for more than 60 percent of the eleven thousand jobs existing in maquila plants (Masi, 2017, 17).

TABLE 6.4 Paraguay's Share of Mercosur FDI
Foreign direct investment in Paraguay as a share of total
Mercosur investment; percent millions of dollars.

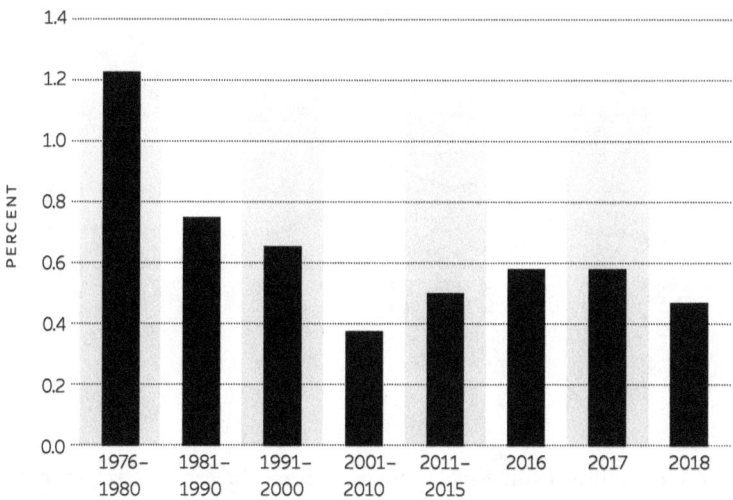

Source: World Bank Development Indicators (2019).

The Horacio Cartes administration (2013–2018) promoted the maquila as an engine of growth and development, and some eighty new plants were established. With Paraguayan labor costs about half of those in Brazil, it is not surprising that most of these plants were established by Brazilian investors, with Brazil the destination for most maquila exports (70 percent). This is leading some to call Paraguay the "China of South America" (Douglas and Malinowski 2017). Still, projects approved under the maquila arrangement accounted for only 14 percent of all foreign direct investment (FDI) entering Paraguay between 2013 and 2016 (Masi 2017, 18).

Foreign Direct Investment

Investment in manufacturing is essential for economic development and the growth of competitive industries in emerging economies. With the advent of Mercosur, it was hoped that both foreign and domestic investors would seize the opportunity to locate production in Paraguay and sell into the entire four-country

TABLE 6.5 Paraguay Real Gross Domestic Product
Growth of the Paraguayan economy in constant 2010 USD: 1960–2018.

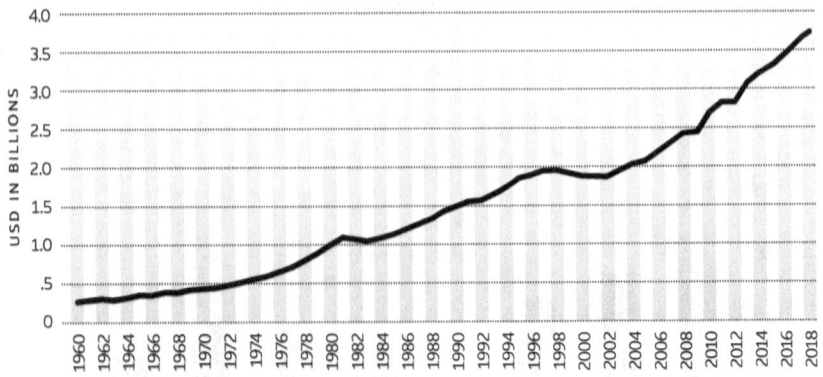

Source: World Bank (2019).

market, but there is little evidence of that taking place. Investment as a share of Paraguay's economy has remained relatively flat over the period, and investment coming from abroad has always been meager, however locally significant.

Since Mercosur was expected to facilitate the integration of Paraguayan manufacturing into international supply chains, an increase in the inflow of capital from foreign countries might be expected. This would suggest that international investors, regional or extraregional, identified Paraguay as a potential low-cost location for investments that would serve the growing Mercosur region.

GROWTH AND INCOME DISTRIBUTION

Expanding trade and growing investment should lead to a growing economy. Indeed, the Paraguayan economy has grown, even adjusting for inflation (see table 6.5). When adjusting for population growth, however, growth was disappointing. In the first decade after the Treaty of Asuncion, per capita growth was modest as Paraguay endured a banking crisis. In the next decade, Paraguayan per capita income grew much more quickly and in line with its Mercosur partners, but in the last decade (2008–2018) per capita income continued to grow in Paraguay, but more slowly than in other Mercosur countries (see table 6.6). In the absence of a proactive development strategy, the economy experienced boom-and-bust cycles associated with commodity prices and climatic conditions.

This sort of growth suggests greater employment and higher productivity.

TABLE 6.6 Paraguay and Mercosur Gross Domestic Product
Per capita income in current USD, Paraguayan and Mercosur compared.

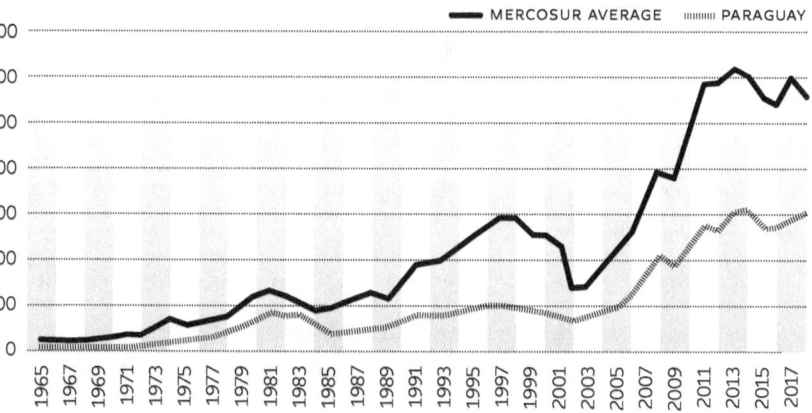

Source: World Bank Development Indicators (2019).

That, in turn, should lead to higher wages and better salaries associated with higher levels of skill development. Here, the data reveal something different. The distribution of income suggests that rather than spurring the growth of a middle class based on formal employment in export-driven manufacturing, the economy is concentrating income among the wealthiest 20 percent of Paraguayans. The top 20 percent of income earners have increased their share of the economy by almost a quarter, holding more than half of all income. Those at the bottom of the income ladder have seen their incomes fall by one-third between 1990 and 2014, and this after even deeper losses in the period of economic stagnation from 1995 to 2005. Even years of exceptionally high growth were also associated with a worsening of income distribution (see table 6.7).

This pattern of high growth and worsening income distribution is consistent with the rapid expansion of mechanized agriculture (soy and corn) taking place in eastern Paraguay, and the extension of soybean farming and cattle ranching into the Gran Chaco of western Paraguay. While planted acreage quadrupled between 1991 and 2010, output has quintupled thanks to double cropping and the economies of scale associated with mechanization. As a result of these recent trends, the World Bank reports that "1.1 percent of the rural establishments own 80 percent of the land, and 82 percent of farmers, who have less than 20 hectares each, occupy only 6 percent of the total area" (Arce and Arias 2015, 1.3).

TABLE 6.7 Distribution of Income

	1990	1995	1999	2003	2005	2008	2011	2014	2017
GINI index	40.8	58.2	54.6	54.9	51.4	50.7	52.3	50.7	48.8
Share of income held by lowest 20% of population	5.8	2.4	2.8	3.4	3.9	4.1	3.5	4.0	4.6
Share of income held by highest 20% of population	47.1	61.8	58.6	59.4	56.3	55.7	56.7	55.6	54.0
Real GDP growth rate	4.1	6.8	-1.4	4.3	2.1	6.4	4.3	4.9	5.0

Data Source: World Development Indicators (2019). A higher GINI index is associated with a less equal distribution of income. Last Updated Date: 10/28/19

After twenty-five years, it is difficult to disentangle the effects of Mercosur from other global phenomena. Quite unexpectedly, China joined the world's market economies in 2004, and the demand for commodities and minerals rose dramatically. Genetically engineered seeds changed farming practices and favored large-scale production over small farms. The Argentine economy faced a prolonged period of economic challenges characterized by slow growth and an overvalued exchange rate. Rising incomes in many countries, from Chile to Kazakhstan to Russia, increased the demand for Paraguayan beef. At the same time, the Argentine and Brazilian economies have recently become much less reliable economic partners as they have both faced a prolonged set of economic challenges. These are all changes that would seem to increase the concentration of income and dilute the impact of Mercosur on the Paraguayan economy.

It does seem clear, however, that Mercosur has led Paraguay to increase its commercial connections with neighboring countries. Some subtle changes in trade data suggest that Mercosur's impact on Paraguay's industrial sector may be growing and that, slowly, it may be putting downward pressure on the reexport trade. While industrial exports are insignificant in absolute terms, more than half of all Paraguayan industrial exports go to Mercosur markets (Servín 2010), and the growth in maquila plants suggests that this may trend toward more integrated production across borders. It is difficult to believe that this could not have taken place more quickly with appropriate industrial policies in place.

Alternatively, should other Mercosur countries have done more to ensure the integration of Paraguay into their industrial production? Recent moves by the Brazilian government to promote manufacturing linkages with Paraguay suggest that this might have been very effective.

Beyond the Treaty of Asunción

Mercosur is part of an enduring vision of a larger, unified Latin America. The Treaty of Asunción provided for both the addition of new members and the ability of the group to join other regional integration projects.[9] Since the 1990s, new members have been added and existing memberships have been challenged. A regional market of about US$641 billion in 1991 has grown to include six countries representing a market of about $3.15 trillion. This is roughly the same size as the German economy, one of the top five in the world.

The treaty also provided an ambitious agenda for deepening integration over time. It envisioned the free movement of not only goods and services but also factors of production. And while it made immediate provisions for tariff reductions, it also created long lists of exceptions and a number of exemptions from the common external tariff (CET). These would be the subject of automatic elimination over time as well as ongoing negotiation. The inability of the member countries to establish a more coherent CET has been the subject of much discussion and Mercosur pessimism. And while the treaty anticipated coordinated macroeconomic and sectoral policies and even the creation of a common currency, such a level of economic integration still seems to lie far in the future.

Regional integration agreements are often evaluated or discussed in terms of their tendency to broaden their scope or deepen their reach. For Paraguay, the ability of Mercosur to expand the scope of its market has been key to defining the success of the agreement. This small economy, far from major world markets, appreciated the potential advantage in opening borders to trade and investment. Coordinating sovereign prerogatives with its larger neighbors was more problematic. Centuries of fighting incursions from neighboring countries has made it difficult to set aside hard-won victories in exchange for the potential benefits that might materialize from greater interdependency. The next section of this chapter will examine the broadening and deepening of Mercosur since the 1990s from Paraguay's perspective.

Broadening the Opportunities

The Treaty of Asunción left Bolivia and Chile on the margin of what promised to be a large and growing integrated market. While the Bolivian government was enthusiastic about an agreement with Mercosur as it sought to strengthen its relationship with Brazil (particularly in the energy sector), the issue was more complicated for Chile. In the 1980s, under the guidance of the Chicago Boys, Chile had brought its average tariff rate down to 11 percent, much lower than even the anticipated Mercosur tariffs for extraregional products. Full membership in Mercosur for Chile, which would require raising tariffs again, seemed out of the question. Still, Chilean firms were anxious to seize the opportunity to increase exports, particularly of manufactured products, and an agreement with Mercosur offered Chile a way to engage with the region after years of isolation under the military dictatorship of Augusto Pinochet. The Mercosur countries were keen to include Chile, as it offered Mercosur a window to the Pacific and emerging Asian markets.

Both countries signed economic complementarity agreements (ECAs) with Mercosur in 1996, and Bolivia became a full member in 2016. Mercosur and the Andean Group signed an ECA in 2002 that provided for the creation of a free trade area between the two regions (Porrata-Doria 2005). These agreements with additional Latin American countries and groups have provided small but important contributions to Paraguay's export portfolio. William Swanson (2012) reported that almost half of all exports to these markets consisted of chilled beef. María Belén Servín (2010) found that several of the Andean countries were important markets for Paraguayan pharmaceutical exports.

For a time, the only alternative to Mercosur for Paraguay might have been the US-led proposal for a Free Trade Area of the Americas. Often considered but always rejected by Paraguay and Uruguay, this regional integration initiative calls for the creation of a free trade area for the hemisphere and builds on the concept of NAFTA, seeking to add countries to the existing trilateral free trade agreement. To date, the Mercosur countries have preferred to work toward the deeper integration of a common market, although the slow pace of progress toward that objective has led individual Mercosur countries occasionally to consider the option.

More recently, the creation of the Pacific Alliance offered a new regional integration opportunity. Formed in 2012 by Chile, Colombia, Mexico, and Peru for the immediate purpose of creating a free trade area, the initiative reflects the changing political dynamics of the region. All four governments at the founding of the alliance were more market oriented and export driven than the Mercosur countries. While the long-term vision for the Pacific Alliance includes the free movement of capital and labor, its current orientation seeks to promote economic growth by increasing exports to growing Asian markets. While the Pacific Alliance has moved quickly to increase intraregional trade and even created a single, stronger stock exchange, it is about half the size of Mercosur in economic terms. This will be an important consideration for countries as they consider how to align their economic futures with the regional groupings.

The European Union has always been the model for Mercosur, and yet integration with Europe seems to have eluded both parties. Agriculture is the issue that seems intractable, as the EU has preferential agreements with former European colonies under the Lomé Convention, and Mercosur's most likely exports, at least initially, would be agricultural. Still, the EU has consistently provided support for many projects in the Mercosur countries, and relations between individual members and the EU are good.[10] Recent events on both sides of the Atlantic may have set the stage for progress on an EU-Mercosur agreement. The deep recession in Brazil in 2016 and 2017 and the rise of neoliberal governments in Argentina, Brazil, and Paraguay have created a sense of urgency within Mercosur and a willingness to negotiate more seriously. At the same time, the exit of the United Kingdom from the EU has made British negotiators more interested in reaching an agreement with Mercosur, an economy that is approximately the same size as that of the UK.

In all, since the 1990s, Mercosur has signed some twenty-two preferential trade agreements including with countries as far away as India, Israel, Egypt, and the South African Customs Union.[11] It is unlikely that Paraguay, acting alone, could have negotiated this kind of access for its products in so many different markets. As a small country with limited diplomatic resources, Paraguay might not have commanded the attention of richer countries on other continents, but these markets appear to offer Paraguay an important opportunity for its incipient industrial sector.

STEPPING BEYOND FREE TRADE

Since the 1990s, the legacy of openness and institutional weakness has hampered the ability of Paraguayan economic actors to seize opportunities or reposition themselves against foreign competition. As a result, the impact of Mercosur on trade, investment, and overall economic activity is idiosyncratic and probably less than it might have been. Yet Mercosur remains as much an issue of international relations as of economic development. Andrés Malamud notes that "the project has fostered domestic democratic stability and lasting peace among its members. In a region historically characterized by authoritarianism and military rule, this accomplishment alone justifies integration issues" (2005, 426). At critical junctures, Mercosur countries have played a decisive role in sustaining the democratic transition in Paraguay.

One of the early threats to the democratic process taking root in Paraguay was an attempted coup by General Lino Oviedo in April 1996, followed three years later by another presidential crisis (Abente Brun 2009). In each case, pressure from Mercosur partners ensured support for nonviolence and helped to stabilize volatile situations. In 2012, Mercosur partners tried mightily to avert a "legislative coup" but were unable to keep the Paraguayan Congress from concluding a flawed and hasty process that removed from office the first democratically elected president from an opposition party in some sixty years, Fernando Lugo. Unable to stop the process, Mercosur countries voted to suspend Paraguay's Mercosur membership for this violation of democratic principles.[12] Losing its vote during suspension, Paraguay was unable to block the admission of Venezuela to Mercosur, which proceeded in 2012. After democratic elections in April 2013, Paraguay was reinstated to full Mercosur membership. Ironically, Paraguay would vote, along with the majority, to suspend Venezuela in 2017 for violations of democratic rights in that country.

While Mercosur has not, in fact, become the Common Market of the South, it has taken steps that incrementally increase regional integration and gradually change the economies and societies of the region substantially. Therefore, Mercosur is far from being an "incomplete customs union." Indeed, it resembles more an "incomplete free trade area with some degree of harmonization of member states' extra-zone commercial policies" (Bouzas, Motta Veiga, and Torrent 2002, 131). A review of Paraguayan trade practices and performance confirms the veracity of such a view. Still, Mercosur has advanced toward a common market in other dimensions that are often overlooked. In reviewing its accomplishments since the 1990s, the Mercosur secretariat identifies the following:[13]

- Citizens of all of the Mercosur countries can now travel to other Mercosur countries (including Colombia, Chile, Ecuador, and Peru) with only a government-issued photo ID. No passport or visa is required.

- Citizens of Argentina, Brazil, Paraguay, Uruguay, Bolivia, Chile, Peru, Colombia, and Ecuador may apply for residency in any of the other countries simply by presenting minimal required documentation. A two-year residency is automatically awarded; at the end of the period, citizenship in the country of residency may be obtained.
- Citizens from the four original countries (Argentina, Brazil, Paraguay, and Uruguay) who have worked in one or more of the other countries mentioned may collect pension benefits to which they would have been entitled if they had been legal residents in that country.
- Mercosur has created a fund to address the asymmetries that exist among member nations and across various regions. The Fondo para la Convergencia Estructural del Mercosur (FOCEM) was created in 2004 and in 2015 was extended for ten years.
- Mercosur license plates are becoming available, and the harmonization of vehicle registration across the countries of Mercosur is underway.
- To improve health within the region, member countries and Chile, Peru, and Surinam have created a coordinated buying group to improve their bargaining power in the purchase of expensive drugs.
- Two Mercosur units focus on human rights including the rights of children, the elderly, and members of the LBGT community. These units also continue investigations into human rights violations during periods of military dictatorship in the region.

For Paraguay, protections for migrants are particularly important. For many decades, Paraguayans have left the country for work in Argentina and Brazil, primarily (Sala 2008). Extending rights and formalizing their status in the countries where they work is an important step in ensuring their safety and fair treatment (Sala 2017). Mercosur, working in collaboration with the International Organization for Migration, has been regularizing residency documents, work permits, and other forms of documentation, especially in the border areas.

The creation of the Fondo para la Convergencia Estructural del Mercosur (FOCEM; Structural Convergence Fund) in 2006 was a significant achievement for Paraguay. The issue of asymmetries had plagued Mercosur from the start, and remedying this had long been a priority on the Paraguayan negotiating agenda (Masi, Terra, et al. 2008). For Paraguayan producers, trapped in a landlocked country, improved road, rail, and river transport is essential to achieving competitiveness. Perhaps more important for the region as a whole, however, were the vast differences among the countries, and among regions within the larger countries, in terms of standards of living and access to basic social services. The creation of FOCEM was an attempt to both recognize these serious asymmetries in terms of size and wealth among countries while at the same time addressing regional inequalities within countries and the institutional weaknesses that were common to all.

Under FOCEM, Mercosur member countries contribute to the fund in proportion to their size and wealth and draw from it in reverse proportion. Projects eligible for FOCEM funding must fall within one of the following categories: infrastructure, competitiveness (value chain enhancements), social cohesion (health, education, housing), and institution strengthening. Paraguay has been the major beneficiary of FOCEM funding; between 2005 and 2015, FOCEM allocated $753 million to projects in Paraguay, almost half the FOCEM budget. These projects in Paraguay include: (1) infrastructure such as transmission lines and improvements to roads and streets around Asunción; (2) funding to fight hoof-and-mouth disease in cattle; (3) housing projects for the very poor and potable water for indigenous communities; and (4) along with the other Mercosur countries, technical cooperation to enhance the protection of human rights.

While progress continues, a real common market has been difficult to achieve. Deepening economic integration requires greater interdependency, stronger rules and stricter adherence to them, and a willingness to pool sovereignty or at least cede some political autonomy (Doctor 2013, 522). All of this would require a greater level of trust and commitment than currently exists. From the perspective of Paraguay, a small, landlocked country, such trust would be difficult to achieve given the political turmoil that seems to roll through the region periodically. With certain kinds of "dependencies" seemingly locked in and the disproportional weight of Brazil in the region's deliberations, the preconditions for deepening integration are absent. The creation of a supranational organization, following the European model, might help to overcome differences and provide more sustained leadership, but that runs counter to some long-held, fundamental tenets of foreign policy in the region (Rachid and Ramírez 2008). A more likely path in the near future may be small steps driven by presidential initiatives.

Conclusion

There is no doubt that the state of Mercosur after twenty-five years falls far short of that imagined by the founders in the Treaty of Asunción. Given the vast differences among the member countries, it should not come as a surprise that progress toward the ambitious goal of a common market has been slow. Brazil may be the largest member of the project, but it is not the richest. While Uruguay is the smallest country in Mercosur in terms of size and population, it has the highest per capita income. Twenty-five years into the process of integration, Paraguay's economy is only half the size of Uruguay's and less than 1 percent of Brazil's. It is by far the poorest country in the region with a per capita income about one-quarter of that of other members, and, according to the World Bank's Human Development Indicators, it ranks far behind Argentina and Uruguay and close to Brazil. While almost half of Paraguay's exports depend on Mercosur partners, only 10 percent of Brazil's exports go to Mercosur countries while twice as much goes to the European Union.

That said, the economies and societies of the member countries are much different today than they would have been without Mercosur. For Paraguay, this is particularly true. Democracy seems to have taken hold in Paraguay, though still challenged periodically by powerful players with authoritarian tendencies. Funding for vital infrastructure and regional improvements in phytosanitary standards have increased exports and set the stage for greater prosperity. The economy continues to be the most open of the member countries, and Mercosur has expanded Paraguay's global trading horizons. Extraregional agreements have opened markets for Paraguay that it might have been unable to access alone, and these markets are important. Not only do they enable Paraguay to diversify its markets, they also permit new products to be exported, particularly manufactures. There are some signs that, after twenty-five years, supply chain integration is beginning to take place. This may have been the result not so much of market forces but rather of an explicit drive in both countries to see Paraguay as "Brazil's China."

While the advent of Mercosur was indeed a monumental shock to the Paraguayan economy, the quarter century that followed has brought with it enormous changes. The emergence of China as a provider of many low-cost manufactured goods coupled with its global demand for raw materials has had a profound effect on Latin American economies. Closer to home, the persistent economic problems of Argentina, its overvalued currency and recourse to surcharges and import licenses, has made Paraguay's reliance on Brazil almost inevitable. As a result, it is difficult to discern the impact of Mercosur in isolation. What seems to be clear is that it has provided many opportunities, and only some of them have been fully exploited.

Notes

1. This section draws substantially from an earlier paper by the author; see Birch 1996.
2. For an excellent analysis of this period, see Nickson 1981.
3. Work on Yacyretá, a hydroelectric facility near the Paraguayan town of Encarnación on the lower Paraná River along the border between Paraguay and Argentina, was expected to begin in the early 1980s as construction activity at Itaipú was ending. The Yacyretá project is much smaller than Itaipú, but other hydro projects along the Paraná were also under consideration.
4. This section draws heavily from an earlier paper (Birch 2014, 271–75).
5. The 1960 Treaty of Montevideo created LAFTA, bringing together seven Latin American countries including Paraguay (later adding four more) for the purpose of lowering tariffs on products moving among member countries. In 1980, the second Treaty of Montevideo expanded membership to include a total of thirteen countries, forming the Latin American Integration Association (LAIA). While creating more flexibility in terms of the integration process, the LAIA also adopted the more ambitious goal of creating a Latin American common market.
6. When Paraguay was suspended from Mercosur in July 2012 in the wake of the impeachment of President Fernando Lugo, references to the Triple Alliance resurfaced immediately and fanned nationalistic indignation. Luis María Argaña, a leading Colorado Party politician and vice president at the time of his assassination in 1999, was an outspoken critic of Paraguay's membership in Mercosur.
7. The author would like to recognize the invaluable assistance provided by Laura Hales in the construction of the graphs and tables referenced in this section.
8. A private think tank in Asunción has been working to improve government statistics. It has a database that is available for public use at https://mega.nz/file/YWIBQTwA#zwUJUlhk51Zb _umslKsXS39cvW1CjamtVnSuodol9Ac.
9. The Rose Garden Agreement (1991) provides that the four Mercosur countries will negotiate as a group their entry into other regional trade agreements, thus strengthening their hand in negotiations with larger, more powerful economic groups.
10. This is especially true after the withdrawal of the United Kingdom from the EU. Tensions between Argentina and the UK have persisted in the aftermath of the Falklands (Malvinas) War (1982).
11. Lucas Arce (2010) notes that the major exports to these markets are beef, leather products, wood, oilseeds, and chemicals.
12. The Treaty of Ushuaia of 1998 is sometimes referred to as the "democratic clause" of the Mercosur agreements.
13. See http://www.mercosur.int/innovaportal/v/7497/2/innova.front/25-aniversario.

Bibliography

Abente Brun, Diego. 2009. "Paraguay: The Unraveling of One-Party Rule." *Journal of Democracy* 20, no. 1 (January): 143–56.

———. 2011. "Hacia una democracia de calidad." In *El reto del futuro: Asumiendo el legado del bicentenario*, edited by Dionisio Borda and Diego Abente Brun, 25–56. Asunción: Centro de Análisis y Difusión de la Economía Paraguaya.

Arce, Carlos, and Diego Arias. 2015. "Paraguay Agricultural Sector Risk Assessment: Identification, Prioritization, Strategy, and Action Plan." Agriculture Global Practice Technical Assistance Paper. World Bank, Washington, DC.

Arce, Lucas. 2010. "Tendiendo costosos puentes: Paraguay en el Mercosur." *Civitas* 10, no. 1: 118–33.

Baer, Werner, and Melissa Birch. 1984. "Expansion of the Economic Frontier: Paraguayan Growth in the 1970s." *World Development* 12, no. 8 (August): 783–98.

———. 1987. "International Economic Relations of a Small Country: The Case of Paraguay." *Economic Development and Cultural Change* 35, no. 3 (April): 601–27.

———, eds. 1994. *Privatization in Latin America: New Roles for the Public and Private Sectors*. Westport, CT: Praeger.

Beittel, June S. 2010. "Paraguay: Political and Economic Conditions and U.S. Relations." Congressional Research Service, Washington, DC.

Birch, Melissa. 1992. "Pendulum Politics: Paraguayan Economic Diplomacy, 1940–1975." In *Changing Boundaries in the Americas: New Perspectives on the US-Mexican, Central American, and South American Borders*, edited by Lawrence A. Herzog, 203–28. San Diego: Center for U.S.-Mexican Studies, University of California, San Diego.

———. 1993. "El legado económico de los años de Stroessner y el desafío por la democracia." In *Paraguay en Transición*, edited by Diego Abente Brun, 31–49. Asunción: Centro de Análisis y Difusión de la Economía Paraguaya.

———. 1996. "Economic Policy and the Transition to Democracy in Paraguay." In *Economic Policy and the Transition to Democracy: The Latin American Experience*, edited by Juan Antonio Morales and Gary McMahon, 166–90. London: Macmillan.

———. 2000. "Mercosur: The Road to Economic Integration in the Southern Cone." *International Journal of Public Administration* 23, nos. 5–8: 1387–413.

———. 2005. "La agenda económica inconclusa: (Re)creando las bases para el desarrollo económico." In *Estado, economía y sociedad: Una mirada internacional a la democracia paraguaya*, edited by Diego Abente Brun and Fernando Masi, 75–108. Asunción: Centro de Análisis y Difusión de la Economía Paraguaya.

———. 2014. "Paraguay and Mercosur: The Lesser of Two Evils?" *Latin American Business Review* 15, nos. 3–4: 269–90.

Borda, Dionisio. 2011. "La economia política del crecimiento, pobreza y desigualdad en el Paraguay (1968–2010)." In *El reto del futuro: Asumiendo el legado del bicentenario*, edited by Dionisio Borda and Diego Abente Brun, 57–113. Asunción: Centro de Análisis y Difusión de la Economía Paraguaya.

Bouzas, Roberto. 2003. "¿Puede sobrevivir el Mercosur?" *Perfiles Latinoamericanos* 11, no. 23 (December): 231–42.

Bouzas, Roberto, Pedro da Motta Veiga, and Ramon Torrent. 2002. "In-Depth Analysis of Mercosur Integration, Its Prospectives and the Effects Thereof on the Market Access of EU Goods, Services and Investment." Working paper, Observatory of Globalization, University of Barcelona, Science Park of Barcelona. Available at https://www.sciencespo.fr/opalc/sites/sciencespo.fr.opalc/files/in-depth%20analysis%20of%20mercosur%20integration.pdf.

Cuenca García, Eduardo, Margarita Navarro Pabsdorf, and Estrella Gómez Herrera. 2013. "The Gravity Model Analysis: An Application on Mercosur Trade Flows." *Journal of Economic Policy Reform* 16, no. 4: 226–348.

Doctor, Mahrukh. 2013. "Prospects for Deepening Mercosur Integration: Economic Asymmetry and Institutional Deficits." *Review of International Political Economy* 20, no. 3: 515–40.

Douglas, Bruce, and Matthew Malinowski. 2017. "Brazil Worries the 'China of South America' Is Eating Its Lunch." Bloomberg News, January 29. Available at https://www.bloomberg.com/news/articles/2017-01-09/brazil-worries-the-china-of-south-america-is-eating-its-lunch.

Guillén, Stella. 2012. "La nueva base de datos de exportación del Paraguay: La reconstrucción, 1995–2011." Centro de Análisis y Difusión de la Economía Paraguaya, Asunción.

Hudgins, Edward L. 1997. "Mercosur Hasn't Caused Trade Diversion." Cato Institute, March 25. Available at https://www.cato.org/publications/commentary/mercosur-hasnt-caused-trade-diversion.

Kaltenthaler, Karl, and Frank O. Mora. 2002. "Explaining Latin American Economic Integration: The Case of Mercosur." *Review of International Political Economy* 9, no. 1: 72–97.

Malamud, Andrés. 2005. "Mercosur Turns 15: Between Rising Rhetoric and Declining Achievement." *Cambridge Review of International Affairs* 18, no. 3 (October): 421–36.

Masi, Fernando. 2011. "Los desafíos de una nueva insercion externa del Paraguay." In *El reto del futuro: Asumiendo el legado del bicentenario*, edited by Dionisio Borda and Diego Abente Brun, 115–53. Asunción: Centro de Análisis y Difusión de la Economía Paraguaya.

———. 2012. "El comercio fronterizo en alerta." *Economia y Sociedad: Analysis de Coyuntura Mensual*, 19–21. Centro de Análisis y Difusión de la Economía Paraguaya, Asunción

———. 2017. "Maquila en Paraguay: Ni boom ni crash." *Economía y Sociedad*, no. 51 (June): 16–18.

Masi, Fernando, María Inés Terra, et al. 2008. "Asimetrías en el Mercosur: ¿Impedimento para el crecimiento?" *Red Mercosur* 1, no. 12 (Autumn).

Nickson, R. Andrew. 1981. "Brazilian Colonization of the Eastern Border Region of Paraguay." *Journal of Latin American Studies* 13, no. 1: 111–31.

Porrata-Doria, Rafael A., Jr. 2005. *Mercosur: The Common Market of the Southern Cone.* Durham, NC: Carolina Academic Press.

Rachid, Leila, and Rubén Ramírez. 2008. *Política exterior de la República del Paraguay: Herramienta para el desarrollo en un mundo globalizado; Memoria de gestión, 2003–2008.* Asunción: Ministerio de Relaciones Exteriores.

Richards, Donald G. 2009. *Export-Led Stagnation in Paraguay: A Time Series Approach.* Asunción: Centro de Análisis y Difusión de la Economía Paraguaya.

Rodríguez, José Carlos. 2001. "Una ecuación irresuelta: Paraguay-Mercosur." In *Los rostros del*

Mercosur: El difícil camino de lo comercial a lo societal, edited by Gerónimo de Sierra, 361–72. Buenos Aires: Consejo Latinoamericano de Ciencias Sociales.

Ruíz Díaz, Francisco. 2012. "El dilema de Tarzán: Una aplicación a las relaciones comerciales de Paraguay con el Mercosur." Centro de Análisis y Difusión de la Economía Paraguaya, Asunción.

Sala, Gabriela Adriana. 2008. "Perfil educativo y laboral de los nuevos y viejos migrantes regionales censados en Argentina y Brasil." *Migraciones Internacionales* 4, no. 4 (December): 73–106.

———. 2017. "Reorientación de la política previsional argentina y acceso de los migrantes limítrofes a la seguridad social." *Migraciones Internacionales* 9, no. 1 (June): 119–49.

Servín, María Belén. 2010. "Políticas regionales de innovación en el MERCOSUR: Obstáculos y oportunidades en la industria farmacéutica en Paraguay." International Development Research Centre. Centro de Estudios sobre Ciencia, Desarrollo y Educación Superior (Centro Redes), Buenos Aires.

———. 2011. *Boletin de Comercio Exterior*, no. 1 (January–November). Centro de Análisis y Difusión de la Economía Paraguaya, Asunción.

Swanson, William. 2012. "Exportaciones industriales." *Observatorio de Economía Internacional*. Centro de Análisis y Difusión de la Economía Paraguaya, Asunción.

United Nations. 1994. *Open Regionalism in Latin America and the Caribbean: Economic Integration as a Contribution to Changing Production Patterns with Social Equity*. Santiago: Economic Commission for Latin America and the Caribbean.

World Bank. 1992. *Paraguay: Country Economic Memorandum*. Washington, DC: World Bank.

World Trade Organization. 2012. "Paraguay: Country Profile" (WT/TPR/S/245). Available at https://www.wto.org/english/tratop_e/tpr_e/tp345_e.htm.

Yeats, Alexander J. 1998. "Does Mercosur's Trade Performance Raise Concerns about the Effects of Regional Trade Arrangements?" *World Bank Economic Review* 12, no. 1 (January): 1–28.

CONTRIBUTORS

MELISSA H. BIRCH is an associate professor and the executive director of the Institute for International and Global Engagement at the University of Kansas at Lawrence. She holds a bachelor of arts degree in anthropology and Latin American studies from New College (Sarasota, Florida) and a master of science and PhD in economics from the University of Illinois. Her research and teaching interests focus on the managerial challenges of business in Latin America.

PAOLA CANOVA is an associate professor in the Department of Anthropology at the University of Texas at Austin and an affiliate faculty member in the Teresa Lozano Long Institute of Latin American Studies. She received her doctorate from the University of Arizona. Her research interests include gender and sexuality, indigeneity, ethics, political ecology, Latin America, and Paraguay. She is the author of *Frontier Intimacies: Ayoreo Women and the Sexual Economy of the Paraguayan Chaco* (2020) and a coeditor of *Reimagining the Gran Chaco: Identities, Politics, and the Environment in South America* (2021).

SARAH PATRICIA CERNA VILLAGRA is a professor at the Consejo Nacional de Ciencia y Tecnología in Mexico and the Centro de Estudios Sociológicos at the Colegio de México. She received a doctorate in law and government and a master's degree in political science from the Universidad de Salamanca, Spain. She also received a doctorate in political and social sciences from the Universidad Nacional Autónoma de México. Her research interests include political systems, elections, representation of women in politics, and gender and politics.

BARBARA A. GANSON, professor of history at Florida Atlantic University in Boca Raton, is a specialist in the field of ethnohistory. She received her master of arts in Latin American studies and PhD in history from the University of Texas at

Austin. She is the author of an award-winning book, *The Guaraní under Spanish Rule in the Rio de la Plata* (2003). In 2017, she published the first bilingual edition of Jesuit missionary Antonio Ruiz de Montoya's *Conquista espiritual hecha por los religiosos de la Compañía de Jesús en las provincias del Paraguay, Paraná, Uruguay y Tape* (1639) with Clinia M. Saffi (Institute of Jesuit Sources, Boston College, 2017). She is an honorary member of the Centro de Estudios Antropológicos of the Universidad Católica "Nuestra Señora de la Asunción."

RENÉ HARDER HORST, the I. G. Greer Distinguished Professor of History at Appalachian State University, received his master of arts and PhD in history from Indiana University. Harder Horst is the author of *The Stroessner Regime and Indigenous Resistance in Paraguay* (2007), which details the complexities of Paraguay's political culture and the impact of development programs on its Native peoples and peasants. He is currently working on a collaborative book on John Belaieff, the White Russian general who, in exile, helped direct Paraguay's military victory over Bolivia in the Chaco War (1932–1935). He is also working on a book on Native experiences in Paraguay following the end of the Stroessner regime in 1989.

ROQUE JAVIER MERELES PINTOS is a graduate student of political science at the Universidad Nacional de Asunción, Paraguay, where he received his bachelor's degree in communications. He is a journalist by profession and a political editor for the Agencia de Información Paraguaya.

RICHARD K. REED is an anthropologist and professor at Trinity University in San Antonio. Over the past fifteen years, he has been working with Guaraní villages on the frontier of expanding colonization and agriculture in Paraguay. Two of his books are *Prophets of Agroforestry* (1995) and *Forest Residents and Forest Managers* (1997). He studies the effects of deforestation on indigenous groups in the forests of South America.

EDUARDO TAMAYO BELDA is a doctoral student in the contemporary history program at the Universidad Autónoma de Madrid. He has a master's degree in political science from the Universidad Nacional de Asunción and the equivalent of a bachelor's degree in history from the Universidad Autónoma de Madrid.

BRIAN TURNER, professor and chair of the Department of Political Science at

Randolph-Macon College in Ashland, Virginia, teaches courses in the politics of Latin America, Africa, and China; and in international studies. He is active in the Middle Atlantic Council of Latin American Studies, currently serving as treasurer; and in the American Association of University Professors, currently serving on the National Executive Committee. His research focuses on Latin America, with a concentration on Paraguay.

SARA MABEL VILLALBA PORTILLO is a graduate of the Universidad Católica de Asunción, Paraguay. She received her doctorate in contemporary political processes from the Universidad de Salamanca, Spain. She is a member of the Programa Nacional de Investigadores of the Consejo Nacional de Ciencia y Tecnología, Paraguay. She teaches political science and sociology at the Universidad Nacional de Asunción.

INDEX

Page numbers in *italic* text indicate illustrations.

Abdo Benítez, Mario, 100–102
Abente Brun, Diego, 95
abolishment, of slavery, 8
Academy of the Guaraní Language (Academia de la Lengua Guaraní), 13
Acha, Sebastian, 130n9
activism, 94; Indigenous, 22–24; political, 31
Act of Buenos Aires (1990), 141
agriculture, 1, 11, 25, 44, 50n2, 137–38; exports from, 144; Guaraní, 39; mechanized, 148, 150; Mennonite, 57; soybeans and, 41–42
agroforestry, 27–28
Alder Ibánez, José Luis, 131n15
Alfonsín, Raúl, 141
Alianza list, 117
Alianza Patriótica para el Cambio (APC) (electoral alliance), 77, 94–97
Alliana, Pedro, 73
Alto Paraguay (department), 68n8, 114, 122
Alto Paraná (department), 27
American Convention on Human Rights, 91
los ancianos (elders), 28
ANR. *See* Asociación Nacional Republicana–Partido Colorado
APC. *See* Alianza Patriótica para el Cambio
Argaña, Luis María, 86, 158n6
Argentina, 10, 138; Buenos Aires, 7, 14, 40, 141; occupation by, 8; trade with, 141; women in politics in, 113
Argentine-Brazilian Integration Act (1986), 141

Article 125, constitution, 92
Asociación Nacional Republicana–Partido Colorado (Colorado Party) (ANR), 8, 10, 29, 73–77, *75*, 80–81; candidates for, 131n13; democracy and, 85–86; final years of, 84–85; gender quota and, 110, 124; Mercosur and, 142; return to power, 94, 95, 97, 99–102; traditionalist group, 103n8; women in, 116–17, 120
assassination attempt, of Ramírez, 21–22
Asunción, 2, 3, 48; US embassy, 82–83
authoritarian rule, 7, 21, 77, 86, 95
"Authorized Indian," 31–32
Avá Guaraní, 27, 50n1
Ava-ka'ë (Guaraní), 37
Avanza País (political party), 120, 128
Ayolas, Juan de, 2
Ayoreo, 53–55; exploitation of, 61–62; land for, 60–62, 64–65; Mennonites and, 55–56, 57–58, 62–63; in urban spaces, 60–62, 63–65, 66–67

ballot structures, 112–13
Barbados Symposium on Interethnic Conflict in South America, 23–24
battle of Cerro Porteño, 7
beggars, 46, 49
Belgrano, Manuel, 7
Beloved Fatherland Party (Partido Patria Querida), 95

Benitez Diaz, Eusebia María, 122
Birdwatchers (Terra Vermelha) (film), 12
Bolivia, 9, 32, 58, 151, 152
bourgeoisie, fraudulent, 80–81, 82
Brazil, 3, 10, 37–38, 138, 141, 157; energy sovereignty and, 97; exports to, 144; occupation by, 8; trade with, 150
bridges, building, 40
Broad Front (Frente Guasú), 97
Buenos Aires, 7, 14, 40; Act of Buenos Aires (1990), 141
bureaucracy, fraudulent, 103n5
Buschegger, Henry, 58
Bush, George H. W., 24

Caaguazú (department), 26
Campo Loro, 59
Campos Morombí, 25, 104n15
candidate list, 115, 125–26; corruption of, 110; legal immunity (fueros), 114, 126
candidates, electoral, 115, 116–17, 120
Canindeyú (department), 121, 122, 131n12
capital accumulation, 59
Cario-Guaraní, 2, 3
Carter, Jimmy, 103n7
Cartes, Horacio, 73, 99–102, 104n17, 146
Casa Pasajera, 53, 61–63, 64–65, 67
Casco, Rocío, 128
Castiglioni, Luis, 95–96
Catholic Church, 28, 29, 91
Catholic missionaries, 3–4, 18n37
census: 1846, 7; Indigenous, 32, 50n1; 1647, 5; 2012, 11
Cerro León, 56, 68n10
Cerro Potý settlement, 47–50
CET. *See* common external tariff
Chaco region, 2, 11, 56, 63, 117, 119
Chaco War, 9
Chaidi 2, 64–65
Chamber of Deputies, 114, 116–17, *118*, 124, 126, 130n10
Charlevoix, Pierre François Xavier de, 16n6
Chase Sardi, Miguel, 23, 57

Chaves, Federico, 79, 82
children, illegitimate, 8, 17n22
Chile, 152
China, 157
Christianization, 3
Ciudad del Este (district), 14, 44, 122
Civil War, 79, 103n4
closed-list systems, 112–13, 114
Cold War, 83
Colombia, Indigenous rights in, 32
Columbus Quincentenary, 28
El comisario del Valle Lorito (play), 14
"commercialization," of candidate lists, 126
Commission on Social and Gender Equity, 126
common external tariff (CET), 151
Common Market of the South (Mercosur), 87, 99, 135–36, *140*, 140–42, 150–54, 157; democracy and, 154; exports to, 143–44, *144*; FDI and, *147*, 147–48; FOCEM and, 155–56; imports from, *145*, 145–46, *150*; Rose Garden Agreement (1991), 158n8; secretariat for, 154–55; Treaty of Ushuaia (1998), 158n11
communism, 83, 138
Concepción (department), 122
Congress, 89, 96, 99, 129; women in, 116–17, *118*, 130n10
constitutional assembly, 29
constitutionalism, Latin American, 88
Constitution of 1992, Republic of Paraguay, 8; Article 125, 92; Article 118 and 119, 114; articles to protect Indigenous in, 30; indigenous rights and, 92; Law 1/89, 91; new, 31–33, 87; 1992 national, 87–93, 104n11, 113
control, "outside power organs" as, 93
Coordinadora Colorada Campesina (ANR faction), 125
Corredor Vial Bioceánico, 64
corruption, 126
coup d'état, 13, 83, 84–86, 104n11; against Chaves, 79; by Oviedo, 154; against Stroessner, 77

crisis of representation, 129
cultural heritage, indigenous, 27–28
Curuguaty massacre, 98, 104n16
Cusicanqui, Silvia Rivera, 31

dams. *See* hydroelectricity
debt crisis, 135, 140–41
decentralization: political, 76, 119; territorial, 90–91
Declaration of Barbados, 23, 68n11
deforestation, 11, 40–41, *42*; environmental impacts, 42, 44–45; Guaraní and, 43–46
democracy, 1, 13, 14, 25, 81; ANR and, 85–86; direct mechanisms of, 92–93; Indigenous people and, 28–31; political parties, 74–75; Stroessner and, 81–82; threats to, 154; transition to, 86–87, 88, 135, 139–43
departamentales, juntas, 119–20, *120*
departamentos and distritos, 130n8
Departmental Councils (juntas), 119–20
descriptive representation, 111–13
development. *See* economic development
D'Hondt method, 76, 114
Diálogo Nacional, 25
dictatorship, in Paraguay, 24–27, 84–86, 135
displacement, of Guaraní, 45–47, 48
district magnitude, 112
distritos and departamentos, 130n8
drugs, 46–47
Duarte Frutos, Nicanor, 94, 95

Eastern Paraguay, 40, 50n1, 137–38
Ebetogue community, 61
economic complementarity agreements (ECAs), 152
economic development, 69n13, 93–94, *95*, 105, 141; under Stroessner, 136–39
economic growth, 1, 136, 148; Itaipú dam and, 137–38; open-economy strategy for, 139
economic policy, 139–43
economy, 59, 157; impact on, 143; performance of (1999-2008), *95*

Effective Number of Parties formula, 77, *78*; evolution of (1989-2018), *79*
elders (*los ancianos*), 28
elections, 113; Chamber of Deputies (1993-2018), *118*; gubernatorial, 122, *123*; mayoral, 122, *123*; methodology, 115–16; municipal, 90–91, 103n2, 120–21, *121*; national, 90–91; primary, 114; procedures of, 90–91; Senate, *118*, 125; 2018 presidential, 101, 102; of women, 117–19, 122, 123–26
electoral candidates, 115, 116–17, 120
electoral reform, 126
electoral system, 113–14; women and, 112
electricity, 10
emigration, 96
encomienda, 3
Enenlhit, 19, 21, 30
energy sovereignty, 97
environmental impacts, of deforestation, 42, 44–45
equity, gender, 116
erosion, 42
Estigarribia, José Félix de, 9
Etacore, Chome, 64
Ethnos 360. *See* New Tribes Mission (NTM)
EU. *See* European Union
Eurocentrism, 56
European Electoral Observer Mission, 122
European Union (EU), 153, 158n9
Evueví (Payaguá), 11
executive positions, women in, 122–23
exports, 146, 152, 158n10; to Brazil, 144; growth of (1980-2016), *140*; to Mercosur, *140*, 143–44, *144*
exports to Mercosur by country, 1980–2016, *144*

FDI. *See* foreign direct investment
Febrerista Party, 9
female weaver (*hilandera*), 2–3
Fernheim colony, 53, 56–59, 61, 68n1
Ferreira, Olga, 127–28
Figueredo Amaro, Ana María, 131n15

Filadelfia, 53–54, 56, 57, 60, 65–67
Filártiga, Joel, 13
Filizzola, Carlos, 128
Flores, Nemecio, 26–27
Flores, Severo, 23, 24, 30
Fondo para la Convergencia Estructural del Mercosur (FOCEM), 155–56
foreign direct investment (FDI), 146, *147*, 147–50
the forest: changes in, 40–42; Guaraní and, 38–40
forestry: agro-, 27–28; deforestation, 11, 40–41; logging, 41
formula, Effective Number of Parties, 77, *78*, *79*
Francis (Pope), 109
Franco, Federico, 98, 99
Franco, Rafael, 9
Franco, "Yoyito," 125
fraudulent bourgeoisie, 80–81, 82
fraudulent bureaucracy, 103n5
freedoms, fundamental, 91–92
free trade, 153–56
Free Womb Law (1842), 7
Frente Guasú (Broad Front) (political party), 97
fundamental freedoms, 91–92

GDP. *See* gross domestic product
gender: politics and, 110–15; success rates by, 115–16
gender equality index, 110
gender equity, 116
gender imbalances, *121*
Gender Office (Unidad de Género), 115
gender quotas, electoral, 109–15, 126, 129; laws, 116, 124; in municipal elections, 120–21
gender-sensitive legislation, 127–28, *128*
gender separation, 4, 16n9
General Artigas (district), 121
"Global Gender Gap Report 2017" (WEF), 110
global markets, 139, 142, 143
Gobernación de Boquerón, 64
Gómez Florentín, Carlos, 82

Gondra Pereira, Manuel, 8, 17n24
Gorbachev, Mikhail, 24
governors (of departments), 90–91, 113, 119
gross domestic product (GDP), 1, 93, *95*, *149*
growth: of exports to Mercosur (1980-2016), *140*; of the Paraguayan economy in USD: 1960–2016, *149*
Grünberg, Georg, 23
Grupo de Apoyo, 104n14
Guaidó, Juan, 102
Guaraní, 3–5, 11, 28, 37–38; agriculture of, 39; Avá, 27, 50n1; Cario-, 2, 3; deforestation and, 43–46; displacement of, 25, 45–47, 48; forest, 38–40, 46–47; independence of, 12, 39; language of, 5–6, 12–13, 18n37; Mbyá, 25, 26–27, 43, 50n1; new technologies and, 5; Paĩ Tavyterã, 25–26, 50n1; young, 46–47
Guaraní-Kaiowá, 12
gubernatorial elections, 122, *123*
Guevara, Isabel de, 2
Guidai Ichai (New Community), 65–67

Halley Mora, Mario, 14
HC. *See* Honor Colorado
Herken, Juan Carlos, 103n5
hilandera (female weaver), 2–3
Honor Colorado (HC), 73, 74
Humanist Party, 122
human rights, 80, 155
hunting, 39
hydroelectricity, 1, 11, 94, 138, 139, 146; Itaipú Dam, 44–45, 102, 137; protests of, 22; Yacyretá Dam, 45, 158n3
"hypermarginality," 54

Ibáñez, José Luis Alder, 131n15
identity, pan-Indigenous, 20, 29
illegitimate children, 8, 17n22
immigration, 8–9
impeachment, 87, 90; of Lugo, 98–99
imports, from Mercosur, *145*, 145–46
import-substitution industrialization (ISI) strategy, 137, 139, 140, 142

income distribution, 148
independence: of Guaraní, 12, 39; of Paraguay, 7–10, 104n12, 135
INDI. *See* Instituto Paraguayo del Indígena
Indigenous organizations, creation of, 28
Indigenous peoples: activism of, 22–24; awakening of, 22; census for, 32, 50n1; land of, 31, 43–44, 50n2; resistance by, 27–28; rights of, 20, 30–33, 92; urbanity and, 56–59. *See also specific topics*
indigenous refugees, 46–50
Indigenous Rights Law 904 (1981), 31, 33
indigenous settlements, map of Paraguay, *ii*
Institute of Rural Welfare (Instituto de Bienestar Rural), 25
Instituto Paraguayo del Indígena (INDI), 49, 63
La instrucción pública en la época colonial (Massare de Kostianovsky), 16n9
international connections, 22–23, 24–25, 82–84
international law, 91
International Organization for Migration, 155
investment, in manufacturing, 147
Irala, Domingo de, 2
ISI strategy. *See* import-substitution industrialization
Itaipú Dam, 44–45, 102, 137
Itaipú (department), 45, 86, 94, 137, 138
Itanaramí, 37, 38, 40

jaguar, 11
Jesuits, 4–5, 6
John Paul II (Pope), 19, 20, 21
Judicial Council, 93
judicial power, 90
juntas departamentales, 119–20, *120*
juntas municipales, 120–21, 130n11

Kissinger, Henry, 103n6
Kunajeju (Guaraní), 37
Kuña Pyrenda (political party), 122

labor relations, 56–59, 60
LAFTA. *See* Latin American Free Trade Area

LAIA. *See* Latin American Integration Association
Lali-puku (Guaraní girl), 37, 40, 48, 49–50
land, 41, 137–38; Ayoreo, 60–62, 64–65; Indigenous, 31, 43–44, 50n2; "social rule of law" concept and, 89; violence over, 25–27
landfill, scavenging in, 49
landscape, physical and cultural, 10–15
languages: Guaraní, 5–6, 12–13, 18n37; Plattdeutsch, 8–9; Spanish, 6, 12; Tupí-Guaraní, 3
Latin American constitutionalism, 88
Latin American Free Trade Area (LAFTA), 140, 158n5
Latin American Integration Association (LAIA), 158n5
laws: Free Womb Law (1842), 7; gender quota, 116, 124; Indigenous Rights Law 904 (1981), 31, 33; Law 1/89, 91; Law of the Maquila, 146
legislation, gender-sensitive, 127–28, *128*
literacy, 6–7
logging, 41
López, Carlos Antonio, 7–8
López, Francisco Solano (General), 8
Lugo, Fernando, 77–78, 94–99, 102, 104n17, 154

Malamud, Andrés, 153
manufacturing, investment in, 147
map of Paraguay, indigenous settlements, *ii*
Marandú Proyect, NGO, 23
March for Territory and Dignity, 32
markets, global, 139, 142, 143
Maskoy people, 28
massacre, Curuguaty, 98, 104n16
Massare de Kostianovsky, Olinda, 16n9
Mata Atlantica, 38
mayoral elections, 122, *123*
mayors (intendentes), women as, 122
Mbyá Guaraní, 25, 26–27, 43, 50n1
MCC. *See* Mennonite Central Committee
McLeod de Zacarias, Sandra, 122
"mechanical arts," 16n12
mechanisms, of democracy, 92–93

mechanized agriculture, 148, 150
media, 97–98
meeting, pan-Indigenous (1991), 29
Mendoza, Pedro de, 2
Mendoza de Acha, Ana María, 130n9
Mendoza Diaz, Mirta Ramona, 122
Mennonite Central Committee (MCC), 55, 56, 68n5
Mennonites, 8–9, 53–54, 60–61; Ayoreo and, 55–56, 57–58, 62–63; colonies, 68n3; labor relations and, 57–59
Mercosur. *See* Common Market of the South
methodology, of elections, 115–16
Mexican political regime, 76, 103n3
migration, 137; Ayoreo, 57–58; International Organization for Migration, 155; urban, 12, 14, 58–59, 61
military, 80, 81, 82, 86, 87
Miño, Dolores de, 130n10
minorities, representation of, 111–12
Misiones (department), 117
missionaries: Catholic, 3–4, 18n37; NTM, 56, 57, 58–59, 68n7, 68n9; Salesian, 55, 56, 68n7; Spanish, 7
Montecito settlement, 60–61
multiculturalism, 92
Municipal councils (*municipales, juntas*), 120–21, 130n11
municipal elections, 90–91, 103n2, *121*; gender quota and, 120–21

NAFTA. *See* North American Free Trade Agreement
ñanduti (spider-web lace), 3
National Constituent Convention, 92, 104n13
national elections, 90–91
National Security Doctrine, 82–84
Native rights movement, 23
Ñeembucú (department), 121
New Community (Guidai Ichai), 65–67
new technologies, Cario-Guaraní and, 5
New Tribes Mission (NTM), 56, 57, 58–59, 68n7, 68n9

1992 national constitution, 87–93, 104n11, 113
niños de la calle (street children), 46, 47
Nivaclé Indigenous people, 19
nomadic indigenous peoples, 2
North American Free Trade Agreement (NAFTA), 135, 152
Notario, Teresa, 122
NTM. *See* New Tribes Mission

OAS. *See* Organization of American States
Ocampos, Marlene, 122
Ombudsman's Office, 93
One Man's War (film), 13
open-economy strategy, 139
open-list systems, 113, 130n9
Operación Cóndor, 83, 103n6
opposition, to Stroessner, 84–85
Organization of American States (OAS), 10
"outside power organs," as control, 93
Ovelar, Blanca, 95
Oviedo, Fabiola, 128
Oviedo, Lino César, 25, 77, 86, 100, 154

Pacific Alliance, 152–53
Paï Tavyterã Guaraní, 25–26, 50n1
Paiva, Félix, 9
Pan Indigenous Identity, 29
Pan-Indigenous meeting (1991), 29
Paraguarí (department), 121
Paraguayan Communist Party, 82
Paraguayan War, 8, 74, 109. *See also* War of the Triple Alliance
"Paraguay" meaning, 3, 16n6
Paraguay River, 2, 3, 7, 10–11, 48
Paraguay's per capita income in constant USD (2010), 1965–2015, *149*
Paraná River, 3, 11, 44, 45, 158n3
Paravicino, José Cayetano, 6
parity rule, 131n16
Partido Encuentro Nacional (PEN), 117
Partido Liberal Radical Auténtico (PLRA), 8, 29–30, 73, 74, *75*, 79, 94; gender quota and,

110; Senate elections and, 125; women in, 119, 120
Partido Patria Querida (Beloved Fatherland Party) (PPQ), 95, 117, 127, 130n9
Partido Unión Nacional de Ciudadanos Éticos (PUNACE), 128
patriarchal cultures, 112
Payaguá (Evueví), 11
PEN. *See* Partido Encuentro Nacional
Peña, Santiago, 100–101
"pendulum politics," 136, 141
performance of Paraguayan economy (1999-2008), 95
Philip V (King), 6
physical and cultural landscape, 10–15
Pilar (district), 121
Plattdeutsch language, 8–9
PLRA. *See* Partido Liberal Radical Auténtico
pluriculturalism, 32
policy, economic, 139–43
political activism, 31
political parties: HC, 73, 74; Paraguayan Communist Party, 82; PEN, 117; PPQ, 95, 117, 127, 130n9. *See also* Asociación Nacional Republicana; Partido Liberal Radical Auténtico
political systems, Paraguay, 73–75, 81; organization of, 76; party system, 76–79
politics: decentralization in, 76, 119; gender and, 110–15; "pendulum politics," 136, 141; women in, 111–13
Pope Francis, 109
Pope John Paul II, 19, 20, 21
Posorajai, Ikevi, 68n7
poverty, 1, 12
PPQ. *See* Partido Patria Querida
Presidente Hayes (department), 117–18
presidential elections, 2018, 101, 102
primary elections, 114
prostitution, 46, 47
Proyecto Liberal de Renovación y Abertura (PLRA faction), 125
public policy, 127–28

public power, voting, 89–90
Puerto Casado, 21, 28, 31
Puerto María Auxiliadora, 68
PUNACE. *See* Partido Unión Nacional de Ciudadanos Éticos

quota. *See* gender quotas, electoral

racism, 43
railroad, building of, 7
Ramírez, René, 19–20, 28, 29–31; assassination attempt, 21–22
Reagan, Ronald, 83–84
Reconciliación Colorada (ANR faction), 124
reelection rules, 89, 100
reform, electoral, 126
refugees: indigenous, 46–50; Mennonite, 55
representation: descriptive, 111–13; of minorities, 111–12; symbolic, 129; of women, 127–28, 129–30
resilience, Indigenous, 49–50
resistance, Indigenous, 27–28
Riacho Mosquito, 19, 28, 29, 30–31
rights: human, 80, 155; of Indigenous people, 20, 30–33, 92; voting, 9, 114; of women, 128
Río de la Plata region, 2
roads, building, 40, 44, 69n13
Roa Rojas, María Digna, 124–25
Rodríguez, Andrés (President), 10, 29, 79, 84, 86
Rodríguez, Karina, 128
Rodríguez de Francia, José Gaspar, 7, 135
Rose Garden Agreement (1991), 158n8
Ruiz de Montoya, Antonio, 18n37
running water, 10

Saguier Caballero, Hugo, 43
Salesian missionaries, 55, 56, 68n7
San Pedro (department), 94, 120, 124
Santacruz, Alberto, 23, 24
Sapucaí (district), 121
Sartori, Giovanni, 77
Schwindt-Baye, Leslie, 129

Second Meeting of Barbados, 23–24
Secretariat of Women (Paraguay), 112, 114
Senate elections, 118, 125
senators, women, 125
separation, gender, 4, 16n9
Shaw, George P., 82
slavery, 7, 8
"social rule of law" concept, 89
socioeconomics, 75
Solalinde de Romero, Ada Fatima, 124
Sommerfield Colony, 26
Soto, Lilian, 122
sovereignty, 97, 104n12, 151
Soviet Union, 24
soybeans, 41–42
Spanish expansion, 2–7
Spanish language, 6, 12
Spanish missionaries, 7
spider-web lace (*ñanduti*), 3
Stahl, Wilmar, 58, 68n4
street children (*niños de la calle*), 46, 47
Stroessner, Alfredo, 1, 10, 13–14, 20–21, 33, 74; ANR and, 76; coup d'état against, 77, 85; democracy and, 81–82; dictatorship of, 24–27, 135; economy under, 136–39; opposition to, 84–85; regime of, 79–82
study, on trade, 145
success rates, by gender, 115–16
Superior Electoral Tribunal (Paraguay), 96, 114
symbolic representation, 129
Symposium on Inter-Ethnic Conflict in South America, 68n11

Takuaguy Oygue, 25, 26
taxes, 93–94, 102
Terra Vermelha (*Birdwatchers*) (film), 12
territorial decentralization, 90–91
Thierry, Robert, 83
Third Democratic Wave, 103n10
trade, 135–36, 140, 143–47; with Argentina, 141; with Brazil, 150; free, 153–56; global, 141; study on, 145. *See also* Common Market of the South (Mercosur)

traditionalist group, ANR, 103n8
Treaty of Asunción, 143, 145, 151–52
Treaty of Madrid (1750), 5
Treaty of Montevideo, 158n5
Treaty of Ushuaia (1998), 158n11
Tribunal Superior de Justicia Electoral, 115
Triple Alliance, 158n6
Troche de Gallegos, María Evangelista, 122, 125
Tupí-Guaraní language, 3

UK. *See* United Kingdom
UNACE. *See* Unión Nacional de Ciudadanos Éticos
UNAP. *See* Union de Nativos Ayoreo del Paraguay
UNASUR. *See* Union of South American Nations
Unidad de Género (Gender Office), 115
Union de Nativos Ayoreo del Paraguay (UNAP), 64
Unión Nacional de Ciudadanos Éticos (UNACE), 73, 77, 117
Union of South American Nations (UNASUR), 99
United Kingdom (UK), 153, 158n9
United States (US), 79, 82, 83–84, 103nn6–7, 152
urbanity, 66–67; forest Guaraní and, 46–47; Indigenous, 56–59; as strategy, 63–65
urban migration, 12, 14, 58–59, 61
urban spaces, Ayoreo in, 60–62, 63–65, 66–67
US. *See* United States
US embassy, Asunción, 82–83

Van Cott, Donna Lee, 21
Venezuela, 102
Villagra, Cerna, 128
Villalba, María Cristina, 122
violence, over land, 25–27
voting, public power, 89–90
voting rights, 9, 114

War of the Triple Alliance, 74, 137, 142, 158n6
wars: Chaco, 9; Civil War, 79, 103n4; Cold War, 83; Paraguayan, 8, 74, 109

Wasmosy, Juan Carlos, 32–33
water, running, 10
WEF. *See* World Economic Forum
Wenner-Gren Foundation, 68n1
women, 109–10; in ANR, 116–17, 120; in Congress, 116–17, *118*, 130n10; elections of, 117–19, 122, 123–26; electoral system and, 112; in executive positions, 122–23; gender quotas and, 111–13; in juntas departamentales, 119–20, *120*; in juntas municipales, 120–21; as mayors, 122; in PLRA, 119, *120*; representation of, 127–28, 129–30; senators, 125
women's rights, 128
work balance, 12

workers, 25, 57, 128, 138
World Economic Forum (WEF), 110–11

Xarayes lake, 16n6

Yacyretá Dam, 45, 158n3
Yasy Cañy (district), 121
Ybycuí (district), 7, 13, 122
yerba mate, 39–40
Yore, Fatima Myriam, 82

Zonade Integración del Centro Oeste de América del Sur (ZICOSUR), 69n13
Zwingli, Huldrych, 68n3

www.ingramcontent.com/pod-product-compliance
Lightning Source LLC
Chambersburg PA
CBHW020934230426
43666CB00008B/1681